more praise for
THE BOOK OF MU

"This book brings us eyebrow-to-eyebrow with
an unprecedentedly rich convocation of masters."
—Franz Metcalf, author of *What Would Buddha Do?*

"Words come alive in this wonderful collection,
filled with laughter, tears, and wisdom."
—Mark Unno, author of *Shingon Refractions*

"The most important of all koans finally gets the attention it deserves.
For those considering koan study, or just curious about this
unique spiritual practice, this is a very valuable book."
—David R. Loy, author of *Money Sex War Karma* and
The World Is Made of Stories

"Useful, insightful, and lovely!"
—Rafe Martin, author of *The Banyan Deer*

"Highly recommended."
—Noah Levine, author of *Heart of the Revolution*

"A book that people will want to read and return to again and again."
—Jeremy D. Safran, editor of *Psychoanalysis and Buddhism*

"Sure to inspire many Zen students and practitioners."
—*Buddhadharma*

"Like a love affair, the koan Mu will tear you open, if you let it. This
book of caring, meticulous essays is a gentle shepherd, escorting both
initiated and uninitiated readers to where we can hear Zen's great
monosyllable beginning to resound on its own."
—Kate Wheeler, editor of *Nixon Under the Bodhi Tree*
and Other Works of Buddhist Fiction

"Mu" by Shodo Harada

THE BOOK OF MU

ESSENTIAL WRITINGS
ON ZEN'S MOST IMPORTANT KOAN

edited by
James Ishmael Ford
and Melissa Myozen Blacker

foreword by
John Tarrant

Wisdom Publications • Boston

Wisdom Publications
199 Elm Street
Somerville MA 02144 USA
www.wisdompubs.org

Library of Congress Cataloging-in-Publication Data
The book of mu : essential writings on zen's most important koan / edited by James Ishmael Ford and Melissa Myozen Blacker ; foreword by John Tarrant.
    pages cm
Includes bibliographical references and index.
ISBN 0-86171-643-4 (pbk. : alk. paper)
1. Koan. 2. Zhaozhou, Shi, 778-897. I. Ford, James Ishmael. II. Blacker, Melissa Myozen, 1954–
BQ9289.5.B65 2011
294.3'85—dc22
                        2010052125
ISBN 978-0-86171-643-2
eBook ISBN 978-086171-609-8

15 14 13 12 11
5 4 3 2 1

Cover design by Gopa&Ted2. Interior design by LC. Set in Aldus 10.5/14. Cover image: "Blizdog" by Kate Hartland, www.cathyhartland.com.

Calligraphy on p. ii is from *Moon by the Window* by Shodo Harada. Calligraphy on p. 34 is "Mu" by Soen Nakagawa, used by permission of the Cambridge Buddhist Association. Calligraphy on p. 120 is by Taizan Maezumi. Calligraphy on p. 309 is by John Daido Loori, private collection.

Wisdom Publications' books are printed on acid-free paper and meet the guidelines for permanence and durability of the Production Guidelines for Book Longevity of the Council on Library Resources.

Printed in the United States of America.

♻ This book was produced with environmental mindfulness. We have elected to print this title on 30% PCW recycled paper. As a result, we have saved the following resources: 30 trees, 9 million BTUs of energy, 2,840 lbs. of greenhouse gases, 13,680 gallons of water, and 831 lbs. of solid waste. For more information, please visit our website, www.wisdompubs.org. This paper is also FSC certified. For more information, please visit www.fscus.org.

To
Jan Seymour-Ford,
David Dae An Rynick,
and Rachel Blacker Rynick

Contents

Acknowledgments

THE LIST OF THOSE to whom we owe acknowledgment is vastly too long to enumerate here. The treasure-trove of Western Zen is amazingly rich and we are grateful for everyone who contributed to this book. We especially thank those who provided texts that we ended up not being able to use, mostly due to the fact that this book began to get unmanageably long. We must, of course, thank our teachers, formal and informal, transmitted in lineage and not. This list is also very long but has to include Robert Aitken, Richard Clarke, Randy Huntsberry, Jon Kabat-Zinn, Philip Kapleau, Jiyu Kennett, Seung Sahn, Saki Santorelli, and Jim Wilson. Most of all we thank John Tarrant, an astonishing master of the koan way, teacher, and friend. And we want to thank our students, friends, and companions at the Boundless Way Zen sangha who've taught us more than they can know.

Our spouses, Jan Seymour-Ford and David Rynick, both old Zen hands, well familiar with that tricky dog and his many companions, were our good friends and necessary guides along the way of putting this book together. They knew when to say "get back to work" and when to say "time to go to bed." Thank you!

Melissa especially wants to thank her daughter, Rachel Blacker Rynick, who daily demonstrates the spirit of Mu through her joy in singing and in living passionately.

And, last, we must thank Josh Bartok at Wisdom Publications for first inviting us to this project and then providing that true professional hand every time we needed it. Endlessly encouraging, he has kept us on task with patience and discipline.

James Ishmael Ford
Melissa Myozen Blacker

Boundless Way Temple
Worcester, Massachusetts

FOREWORD:
THE GREAT KOAN, YOUR DOG

John Tarrant

A KOAN BRINGS ABOUT a change of heart—its value is to transform the mind.

The problem we are trying to solve with a koan is this:

The mind we work with every day evolved to flee saber tooth tigers, hunt mammoths, not kill each other too often, share food, gossip, make babies and develop theories of the universe. To manage all this, the mind makes hypotheses, wondering, "Is that a stick on the path or is it a snake?" or "Is that boy or girl hot?" or "Do I have egg on my face?" or "What will the cancer biopsy numbers be when they come in?"

So we wander along, having thoughts, believing them, acting on them, dealing with the results we get. We scheme and plot, fear and want, trying to wrestle our states of mind into a comfortable shape. People think, "I want not to be crazy when I see my mother," or "I don't want to feel jealous, or afraid," and it's hard work and painful to be always two inches to the left of where we want to be. Adjusting our states of mind is a gymnastic workout that never ends. Our minds are still in beta and we live at some distance from our actual lives.

Koans take account of the confusion and cross-purposes that are a feature of the mind. They lead us to rest in our uncertainty, including what's happening now and what we want to flee.

Koans offer the possibility that you could free the mind in one jump, without passing through stages or any pretense at logical steps. In the territory that koans open up, we live down a level, before explanations occur, beneath the ground that fear is based on, before the wanting and the scrambling around for advantage, before there is a handle on the problem, before we were alienated from the world.

A koan doesn't hide or even manage fear or despair or rage or anything that appears in your mind. Instead, with a koan you might stop finding fault with what your mind presents, stop assuming you already know what your thoughts and feelings are about and how they need to be handled. At some stage my thoughts stopped being compelling and I found a joy in what was advancing toward me. Everyone thinks you need a patch of earth to stand on or you will fall down. Your patch of earth might be someone's approval or a certain amount of money. When the koan opens, you don't need somewhere to stand, or a handle on your experience.

The kindness of a koan consists mainly in taking away what you are sure of about yourself. This isn't a sinister trick, and though I found it disorienting it was more relieving than painful. Taking away is the first gift of a koan.

Among the thousands of koans in the curriculum, the koan Mu (as it's known in Japanese), or Wu (Chinese), or No (English) has been used for about 1200 years. It is popular as a first koan, the koan that stands for all koans, the exemplar and representative, confusing, irritating, mysterious, beautiful, and freeing, a gateway into the *isness* of life, where things are exactly what they are and have not yet become problems. It begins by looking at the question of whether we are alienated or whether we participate fully in life. It comes from a long dialogue with an ancient, twinkly, Chinese grandmaster called Zhaozhou. Here is the full version from *The Book of Serenity*, as translated by Joan Sutherland and me:

> A monk asked Zhaozhou, "Does a dog have buddha nature or not?"
> "Yes," replied Zhaozhou,
> "Then why did it jump into that bag of fur?"
> "It knew what it was doing and that's why it dogged."
> Another time a monk asked Zhaozhou, "Does a dog have buddha nature or not?"
> "No."

"All beings have buddha nature. Why doesn't a dog have it?"

"Because it's beginning to awaken in the world of ignorance."[1]

Teachers usually offer the student the one word "No" or "Mu." There is a long history to this tactic and it was how I first encountered the koan, reading about it in books. It offered a completely different way of approaching the world, something that, given the confused state of my mind at that time, seemed worth trying. I took the koan up by myself without a teacher and made all the beginner's errors, treating the koan more or less as a gadget. I tried to discover the use of it, the way a hunter-gatherer would deal with a toaster found by the trail—pulling on the cord, banging it on the ground, using it as a mirror. "This gadget doesn't seem to be working," I said to myself, scheming and plotting. The other error I made was to treat *myself* as a gadget that had to be tuned to receive the koan—more scheming and plotting.

Eventually, I can't really say why, things changed. I allowed myself to spend all my time with the koan even while I did other things. Especially I allowed myself to persevere without quite knowing why. This meant enlarging my idea of koan work and enlarging my idea of what a "me" was. I stopped identifying with what my mind was telling me, including what it was telling me about meditation. At any given moment, no matter what I was doing, or how busy or tormented my mind appeared to be, I didn't have to think that the koan wasn't present.

When the koan started to change me, there was a figure/ground reversal. I no longer had to remember the koan because that process had become autonomous. In the way that a poet learns a craft and then finds that the poem appears beneath or before the level of volition, the koan showed up without being summoned. I still remember how difficulties disappeared, and I sat in the darkness and became as large as the night with the rain raining through my body. The kindness of the universe seemed to have no limit. And in some sense that moment is still going on.

I like the koan being about a dog. It addresses the question of whether we can actually change, whether we defeat ourselves, and the way we often rule ourselves out. I live with a border collie puppy and in the morning she is complete in the world, and amazingly kinetic. Her heart beats quickly, and she hurtles toward me on her big paddy paws—she is now grown enough that occasionally when she leaps and I'm sitting on the floor she descends from above, a surprise, flailing and excited. There is no flaw in her universe. The koan is about me, about my buddha nature in any state I happen to be in. If I think life is hard, that thought is the dog with buddha nature, and peace is exactly inside that thought when it jumps on me. Then the apparent difficulty of life suddenly isn't a difficulty.

The second thing this koan is good for is as a navigation aid in territory without maps. Once the gates in the mind start to open, the koan is pretty much all you have for navigation. The koan helps you to walk through the dim and bright paths that you have never walked before. You don't have to return to knowing things and assessing your value and skill, and working off the nice map you bought along the way. When you feel as if you are in a dark passage or not getting anywhere, all that is necessary is not to believe those thoughts about being lost in twisty passages. The koan is a nice substitute for wrestling around with your fears.

And if you do resort to your maps, you will find that they are temporary, you don't quite believe in them, and the world itself is more interesting than your explanations of it.

Everyone is new to this koan since everyone is new to this moment. You can drop everything you think you know about this koan and everything you are eager to tell others that you have already learned. Then the koan can find the space to meet you.

Lots of people from lots of cultures have been changed by this koan and I find that an encouraging thought. While it is exhilarating to step off the cliff of everything that has already convinced you, it can also be frightening. It can be consoling to know that lots of other people, who like ourselves have no special aptitudes, have found that this koan saved their lives.

With all the difficulties and absurdities of the koan path my own reaction has been gratitude to the ancient teachers who invented this way of changing my mind. They found a way to talk down through the centuries, a language that helps unshape what I see so that I can see that it is the first day of the world. That is an unforgettable gift.

Koans are a great treasure of civilization and their beauty is just beginning to be understood in the west. After an initial promising start in the West, koans came to be considered esoteric and by a couple of decades ago were being neglected as a method. One of the decisions I made at that time was to teach only koans and nothing but koans and to develop new ways of teaching them, ways that might fit Western culture. Along those lines, the teachers in this book are opening many possibilities for us. The koan Mu or No is the quarter horse of Zen practice— resilient, durable, and adaptable. It's been used so often, in so many countries and eras, that there are many different and contradictory ways to encounter it. It is a mysterious guide, a hidden friend, a vial of ancient light, a rodent that undermines the foundations. *The Book of Mu* gathers different ways to accompany this great koan so you can try it for yourself and find what works for you.

I can tell that James Ford and Melissa Blacker have written a good book because word has gotten around and people are already asking me for the manuscript. When you read this book, a practice will leap out at you, and an impulse will rise out of your own heart to meet it. If you follow that practice with all your heart, or even with sort of most of your heart, and listen to how it's going and adapt what you do, and follow some more, this koan will change your life. You will come to your own, unique understanding of freedom. You might get enlightened. That's what this book is for—to give you a practice that works.

Pacific Zen Institute
Santa Rosa, California

Notes

1. The last line of the koan is literally, "It has activity [or karma] consciousness." This is an Indian system of describing layers of the mind. "Activity consciousness" has the sense that through the agency of ignorance an unenlightened mind begins to be disturbed or awakened.

Introduction

James Ishmael Ford and Melissa Myozen Blacker

The koan is not a conundrum to be solved by a nimble wit.
It is not a verbal psychiatric device for shocking the disintegrated
ego of a student into some kind of stability. Nor, in my opinion, is
it ever a paradoxical statement except to those who view it from
outside. When the koan is resolved it is realized to be a simple
and clear statement made from the state of consciousness
which it has helped to awaken.

—from *The Zen Koan,* by Ruth Fuller Sasaki

THE FIRST VOLUME published in this series, *The Art of Just Sitting,* explores the practice of silent illumination, the practice called *shikantaza.* The next one, *Sitting With Koans,* explores koan study generally, the other great practice of the Zen way. This volume takes a single koan—called variously "Zhaozhou's Dog," "the Mu koan," "the Wu koan" (its Chinese variant use), "the No koan," and "the First koan," and often just "Mu"—and gives it focused attention. Even if you read this volume first, we strongly encourage you to explore the other two books to more deeply understand how this one koan fits into the scheme of Zen practice.

As to Mu itself: the Zen teacher Robert Aitken, one of the elders of Western Zen, has said, "I am still working on Mu, a great mystery, though it is no longer alien." The essays, texts, and Dharma talks collected in this book are attempts by Zen teachers from the past and present to point their students toward clarifying, for themselves, this great mystery of Mu. Anyone who has encountered a teacher of koan Zen or been intrigued by the great questions of this human existence—"Who am I?" or "What is the meaning of my life?" or any of the host of other forms these questions can take—has probably encountered Mu.

Mu, a Japanese word meaning "not," "non-," "nothing," "no," was spoken centuries ago in China by a great Zen master, the peerless master

Zhaozhou (called Joshu in Japanese)—and this word continues to resonate down through the ages to our time. And many people have had quite a lot to say about it. In this book, you will find many different ways of meeting and understanding this koan—and many words about this one word.

As most people who have read even a little about Zen may know, the word *koan* comes from the Chinese *gongan,* and means "public case," as in a court document. A koan might be seen as an assertion about reality and an invitation to an intimate response to that assertion. Or perhaps it can be said a koan is an expression of the boundless nature of all things and explores how that boundlessness interacts, informs, and completes the particularities of our lives. Or, perhaps more prosaically, but maybe more usefully, a koan provides a point in Zen to be made clear.

Both of the editors of this volume have been touched deeply and personally by koan practice and in particular by the koan Mu.

My (JF) experience of koan introspection began with one of my teachers suggesting "that silent illumination is a mature practice for mature people, but that for more difficult cases such as the likes of *you,* koans can shake one up and put us on the right path." I spent the first ten years or so of my Zen practice engaged in silent illumination, and today it is again my baseline practice. But it wasn't until I found the koan way that I found myself opened up, my heart broken and restored, and my place in the world revealed.

And I (MB) found Mu after many years of working with a different opening question, the "Who am I?" inquiry. After some time, my teacher asked me to live with Mu for a while, and by carrying this little word with me, as Wumen advises, "day and night," the world opened up to my heart/mind dramatically and exquisitely. To this day, I return to Mu within my main practice of shikantaza as a reminder and as a friend.

THE HISTORY OF KOAN INTROSPECTION

No one knows the precise origin of koan introspection as a distinct spiritual discipline. Some trace its origins in the Taoist tradition of "pure conversation." Rinzai Zen priest and scholar Victor Sogen Hori, the premier writer on koan introspection in the English language today, advances a compelling argument that the distant ancestor of koan study can be found in the Chinese tradition of literary games.

Whatever its origins, it is a practice most closely associated with the Linji or Rinzai branch of Zen, one of the two schools that dominate modern-day Zen. Two teachers in particular gave koan introspection the shape most Western Zen practitioners will encounter: the Chinese priest Dahui Zonggao and the Japanese priest Hakuin Ekaku. Writings from both of these great teachers on the koan Mu are included in this volume.

Dahui, a twelfth-century Linji-lineage master, is often identified as one of the first teachers to exclusively emphasize koan introspection. Having read the *Record of Yunmen* as a young man, he was inspired to undertake the Zen way. His first teacher, Zhan Tangzhun, pointed out that the young monk's inability to achieve awakening was due to his pride and intellectual acumen. In other words, Dahui's understanding of the outside prevented him from entering the inside.

When Dahui's teacher was on his deathbed, he directed him to go to Master Yuanwu Keqin—the master who would be remembered as the compiler of *The Blue Cliff Record*, one of the most important classic collections of koans. Eventually Yuanwu gave his Dharma transmission to Dahui who in 1137 would become abbot of Nengren Temple. While there he began to collect his own multivolume anthology of koans and became a strong advocate of using the koan explored in depth in this volume, "Zhaozhou's Dog." In Dahui's teachings it is possible to see the beginnings of the approach that would flower with the eighteenth-century Japanese master Hakuin.

In the years he was abbot at Nengren Temple, war and famine plagued the country, and more than half the hundred monks in Dahui's monastery died. In 1158 he became abbot at Mount Jing near Hangshou, and it was during these years that Dahui began to publicly criticize what he saw as an overemphasis on silent illumination practice then current among many Zen communities. Instead he held up the possibilities inherent in koan introspection. While he was personally quite close to Hongzhi Zhengjue, the great advocate of silent illumination at that time (who would interestingly request that Dahui serve as his executor upon his death) the famous division between koan introspection and silent illumination began at the temples of these two teachers.

We find it compelling that the masters of these monasteries were in fact friends, each respecting the other while at the same time criticizing a too-one-sided clinging to this practice or that. This friendship and disagreement is a powerful model for us as we engage with our various Zen practices today. Sadly, however, in the ensuing centuries, the division represented by silent illumination and koan introspection would continue to exist, with sectarian narrow-mindedness raging strong.

Over time koan introspection would gradually ossify, losing its dynamism and becoming more an exercise in formalism, mere study, though over the generations surely there were some who continued to find insight through deeply investigating koans. The next major development in koan introspection came in the eighteenth century with the Japanese master Hakuin Ekaku.

Hakuin and his Dharma successors are of particular importance because of Hakuin's systematization of the practice of koan introspection, helping forge it into a reliable tool of training that, when wielded by a skillful teacher, could bring powerful nondual insights to one's practice. Dahui and Hakuin gave koan introspection its unique shape and placed it as a clearly distinct practice within the Zen schools.

THE NATURE OF KOAN INTROSPECTION

So, what is koan introspection? What does it mean to engage a koan as a spiritual discipline within the line of Dahui and Hakuin? These are important questions especially since koans and koan study are some of the perennially misunderstood elements of Zen. Indeed, the practice at the heart of koan introspection is unique to the Zen schools and has no significant corollary anywhere else in the world's spiritual traditions.

Unfortunately a great deal of what has been published in the English language only clouds the matter. This is partially the fault of the Zen tradition itself, which tends to guard the koan way as an esoteric treasure. And it is partially the fault of some European and American commentators who frequently and profoundly misunderstand both Zen and koan study.

The various scholars who have taken up the subject of koan introspection too often seem like the blind men described by the Buddha: investigating an elephant and interpreting the leg, tail, or trunk as if it were the whole. As Sogen Hori writes, these scholars explore Zen's "nondual epistemology, its ritual and performance, its language, [or] its politics," and such perspectives can indeed help clarify how the koan can be engaged at different levels. Some point to the shortcomings of Zen institutions; some examine how koan study can be and in fact is abused or misused—all speak to one truth or another. But none of these considerations captures the essence of koan introspection.

It should be noted that some "pure" Soto Zen teachers also engage with koans, though this is usually in a discursive way, as objects of focused conversation among practitioners. These conversations are for the most part guided by mature practitioners who often have great insight but little or no formal training in koan introspection, and especially may be lacking in the particular knowledge of Master Hakuin's refined system. Without a doubt, contemporary Soto practitioners can profit from this dialogistic engagement, as can we all. We and they may find moments of startling clarity or gentle prodding toward greater depth in our practice through such deep conversations. In fact this dialogistic approach is one (among several) of the more traditional or "orthodox" uses of koans.

The Dahui/Hakuin legacy of koan practice, however, is more dramatic and intimate than the critical engagement of a spiritual literary tradition, even as a practice grounded in the discipline of silent illumination. To distinguish these disciplines, let us consider the emerging use of the term "koan introspection" for the Dahui/Hakuin style of koan engagement. And it is this style that is the primary focus of the selections in this book.

GREAT FAITH, GREAT DOUBT, GREAT DETERMINATION

Traditional Dahui/Hakuin koan introspection is about our possible awakening, our turning in a heartbeat from delusion to awakening. To achieve this, Zen practice requires three things: great doubt, great faith, and great determination, points first articulated by the Linji master Gao-feng Yuanmiao. These become particularly obvious through koan introspection.

The idea of great doubt might seem startling in this context. Matters of religion often seem to be about faith and sometimes, sadly, even about the crushing of doubters. In Zen, however, doubt is the universal solvent, cast upon every thought, every emotion, every idea. It is meant to be a relentless and intense wondering. As such, this "great doubt" must not be confused with a merely dismissive variety of skeptical doubt. We can catch a hint of the true meaning of great doubt in a reply from Robert Aitken when asked what he thought about contemporary deconstructionist philosophy. He replied that it could be valuable so long as it includes the necessary step of deconstructing *itself*. Turning doubt on ourselves, we strive to manifest the truth behind that delightful contemporary bumper sticker "Don't Believe Everything You Think." Although the invitation here is even more radical: Don't believe *anything* you think.

Koans cultivate and make profound use of this great doubt. Contrary to what some might say on the subject, koans are not meaningless phrases meant to break through to a transrational consciousness (whatever we might imagine that phrase refers to). Rather, koans are a direct pointing to reality, an invitation for us to taste water and to know for ourselves whether it is cool or warm. While there is an aspect in koan introspection that is beyond discursive thought, this practice very much includes our experiences of judging and assessing. The fundamental matter includes everything.

In the hallway of James's house hangs a large calligraphy of the character Mu by the Zen teacher John Tarrant. Tarrant Roshi appends a comment to the character: "Mu fills all of space. No one ever falls out of it."

Great faith is discovered within great doubt. It doesn't take much faith to begin a spiritual practice like Zen. All one really needs to begin is a feeling that something positive might come out of the discipline. While this is a belief, it is of a relatively minor sort. Now, when one finds herself or himself on such a spiritual path, there probably is some deeper, perhaps less well articulated, hope—that the dissatisfactions of our lives can be resolved and may be illuminated by this practice. Quickly we discover various intimations that enlarge that meager faith. This evolving faith becomes Great Faith, deserving those capital letters, within our growing openness to what is, and our growing confidence in what we encounter as really being of use on the way. Great Faith starts as curiosity and blossoms into a dynamic engagement, a dance of the soul.

In koan introspection, doubt and faith travel together. Each informs the other. It is our relentless presence to doubt and faith that takes us to the gate of nondual insight. Indeed both the path to the gate and the gate itself are discovered within that relentlessness, that willingness to not turn away. This relentlessness is that Great Determination. Other good words besides determination might be energy or perhaps courage, great energy and great courage.

From an instrumentalist view of koan introspection, words like *Mu* or phrases like "What is the sound of the single hand?" or "What is your original face from before your parents were born?" are often mistakenly assumed to be meaningless. It is assumed that the "point" of such koans is to simply "startle" the discursive mind into some kind of transrational state. But this understanding of koans simply posits a new dualism: a "lower" discursive consciousness and a "higher" nondiscursive state. This is not what koan introspection is about.

Rather, as we push through any koan—experiencing great doubt, great faith, and great determination—we find the exact identity between our ordinary consciousness and fundamental openness. Nondual reality includes subject and object, each itself and freely transposing with the other; first this, now that, sometimes one drops away, sometimes the other, sometimes both drop away, sometimes one emerges from the other, sometimes both emerge together—but we *rest* nowhere. Resting nowhere and moving fluidly among these perspectives is the true practice of koan introspection.

VARIETIES OF KOANS AND KOAN INTROSPECTION

In China and Korea the primary form of koan engagement is through a *huatou* (in Chinese; *wato* in Japanese), which literally means "word head." In this practice, we are given one single koan, which is seen as being useful for a lifetime. Occasionally, for various reasons, a practitioner will take on a second or even more rarely a third case. But the heart of this is found in fully throwing oneself into one koan. This koan becomes a touchstone of our practice: it is a place to put our doubt, to cultivate great doubt, to allow the various revelations of great faith, and to focus our great energy.

In Japan and the Japanese-derived koan lineages in the West, koan introspection has taken on a new dimension. By the eighteenth century, various Japanese Rinzai teachers began introducing what one could rightly call *koan curricula*. These were programs of koan study through which a student might "pass" during the course of many years. While there is some dispute over who actually developed this system, it is usually believed to have culminated in the work of the great master Hakuin Ekaku and his principal students or, at least, in the work of teachers who followed them. This program is used by Japanese Rinzai to this day—and it is the source of the modern reform used in some of the Soto schools that also have an inherited tradition of koan introspection, the so-called Harada-Yasutani curriculum.

It should also be noted that the Korean master Seung Sahn has introduced a collection of koans used in the Kwan Um School that resembles the Hakuin system although its practitioners are uncomfortable with the terms "system" or "curriculum." As the Kwan Um School is perhaps the largest Zen lineage in the West, one may well encounter this new and creative use of koan introspection. Interestingly, Master Seung Sahn was not particularly intrigued with the Mu koan and it does not have the prominence in his school that it does in Japanese-derived koan Zen. Within the Japanese-derived koan schools, koan introspection begins with a step reminiscent of the Chinese original: the beginning student is given a "breakthrough" koan, a case specifically meant to elicit an initial experience of nonduality. The Japanese term for this koan is *shokan*, or "first barrier." A student might spend years struggling with this first koan; only rarely does someone pass through the breakthrough koan quickly. And, usually if one does, that person has been practicing silent illumination for some years prior to taking up this practice.

A breakthrough koan might be "What is your face before your parents were born?" or Hakuin's own question "What is the sound of the single hand?" But most commonly it is Zhaozhou's Mu. This simple koan is the most common of the gateways to koan practice.

The talks and essays that follow explore this koan in great depth, so we won't go into its shape with any detail in this brief introduction.

Instead we'll simply outline some of what one encounters in the way of koan introspection.

We throw ourselves into the great matter, allowing the doubt to rise. At some point we may try critical analysis; at another point, it may become a mantra—chanted, breathed, whispered, yelled. And each time we think we gain some insight, we take it into the interview room where, most probably, our teacher will reject our response.

My (JF) teacher once told me that "awakening is always an accident"—and we (JF and MB) tell our own students this today. There is no obvious causal relationship between nondual insight and anything we might do or not do. But if awakening is an accident, certain practices can help us become accident-prone. Koan practice is particularly effective at this.

If we open ourselves to this great adventure—with due diligence along with our doubt, faith, and energy—eventually it will happen: We are hit by a bus and everything changes. Or, perhaps the bus just grazes us as it passes by. But even that graze is valuable. This is the point of most koans. They give us an opportunity to break out of what we thought the world had been all about for us and encounter it anew.

When one has demonstrated insight into the basic matter, the teacher trained in koan introspection may go on to ask "checking questions," which reveal how nuanced our insight is. In the case of a breakthrough koan, there might be dozens up to a hundred checking questions. As we move through the breakthrough koan into other cases, there are usually several checking questions for each case beyond the central point.

There are a few books to be found that purport to give "answers" to koans. Occasionally, for reasons that completely elude us, people will take other student's answers and present them to their teacher in the interview room as if some formal or official "passing" of a koan were somehow the important thing, and not our own liberation from our own suffering. It doesn't take too many checking questions to reveal the true quality of a student's insight.

There are a number of ways to categorize koans, and over the years various systems developed to help clarify how one may engage them. A contemporary typology developed by Seung Sahn includes ten categories, which are explored in the book *Ten Gates: The Kong-an Teachings of Zen Master Seung Sahn.* Hakuin's system is the most commonly represented in contemporary Western koan studies, although even it has variations. Hakuin suggested there are five types of koan, the Japanese terms for which are *hoshin, kikan, gonsen, nanto,* and *goi jujukin.*

Hoshin means "dharmakaya" ("Dharma body"—*kaya* being the Sanskrit word for "body"). These koans are concerned with our fundamental insight into nonduality. *Kikan,* or "dynamic action" koans, reveal the activity of emptiness. *Gonsen* or "explication of words" are often quite long and involved. Traditionally one is expected to memorize each of these koans and recite them in front of the teacher before actually engaging their points: for many of us simply memorizing the case can take longer than dealing with it face-to-face in the interview.

Nanto koans are "difficult to pass through"—or at least they seem to have been so for old Master Hakuin, who alluded to eight such cases. It isn't precisely clear what this designation really means. Sogen Hori quotes one roshi who remarked bluntly how "the nanto koans have no significance beyond the fact that Hakuin found them difficult to pass through." In our notes from teachers in our lineage, there are occasional references to one koan or another as being "particularly difficult." However, they were not all the ones that we have found problematic—nor are they reliably that for our students. We've come to suspect that all who walk this path each find their own nanto koans.

Goi jujukin koans are actually comprised of two sets of koans. In Japanese Rinzai the koans one first completes are the ten grave precepts of moral and ethical action. One also usually includes the three refuges of Buddha, Dharma, and Sangha as well as the three pure precepts of ceasing from evil, practicing good, and actualizing good for others. Together with the ten grave precepts, these crown the formal study of koans. There can be hundreds of questions derived from the precepts, the exact number varying from one teacher to another. One then finishes with the Five Ranks, an ancient system of categorizations that recapitulate all that one has encountered over the years of koan study. In the Harada-Yasutani curriculum, the order is reversed, culminating in the investigation of the precepts as koans.

In Japan a student of koan Zen also engages a practice of *jakugo,* or "capping phrases." These are literary tags drawn from the range of East

Asian cultures and compiled in various books. Having completed the checking questions for some koan case, one must then find the appropriate phrase to "cap" the case. Capping phrases are largely eliminated in the Harada-Yasutani curriculum. This is also mostly true for the more "orthodox" Rinzai programs followed in the West.

Capping phrases, while undoubtedly useful, are largely extraneous to the larger point of koan work. Rather than helping to open the eye, this discipline invites the student to see how her or his opening to the world has been anticipated in the rich literature of East Asian culture. In the West what seems to be the original spirit of capping has been revitalized where following some cases a student is asked to compose a verse in appreciation. A few teachers have also been experimenting with creating Western capping phrase collections. It is, however, much too early to see where this spirit of experimentation will lead.

The Unfolding of Koan Curricula

The koan curricula of the Harada-Yasutani system (which ultimately derives from Hakuin's disciple's disciple Kosen Takuju) might be described like this: After encountering a breakthrough koan and satisfactorily investigating it and responding to up to a hundred checking questions around that koan, we pass through a collection of brief cases that set the form for future practice. This "miscellaneous collection" may consist of anywhere between twenty and a hundred koans. These are "in-house" collections not usually published, although a Christian Zen master in the Sanbo Kyodan, Elaine MacInnes, has written *The Flowing Bridge*, a luminous collection of comments on the formal Sanbokyodan miscellaneous collection. An excerpt from her book is included in this volume. After this, we generally work through several classic collections, normally the *Gateless Gate*, the *Blue Cliff Record*, the *Book of Equanimity*, and Jokin Keizan's *Record of Transmitting the Light*.

The first two collections are associated with the historic Linji/Rinzai tradition; the last two are traditional Soto collections and represent the reformist and syncretistic inclinations of the Harada-Yasutani curriculum. While the varying traditions deriving from Master Hakuin may use somewhat different collections, the arc of training remains the same.

In Japanese Rinzai, according to Sogen Hori, two curricula are associated with the two principal heirs of Hakuin. In the Takuju school (which as already noted is also the source of the Harada-Yasutani curriculum) after the breakthrough students begin the *Gateless Gate* and then investigate the *Blue Cliff Record*. The third book is the *Shumon Kattoshu*, only recently published in English as *Entangling Vines*. The last collection is the *Chin'u-shu*, "the Collection of Poison Wings," which is not to our knowledge currently available in English.

The other principal line of Hakuin's Zen, through another of his disciples' disciple Ien Inzan, uses its own internally generated list of koans, rather than those found in the traditional collections. This school's style is considered more direct and immediate, if by repute somewhat "rougher" in approach than within the Takuju style.

The two schools have minor stylistic differences. The Inzan school is said to be a bit more dynamic, while the Takuju school is said to be a bit more gentle and meticulous. Nevertheless, we can find teachers of either temperament in either tradition. And each school easily recognizes the work of the other.

In Japan, someone who "completes" formal koan study might have been practicing for thirty years or more. Without the capping phrases, the Harada-Yasutani curriculum is often completed in as little as ten years from "passing" the breakthrough koan, although usually it takes considerably longer. It appears that the Western Rinzai koan curricula can be passed through in about the same amount of time as the Harada-Yasutani.

In fact most people who take up koan study never complete the formal curriculum—and this isn't seen as a problem. Koans are really just invitations to practice. We do koans to deepen and clarify our zazen, to engage the matter of life and death. Truthfully, we never "complete" our koan work. In schools that use a koan introspection curriculum, however, completion of the formal curriculum is often a necessary, if not sufficient, condition for becoming a teacher.

THE KOAN MU

So, we return to our exploration of Mu. As we have said, of all the breakthrough koans, Mu is the koan most commonly encountered, the heart of most Zen practitioner's koan work. Mu is, from this view, arguably Zen's most important koan.

The scholar Andy Ferguson notes the idea of "penetrating the Mu obstruction" appears in Chinese Zen texts as far back as 730 or so, and he adds that "some textual evidence suggests it was part of Bodhidharma's teachings." The earliest reference to a dog in the context of buddha nature dates from the early ninth century, possibly half a century before Zhaozhou took up the matter with his student.

Ferguson translates the text of that earliest known account from an early lamp anthology, the *Ching-te ch'uan-teng lu*:

> A monk asked, "Does a dog have buddha nature?"
> The master said, "Yes."
> The monk said, "Do you have buddha nature?"
> The master said, "No."
> The monk then said, "All beings have buddha nature. Why is it that you alone don't have it?"
> The master said, "Because I'm not all beings."
> The monk asked, "If you're not all beings, then are you Buddha?"
> The master said, "I'm not Buddha."
> The monk said, "Then what are you?"
> The master said, "I'm not a thing."
> The monk said, "Can you be seen or conceived of?"
> The master said, "It [me] is inconceivable and its meaning can't be obtained. Therefore it is called inconceivable."

The koan mu appears in a long form as case 18 in the collection *The Book of Equanimity* (see John Daido Loori's chapter in this book for Mu in that context). But we encounter the koan Mu in its most succinct form in Wumen Huikai's classic collection the *Wumenguan* (or, in Japanese, *Mumonkan*), the "Gateless Barrier." Master Wumen set it as the first case, attaching a brief commentary and then an appreciative verse (reprinted in this volume, as translated by Robert Aitken). The teacher in the koan story, Zhaozhou Congshen, was a ninth-century Chinese Chan/Zen master. After his first awakening at the age of eighteen, he studied Chan with his teacher Nanquan Puyuan until Nanquan's death, and then went on pilgrimage to deepen his practice through the challenge of meeting other teachers. He eventually settled down and taught until his death, apparently at the age of 120, having transmitted the Dharma to thirteen heirs.

Wumen himself lived in the thirteenth century. His teacher Yuelin Shiguan gave him the koan "Wu." Here is the account of his awakening to Wu from Andy Ferguson's *Zen's Chinese Heritage*:

> Wumen worked with this famous koan for six years without progress. Finally, he vowed not to sleep until he penetrated the heart of this Zen gate. Finally, as he stood in the Dharma hall, he heard the bell sound for the midday meal and suddenly realized profound enlightenment. He then wrote a verse that included the following:
>
> *A clear sky and shining sun,*
> *A great thunderclap,*
> *Instantly all beings' eyes are opened,*
> *And the myriad things come together.*
>
> The following day, Wumen entered Yuelin's room to gain confirmation of his experience.
> Yuelin said, "Where did you see these gods and devils?"
> Wumen shouted
> Yuelin also shouted.
> Wumen shouted again.
> In this exchange Wumen's enlightenment was confirmed.

THE BOOK OF MU

History is history, and now is now. Zhaozhou's dog, your own buddha nature, and life itself can only be encountered in this moment. We encourage you to read this volume in any way that supports your investigation into what it means to live a life of freedom and aliveness. You can read it in sequence, or dip into it randomly. There are so many different ways of pointing at Mu, and to the practice of sitting with this apparently simple and seemingly obscure koan. You may find yourself drawn to and inspired by the words or approach of one teacher, and confused by or averse to the words or approach of another. We encourage you to use whatever is useful in encouraging you to discover the truth of Mu for yourself, and let the rest fall away.

All of these many words about this one word are pointers toward your own intimate relationship to the koan Mu, to your own buddha nature. The sincere young monk and the venerable teacher Zhaozhou are alive right now, ready to accompany you on this journey of discovery. They truly are, after all, you yourself.

ON THE TRANSLITERATION OF NAMES

WE'VE TRIED to minimally edit the talks and essays that follow. One consequence is a variety of transliteration choices for proper names. Today the standard form for transliterating Chinese names is Pinyin, however many of these talks were composed when Wade-Giles was the standard. In addition, Japanese Zen has given all the Chinese teachers names easier for the Japanese to pronounce, and several of the following talks use those names. So, Zhaozhou is the Pinyin, Chao-chou is the Wade Giles, and Joshu is the Japanese for the same person. And there are two talks that use the Korean JoJu for Zhaozhou. The following is a table showing the variations for all names used by the various teachers, with their Chinese transliterations in Pinyin and Wade-Giles form, and their Japanese *romaji* transliteration.

PINYIN	WADE-GILES	ROMAJI
Dahui Zonggao	Ta-hui Tsung-kao	Daie Soko
Dongshan Liangjie	Tung-shan Liang-chieh	Tozan Ryokai
Gaofeng Yuanmiao	Kao-feng Yuan-miao	Koho Gemmyo
Hongzhi Zhengjue	Hung-chih Cheng-chueh	Wanshi Shogaku
Linji Yixuan	Lin-chi I-hsuan	Rinzai Gigen
Mazu Daoyi	Ma-tsu Tao-i	Baso Doitsu
Nanquan Puyuan	Nan-ch'uan P'u-yuan	Nansen Fugan
Nanyue Huairang	Nan-yueh Huai-jang	Nangaku Ejo
Wumen Huikai	Wu-men Hui-k'ai	Mumon Ekai
Xingshan Weikuan	Hsing-Shan Wei-K'uan	Ikan Kozen
Yuanwu Keqin	Yuan-wu K'e-ch'in	Engo Kokugon
Yuelin Shiguan	Yueh-lin Shih-kuan	Gatsurin Shikan
Zhaozhou Congshen	Chao-chou Ts'ung-shen	Joshu Jushin

THE KOAN MU: TEXT, COMMENTARY, AND VERSE

Wumen Huikai

Translated by Robert Aitken

THE CASE

*A monk asked Chao-chou, "Has the dog buddha nature or not?"
Chao-chou said, "Mu."*

WU-MEN'S COMMENT

For the practice of Zen it is imperative that you pass through the barrier set up by the Ancestral Teachers. For subtle realization it is of the utmost importance that you cut off the mind road. If you do not pass the barrier of the ancestors, if you do not cut off the mind road, then you are a ghost clinging to bushes and grasses.

What is the barrier of the Ancestral Teachers? It is just this one word "Mu"—the one barrier of our faith. We call it the Gateless Barrier of the Zen tradition. When you pass through this barrier, you will not only interview Chao-chou intimately. You will walk hand in hand with all the Ancestral Teachers in the successive generations of our lineage—the hair of your eyebrows entangled with theirs, seeing with the same eyes, hearing with the same ears. Won't that be fulfilling? Is there anyone who would not want to pass this barrier?

So, then, make your whole body a mass of doubt, and with your three hundred and sixty bones and joints and your eighty-four thousand hair follicles concentrate on this one word "Mu." Day and night, keep digging into it. Don't consider it to be nothingness. Don't think in terms of "has" and "has not." It is like swallowing a red-hot iron ball. You try to vomit it out, but you can't.

Gradually you purify yourself, eliminating mistaken knowledge and attitudes you have held from the past. Inside and outside become one. You're like a mute person who has had a dream—you know it for yourself alone.

Suddenly Mu breaks open. The heavens are astonished, the earth is shaken. It is as though you have snatched the great sword of General Kuan. When you meet the Buddha, you kill the Buddha. When you meet Bodhidharma, you kill Bodhidharma. At the very cliff edge of birth-and-death, you find the Great Freedom. In the Six Worlds and the Four Modes of Birth, you enjoy a samadhi of frolic and play.

How, then, should you work with it? Exhaust all your life energy on this one word "Mu." If you do not falter, then it's done! A single spark lights your Dharma candle.

WU-MEN'S VERSE

> *Dog, buddha nature—*
> *the full presentation of the whole;*
> *with a bit of "has" or "has not"*
> *body is lost, life is lost.*

HISTORICAL PERSPECTIVE:
THE FIRST TEACHERS OF THE KOAN WAY

Three Commentaries

Dahui Zonggao

Translated by J.C.Cleary

1. To Ch'en Li-jen
Contemplating "No"

A MONK ASKED CHAO-CHOU, "Does a dog have buddha nature or not?" Chao-chou said, "No." This one word "no" is a knife to sunder the doubting mind of birth and death. The handle of this knife is in one's own hand alone: you can't have anyone else wield it for you: to succeed you must take hold of it yourself. You consent to take hold of it yourself only if you can abandon your life. If you cannot abandon your life, just keep to where your doubt remains unbroken for a while: suddenly you'll consent to abandon your life, and then you'll be done. Only then will you believe that when quiet it's the same as when noisy, when noisy it's the same as when quiet, when speaking it's the same as when silent, and when silent it's the same as when speaking. You won't have to ask anyone else, and naturally you won't accept the confusing talk of false teachers.

During your daily activities twenty-four hours a day, you shouldn't hold to birth and death and the Buddha Path as existent, nor should you deny them as nonexistent. Just contemplate this: A monk asked Chao-chou, "Does a dog have buddha nature or not?" Chao-chou said, "No."

2. To Chang An-kuo
Contemplating a Saying

Before emotional consciousness has been smashed, the mind-fire burns bright. At just such a time, just take a saying you have doubts about to arouse and awaken yourself. For example: A monk asked Chao-chou, "Does a dog have buddha nature or not?" Chao-chou said, "No." Just bring this up to arouse and awaken yourself. Whatever side you come at it from, that's not it, you're wrong. Moreover, don't use mind to await enlightenment. And you shouldn't take up the saying in the citation of it. And you shouldn't understand it as the original subtlety, or discuss it as existent or nonexistent, or assess it as the nothingness of true nothingness. And you shouldn't sit in the bag of unconcern. And you shouldn't understand it in sparks struck from stone or in the brilliance of a lightning flash. There should be no place to employ your mind. When there's no place for mind, don't be afraid of falling into emptiness—on the contrary, this is a good place. Suddenly the rat enters a hollow ox horn, [that is, discriminating consciousness reaches an impasse] and then wrong views are cut off.

This affair is neither difficult nor easy. Only if you have already planted deep the seeds of transcendent wisdom, and served men of knowledge through vast eons without beginning, and developed correct knowledge and correct views, does it strike you continuously in your present conduct as you meet situations and encounter circumstances in the midst of radiant spiritual consciousness, like recognizing your own parents in a crowd of people. At such a time, you don't have to ask anyone else: naturally the seeking mind does not scatter and run off.

Yun-men said, "When you can't speak, it's there; when you don't speak, it's not there. When you can't discuss it, it's there; when you don't discuss it, it's not there." He also commented saying, "You tell me, what is it when you're not discussing it?" Fearing people wouldn't understand, he also said, "What else is it?"

3. To Tsung Chih-ko
Contemplating "No"

You inform me that as you respond to circumstances in your daily involvement with differentiated objects, you're never not in the Buddhadharma. You also say that amidst your daily activities and conduct you use the saying "A dog has no buddha nature" to clear away emotional defilements. If you make efforts like this, I'm afraid you'll never attain enlightened entry. Please examine what's under your feet: where do differentiated objects arise from? How can you smash emotional defilements in the midst of your activities with the saying "A dog has no buddha nature"? Who is it who can know he's clearing away emotional defilements?

Didn't Buddha say: "Sentient beings are inverted: they lose themselves and pursue things." Basically things have no inherent nature: those who lose themselves pursue them on their own. Originally objects are undifferentiated: those who lose themselves do their own differentiating. (You say) you have daily contact with differentiated objects, and you're also within the Buddhadharma. If you're in the Buddhadharma, it's not an object of differentiation; if you're among differentiated objects, then it's not the Buddhadharma. Pick one up, let one go—what end will there be?

At the Nirvana Assembly [when the Nirvana Sutra was expounded, just before the Buddha's death], the broad-browed butcher put down his slaughtering knife and immediately attained buddhahood where he stood. How could you have so much sadness and sorrow? In your daily activities as you respond to circumstances, as soon as you become aware of being involved with differentiated objects, just go to the differentiating to raise the saying "A dog has no buddha nature." Don't think of it as clearing away, and don't think of it as emotional defilement; don't think of it as differentiation, and don't think of it as the Buddhadharma—simply contemplate the saying "A dog has no buddha nature." Just bring up the word "No." And don't set your mind on it and await enlightenment. If you do, objects and the Buddhadharma are differentiated, emotional defilements and the saying "A dog has no buddha nature" are differentiated, interrupted and uninterrupted are differentiated, and encountering the confusion of emotional defilements so body and mind are unsettled and being able to know so many differentiations are also differentiated.

If you want to remove this disease, just contemplate the word "No." Just look at the broad-browed butcher putting down his knife and saying, "I am one of the thousand buddhas." True or false? If you assess it as false or true, again you plunge into objects of differentiation. It's not as good as cutting it in two with a single stroke. Don't think of before and after: if you think of before and after, this is more differentiating.

Hsuan-sha said this matter "Cannot be limited—the road of thought is cut off. It does not depend on an array of adornments—from the beginning it's been real and pure. Moving, acting, talking, laughing, clearly understanding wherever you are, there's nothing more lacking. People these days do not understand the truth in this, and vainly involve themselves with sensory phenomena, getting defiled all over and tied down everywhere. Even if they understand, sense objects are present in complex confusion, names and forms are not genuine, so they try to freeze their minds and gather in their attention, taking things and returning them to emptiness, shutting their eyes, hiding their eyes; if a thought starts up, they immediately demolish it; as soon as the slightest conception arises, they immediately press it down. Those with a view like this are outsiders who have fallen into empty annihilation, dead men whose spirits have not yet departed, dark and silent, without awareness or knowledge. They're "covering their ears to steal the bell," vainly deluding themselves.

All you said in your letter was the disease Hsuan-sha condemned—the perverted Ch'an of quiescent illumination, a pit to bury people in. You must realize this. When you bring up a saying, don't use so many maneuvers at all—just don't let there be any interruption whether you're walking, standing, sitting, or lying down. Don't discriminate joy and anger, sorrow and bliss. Just keep on bringing up the saying, raising it and raising it, looking and looking. When you feel there's no road for reason and no flavor, and in your mind you're oppressed and troubled, this is the place for each person to abandon his body and his life. Remember, don't shrink back in your mind when you see a realm like this—such a realm is precisely the scene for becoming a buddha and being an ancestral teacher.

And yet the false teachers of silent illumination just consider wordlessness as the ultimate principle, calling it the matter of "the Other Side of the Primordial Buddha," or of "before the Empty Eon." They don't believe there is a gate of enlightenment, and consider enlightenment as a lie, as something secondary, as an expedient word, as an expression to draw people in. This crowd deceive others and deceive themselves, lead others into error and go wrong themselves. You should also realize this.

In the conduct of your daily activities, as you're involved with differentiated objects, when you become aware of saving power, this is where you gain power. If you use the slightest power to uphold it, this is definitely a false method—it's not Buddhism. Just take the mind, so long-lasting, and bring it together with the saying "A dog has no buddha nature." Keep them together till the mind has no place to go—suddenly, it's like awakening from a dream, like a lotus flower opening, like parting the clouds and seeing the moon. When you reach such a moment, naturally you attain unity. Through the upsets and errors of your daily activities, just contemplate the word "No." Don't be concerned with awakening or not awakening, getting through or not getting through. All the buddhas of the three worlds were just unconcerned people, people for whom there is nothing; all the generations of ancestral teachers too were just people without concerns. An ancient worthy said, "just comprehend nothingness in the midst of things, unconcern amidst concerns: when seeing forms and hearing sounds, don't act blind and deaf." Another ancient worthy said, "Fools remove objects but don't obliterate mind; the wise wipe out mind without removing objects." Since in all places there's no mind, all kinds of objects of differentiation are nonexistent of themselves.

Gentlemen of affairs these days, though, are quick to want to understand Ch'an. They think a lot about the scriptural teachings and the sayings of the ancestral teachers, wanting to be able to explain clearly. They are far from knowing that this clarity is nonetheless an unclear matter. If you can penetrate the word "No," you won't have to ask anyone else about clear and unclear. I teach gentlemen of affairs to let go and make themselves dull—this is this same principle. And it's not bad to get first prize in looking dull, either—I'm just afraid you'll hand in an empty paper. What a laugh!

Two Commentaries

Eihei Dogen

Translated by Taigen Dan Leighton and Shohaku Okumura

1. Zhaozhou's Dogs and Dogen's Cats

This single story has a truth to be studied. Do you thoroughly understand this truth?

After a pause Dogen said: buddha nature has a nose to grasp, but a dog does not have a horn [to hold]. [With buddha nature] not avoiding entry into a skin-bag, cats give birth to cats.

2. The Whole Body of a Dog

> *[...] The whole body is a dog, the whole body is Buddha.*
> *Is this difficult to discuss or not?*
> *Selling them equally, you must buy them yourself.*
> *Do not grieve for losses or being one-sided.[1]*
> *Yes and no are two buddha natures,*
> *Not reaching the vitality of living beings.*
> *Although they resemble kumiss[2] and cheese,*
> *This is really like samadhi without thought.*

Notes

1. "Being one-sided" is *henko*, partial or inclined and withered. This might refer to taking only one side, but according to Menzan it may also mean that one side of the body is not working, as in a stroke victim.

2. Kumiss is a drink from fermented mare's milk, used by Asian nomads.

Great Doubt

Hakuin Ekaku

Translated by Philip Yampolsky

THE MASTER FA-YEN of Mount Wu-tsu has said in a verse:

> *The exposed sword of Chao-chou*
> *Gleams brilliantly like cold frost.*
> *If someone tries to ask about it,*
> *His body will at once be cut in two.*

To all intents and purposes, the study of Zen makes as its essential the resolution of the ball of doubt. That is why it is said: "At the bottom of great doubt lies great awakening. If you doubt fully you will awaken fully." Fo-kuo has said: "If you don't doubt the koans you suffer a grave disease." If those who study Zen are able to make the great doubt appear before them, a hundred out of a hundred, a thousand out of a thousand, will without fail attain awakening.

When a person faces the great doubt, before him there is in all directions only a vast and empty land without birth and without death, like a huge plain of ice extending ten thousand miles. As though seated within a vase of lapis lazuli surrounded by absolute purity, without his senses he sits and forgets to stand, stands and forgets to sit. Within his heart there is not the slightest thought or emotion, only the single word *Mu*. It is just as though he were standing in complete emptiness. At this time no fears arise, no thoughts creep in, and when he advances single-mindedly without retrogression, suddenly it will be as though a sheet of ice were broken or a jade tower had fallen. He will experience a great joy, one that never in forty years has he seen or heard. At this time "birth, death, and Nirvana will be like yesterday's dream, like the bubbles in the seas of the three thousand worlds, like the enlightened status of all the wise men and sages." This is known as the time of the great penetration of wondrous awakening, the state where the "ka" is shouted. It cannot be handed down, it cannot be explained; it is just like knowing for yourself by drinking it whether the water is hot or cold. The ten directions melt before the eyes, the three periods are penetrated in an instant of thought, What joy is there in the realms of man and Heaven that can compare with this?

This power can be obtained in the space of three to five days, if the student will advance determinedly. You may ask how one can make this great doubt appear. Do not favor a quiet place, do not shun a busy place, but always set in the area below the navel Chao-chou's Mu. Then asking what principle this Mu contains, if you discard all emotions, concepts, and thoughts and investigate single-mindedly, there is no one before whom the great doubt will not appear. When you call forth this great doubt before you in its pure and uninvolved form you may undergo an unpleasant and strange reaction. However, you must accept the fact the realization of so felicitous a thing as the Great Matter, the trampling of the multi-tiered gate of birth and death that has come down through endless kalpas, the penetration of the inner understanding of the basic enlightenment of all the Tathagatas of the ten directions, must involved a certain amount of suffering.

When you come to think about it, those who have investigated the Mu koan, brought before themselves, the great doubt, experienced the Great Death, and attained the great joy, are countless in number. Of those who called the Buddha's name and gained a small measure of benefit from it, I have heard of no more than two or three. The abbot of Eshin-in has called it the benefits of wisdom or the power of faith in the mind. If you investigate the Mu or the Three Pounds of Flax or some other koan, to obtain True Reality in your own body should take from two or three months to a year or a year and a half.

FOUNDING TEACHERS IN THE WEST

"Mu" by Soen Nakagawa

Teisho on Joshu's Dog

Shaku Soen

Translated by Victor Hori

THERE ARE FORTY-EIGHT KOANS in the *Mumonkan* and this koan on the word *Mu* comes right at the beginning. Why? The reason lies in a dog. Even the title of the *Mumonkan* comes from this *Mu*. For each of the forty-eight cases there is a commentary, but from olden times, people have particularly admired the commentary on Mu because it is very terse and gets the essentials. A monk came to Joshu and asked him, as an example case, "Does a dog have buddha nature or not?" It is clearly stated that in Buddha, all sentient beings without exception are endowed with the wisdom and virtue of the Tathagata. The monk had been laboring under this assumption. If even maggots have buddha nature, then does that barking dog there also have buddha nature, he was asking. In reply, Joshu said "Mu." *Mu* is written with the character which means "No, not have" but is it "no"? Is it the "no" of "yes and no"? Is it the "no" of refusal? What "no" is it? You cannot say it is *bodhi* or *nirvana*. You cannot say it is Buddha or God. Joshu just said *Mu*, that's all. But this monk did not have the least bit of an open eye, so there was no helping him. Since he took Joshu to be saying, "The dog does not have buddha nature," he started to quibble, "Isn't it a basic principle of Buddhism that all sentient beings have buddha nature? Why did the master just now say that the dog does not have buddha nature?" There's nothing you can say to someone like that, but Joshu replied, "It's because it had karmic consciousness"—that's so typical of him.

On another occasion, a monk came to Joshu and asked the same question, "Does a dog have buddha nature or not?" and this time Joshu answered "*U*." [*U* is written with the character for "yes," or "have."]

That's because for some reason, unlike the previous monk, this monk had been laboring under the assumption *Mu* meant "not have," so he too started quibbling, "And why does that which already has buddha nature leap into the body of a dog?" To this Joshu replied, "For the sake of others, it knew yet still transgressed."

If you want to know Joshu's mind when he gave these *wato* one-line responses[1]—from "karmic consciousness" to "it knew yet still transgressed"—first you have to pass Mu, then investigate and clarify them one at a time.

It is just a single word, *Mu*, but in later years many heroic and noble persons shed beads of sweat and tears of blood because of Mu. If you read the *Dentoroku* (*Record of the Transmission of the Lamp*), there were many persons—such as in one period a prime minister, in another period a shogun—though they had precious little free time, who broke their bones over this Mu. You can't apply scholarly studies to this question; you can't interpret it through intellect. If you are trying to deal with it within the realm of discriminatory thought, that is like trying to knock the moon down out of the sky with a stick—utterly beyond reach. There is no other way than to grapple with it directly, penetrate right to the core. Read and thoroughly take to heart Mumon Osho's commentary.

[In the following text, the lines in italic are Mumon's commentary. The regular text is Shaku Soen's lecture on Mumon's commentary line by line.]

To come to Zen, you must pass through the barrier gate of the ancient masters; for wondrous satori, you must exhaust completely the ways of ordinary mind.

For *satori* in this body as it is, neither "fake" (*ansho* 暗照)[2] Zen or "silent illumination" (*mokusho* 黙照) Zen are of any use. You enter the inner chamber of the ancestor buddhas only after you have passed through the one barrier gate. There is *satori* that is not based on seeing the old koancases, but in most cases, this is imitation *satori*. Worldly knowledge handles things through intellectual discrimination, but these are all operations of consciousness. Here however, it is said, "You need to exhaust completely the ways of ordinary mind." The Zen school first of all makes you throw yourself completely into the nondual ultimate itself, into the right-here-and-now of the absolute. Here it does not matter how much you apply the power of intellectual discrimination, you cannot possibly reach this. When you truly "break your bones" over this, when you are trying your utmost no matter what you are doing, then will you finally reach the place where you have exhausted completely the ways of ordinary mind. The Zen phrase "First, the Great Death" is talking about this extreme point. To open the eye of authentic *kensho*, no matter what else you do, you must pass once through the realm of "First, the Great Death."

Those who do not pass through the ancestors' barrier gate and do not exhaust completely the ways of ordinary mind are phantoms lurking in the grasses, hiding in the trees.

Hakuin Osho says that those who have not yet heard his sound of one hand cannot be described as anything other than a walking clot of the dregs and delusions of mind. It does not matter what mysterious principle you have learned, or what hard-to-get *satori* you have attained, if you have not actually passed through the ancestors' barrier gate, if you have not passed through the realm of "First, the Great Death," severing the root of life, they will all turn out to be nothing more than seeds of ignorance and roots of wrong views. He belittles such people as phantoms lurking in the grasses and hiding in the trees.

Tell me, what is the ancestors' barrier gate? Just this one word Mu *is itself the one barrier gate of Zen.*

The 1,700 koans all constitute the barrier gate of the ancestors. To distinguish real *satori* from imitation *satori*, to authenticate the true from the false, we definitely need this barrier gate, the old case koans of the ancestors. At the Hangu Gate, a person imitated the crow of a cock and woke everyone up,[3] but at the checkpoint of Zen, if you merely mouth Zen words, you will not be allowed to pass. First of all, you must attempt to pass through the barrier gate of Mu. It is just a single word but within it, all of the more than 5,000 volumes of the Buddhist canon and the 1,700 koans of the ancestors are contained. That is not all. It also possesses the ten thousand things, the entirety of everything between heaven and earth. So for this reason, when you at once take Mu firmly in hand and make it yours, you will illuminate the many other barrier gates and you will pass right through them one after another. This clarifies the meaning of the title "The Gateless Barrier."

Those who pass through will not only see Joshu intimately but at once will also walk hand in hand with our ancestors of the past, and face them eyebrow to eyebrow. They will see with the same eye and hear with the same ear. Will that not be wonderful?

Hakuin Osho says that Shakyamuni and Amida Buddha are even now in the thick of practice. We should be grateful for these words. If you can chew your way through the one word *Mu*, then it is no sweat at all to get to the level where you meet Joshu Osho. Bodhidharma and Rinzai too are right now fine and healthy. You will understand what it means to be always face to face with them from morning to night. A wave of the hand, a step of the foot, are all the embodiment of the ancestor buddhas; a cough, a spit, a wave of the arm are also appearances of "Why did Bodhidharma come from the west?" You will have a living eye that sees, a living ear that hears—and there will not be the least bit of difference between seeing and hearing the ancestor buddhas and seeing and hearing yourself. Penetrate deeply into this wondrous happiness and for the first time savor its taste.

Don't you want to pass the barrier? Take your 360 bones and your 84,000 pores, make your entire body into a solid mass of questioning and penetrate into this Mu.

Stalwart souls—the type who say, no one more than I wants to see right through Mu—will do whatever it takes. They will take their 360 bones and their 84,000 pores, their entire five-foot body from the top of the head down to the tips of their toenails, and making it one solid mass of questioning, they will target Mu and plow straight into it.

*Practice day and night. Do not interpret Mu as nihilism. Do not inter-
pret it as yes/no dualism. It will be like having swallowed a hot iron ball.
You try to cough it up but you cannot.*

Working on Zen is not just limited to sitting on a cushion. Make no distinction between night and day, between being awake or being asleep,
between eating or shitting, between receiving guests or working: in all
times and in all places, you are in the *samadhi* of Mu. The ancients said
that working on Zen in the midst of action is 100,000,000 times more
valuable than working on Zen while sitting still. If your way of working
on Mu is listless and half-hearted, mistaken thoughts of many kinds will
arise. You will just make guesses—since you can't reason it out, can't put
it into words and can't put your hands on it, you think there is nothing
to do except say *Mu.* Or you think it expounds a principle; or you think
it expresses a meaning—but such answers do not see Mu at all. The dead
practice of those with fox doubt and little faith, though they spend one
billion years on it, is not one bit of use. Put a bullet that has been heated
red hot into your mouth, you cannot swallow it and you cannot spit it
out. When you work on your practice, that's what it should be like. Back
and forth, back and forth, when you finally reach that place where ahead
there is no advance and behind there is no retreat, then for the first time
you will find that a living path appears. Push yourself to the utmost and
at that point there is transformation; transform yourself and you will
pass through—this is the necessary principle. No matter what, once at
least, you must finally push yourself to the limit.

*When you have thrown away all your former wrong knowledge and
mistaken understanding, when you have aged and refined yourself a
long, long time, then naturally inner and outer will come together as one.
Like the dumb person who has had a dream, only you will know what
you have had. Suddenly you will see! Heaven trembles and the earth
quakes.*

The delusions caused by the Three Poisons and the Five Desires, of course,
darken your original nature and hinder your awakening, but to be bound
up by intellectual study and understanding is also similarly a delusion and

a hindrance, so you should totally cast away such intellectual learning and understanding. To cast them out, we use harsh language calling them "wrong knowledge" and "mistaken understanding," but there is no implication here that it has to be done in a short time or a long time, or that it takes a certain number of months or years—we are not worshipping speed here. The essential point is how closely you apply yourself to the work. When you make a totally committed, pure, and sincere effort, then exactly in the way a fruit ripens, your practice ripens too. If there is room for you to catch glimpses of the many venues of the world, if there is even the slightest bit of wandering thoughts, then you cannot call that the state of "becoming one." You must get to that place where here and everywhere there is nothing that is not Mu, where the world in all ten directions is realized as one single Mu. On the way to this point, even though you may not be trying to attain *satori*, nevertheless *satori* of itself happens. Your state of mind at that time is like that of a deaf mute person who has had a dream: it is impossible for you to talk to anyone about it. All you can do is say "Yes, of course" and nod your head in agreement. In your practice, you have aged and refined yourself a long time but the moment of *satori* comes suddenly and takes no time at all. When you get it, you get it all at once. When you look back upon this absolute moment of "First, the Great Death," in plain terms you call it great enlightenment. Heaven trembles and the earth quakes—everything emerges from here. Bukko Kokushi, it is said, entered into the *samadhi* of Mu and did not breathe for one day and one night, and then when he heard the mallet striking the sounding board in front of the head monk's room, he experienced great enlightenment. His enlightenment verse reads:

一搥擊碎精靈窟	With one blow I shatter the cave of the pure spirit
突出那吒鐵面皮	And thrust forth the skin of Nata's[4] iron mask
雙耳如聾口如啞	Two ears like a deaf man's, mouth like a mute
等閑觸着火星飛	If I happen to touch it, sparks fly.

It makes you think how exciting it is to penetrate through.

It is like stealing and taking in hand General Guan's great sword. When you meet the Buddha, you kill the Buddha; when you meet the ances-

tors, you kill the ancestors. On the brink of life and death, you attain utter freedom; facing the six realms and the four births, you live in the samadhi of play.

Wherever General Guanyu wields his Blue Dragon sword, he has no enemies, so it is said. [*Satori* is like] stealing this sword and making it your own. Once the "Blown Hair Sword"[5] of Mu is in your hands, nothing it touches remains uncut. There is a saying "When you meet the Buddha, you kill the Buddha; when you meet the ancestors, you kill the ancestors." Don't misunderstand this saying. Medicine is necessary to cure a disease but once the illness is cured, there is no further necessity for the medicine. If you continue the medicine even after treatment, for sure it will affect your health badly. To drive out delusion, you must rely on *satori*, but once the delusion has been removed, *satori* is no longer needed. After the insight called *satori* is born, inevitably what may be called the dregs of *satori* are also left behind. If you remain constantly attached to *satori*, it is not possible to attain the true realm of the great emancipation and the great peace. The Zen school belittles such attachment to the insight of *satori* speaking of it in such terms as "Buddha-sickness" and "ancestor-sickness." The celebrated sword called *Mu* shreds to pieces "Buddha-sickness" and "ancestor-sickness," delusion and *satori*. Lay even the 84,000 Dharma gates and the 1,700 koans on the palm of your hand and it slices them away. *Samsara* (life-and-death) is just another name for delusion, but it is not that we flee into *satori* because delusion is something fearful; rather we leap into delusion and there attain a great freedom. We do not run away into the mountains leaving the world behind. No, we go about our work cheerfully surrounded by the miles of "red dust" of the world. To do that, you first need to make a firm footing for yourself. The "six realms" [into which one can be reborn] are heaven, humans, *asuras*,[6] hungry ghosts, animals, and hell. The "four births" are [the ways creatures come into existence]: from the womb, from eggs, from moisture, and from transformation. Once you function in the great freedom, you come and go wherever you want to do your work, not just in the world of humans but in hell, the world of animals, etc. You are master of wherever you are—that is how you work. Rinzai said, "Enter hell as if strolling in a pleasure garden."

How then do you strive? Put all your strength and energy onto Mu. *If you do not waver, you will light a Dharma candle.*

Mumon has spoken in great detail to this point, but from here forward, it is a matter of your own personal effort. Ultimately when it comes to how to practice, it is beside the point to get hung up on whether to do it this way or that way. Drive yourself heart and mind totally into Mu; no matter what, go straight ahead forward. When you truly and sincerely make a great effort and do not waver, when you are resolute and harbor no doubt about that great moment of complete *satori*, then with just a tiny thrust forward, the light of your Dharma treasury flares forth in a moment, and illuminates heaven and illuminates earth. You can experience that great happiness.

MUMON'S VERSE

> *A dog! Buddha nature!*
> *All manifest, actual and alive.*
> *But with the slightest touch of yes and no*
> *Dead your body, lost your soul.*

In response to the monk's question, "Does a dog have buddha nature or not?" Joshu's answer, just *Mu*, is "All manifest, actual and alive." He has presented his mind totally, put out all the cash with no part payments. Here Joshu wields his gleaming sword. Here, if you start making intellectual discriminations like "this and that" even a little, it will slash you in two. It is like being deathly ill. If you start saying "Yes" or "No" even just a little, or start wandering around thinking in dualistic terms, at once you lose your life.

Notes

1. The *wato* (話頭) is the key word or phrase in a koan story.

2. For *ansho*, Shaku Soen uses the characters 暗照, but this is not a recognized compound. Quite probably he is referring to the compound 暗證 (*ansho*), which means "fake," "charlatan."

3. Shaku Soen is referring to an event in historical legend. During the Warring states period (476–221 BCE), the nobleman Mengchang Jun (孟嘗君) of Qi had been taken captive by King Zhaoxiang of the neighboring state of Qin. Mengchang Jun managed to escape house arrest and he fled for his home state of Qi. By midnight, he had reached the Hangu Checkpoint (函谷関), which was the last checkpoint in Qin. Once through that gate, he would be safely back in Qi. However the Hangu Checkpoint would not open its gates until the first crow of the cock in the morning. One of Mengchang's followers gave a convincing imitation of a cock crow; this woke up all the cocks, which then started to crow as well. The soldiers inside the checkpoint duly opened the gates and Mengchang was able to pass through and escape to freedom.

4. In early Indian culture, Nata (Skt. Nalakuvara) was a powerful demon-king, depicted with three faces and eight arms, swinging iron clubs with tremendous destructive power. Eventually he was tamed and became a fierce defender of the Buddha.

5. The "Blown Hair Sword" was famous for its sharpness: a hair blown against its blade would be cut into two. See Case 100 of the *Blue Cliff Record*.

6. Asuras are gods who originally lived in heaven. Because they began fighting among themselves, they fell out of heaven into their own realm.

Chao-chou's Dog

Robert Aitken

THROUGHOUT HIS LONG CAREER Chao-chou taught in a simple manner with just a few words. It is said that a light seemed to play about his mouth as he spoke. Dogen Kigen, who freely criticized many of his ancestors in the Dharma, could only mutter in awe, "Joshu, the old buddha."[1] Forty generations of Zen students and more since his time, Chinese, Korean, Vietnamese, Japanese, and now people everywhere, have breathed his one word "Mu," evoking the living presence of the Old Buddha himself.

Thus Mu is an arcanum—an ancient word or phrase that successive seekers down through the centuries have focused upon and found to be an opening into spiritual understanding.[2] When you join that stream you have joined hands with countless pilgrims, past, present, future.

In every usage the word "Mu" means "does not have"—but if that were Chao-chou's entire meaning, there wouldn't be any Zen. [...] Wumen worked hard on Mu for six years. Though he declares that he did not put the cases of his book in any particular order, it nonetheless seems significant that he chose his own first koan as the first for his book. In many Zen Buddhist temples, including our own, the first teisho of every sesshin (retreat) is devoted to Mu. This single syllable turns out to be a mine of endless riches.

The monk's question is about buddha nature, and Chao-chou's "Mu" in response is a *presentation* of buddha nature. Buddha nature is the fundamental subject of Buddhist teaching. It is the nature of our being. Dogen establishes this at the outset of his essay titled "buddha nature": "All beings without exception have buddha nature. The Tathagata abides without change. This is the lion roar of our great teacher Shakyamuni, turning the Wheel of the Dharma, and it is the head and eyeballs of all buddhas and all Ancestors."[3]

"Tathagata" is the term for the buddha coming forth. It identifies each being in the universe as unique and sacred. It is exemplified by the Buddha Shakyamuni, but experienced upon encountering each person or thing as *this! this!* The monk sitting before Chao-chou cannot acknowledge his own Tathagata. At a deep level he is asking, "Do I really have buddha nature as they say?" Chao-chou presents his affirmation with a single word of a single syllable: "Mu."

In his quiet way Chao-chou is also showing the monk how to practice. He is just saying "Mu." This you can take as a guide, inspiration, and model. This is your path and, breath by breath, you will realize the buddhahood that has been yours from the beginning. "*Миииииии.*"

Wu-men unpacks Chao-chou's "Mu" for us most compassionately in his comment, giving one of the few expositions in classic Zen literature of the actual process of zazen up to and including realization. Phrase by phrase it opens the Way. "For the practice of Zen," he begins, "it is imperative that you pass through the barrier set up by the Ancestral Teachers." The oldest meaning of "barrier" in English, and in Chinese and Japanese as well, is "checkpoint at a frontier." There is only an imaginary mark on the earth to distinguish, say, the United States from Canada, yet our two countries have placed checkpoints along its length. There is no line in your essential nature to distinguish insight from ignorance, but in Zen Buddhist practice someone in a little house by the road will say: "Let me see your credentials. How do you stand with yourself? How do you stand with the world?" You present yourself and are told: "Okay, you may pass" or "No, you may not pass."

The barrier is an archetypal element of human growth—an obstacle to be surmounted by heroes and heroines from time immemorial. It is said that Bodhidharma, revered as the founder of Zen in China, faced the wall of his cave in zazen for the last nine years of his life, though he had long ago found that wall, that barrier, to be altogether transparent. For his part, the Buddha saw through his barrier when he happened to glance up and notice the morning star. Down through the ages there have been countless buddhas whose barrier turned out to be wide open after all. You too face that barrier. Confirm it as your own.

"For subtle realization," Wu-men continues, "it is of the utmost importance that you cut off the mind road." This is not an injunction to cut off thoughts. As Yasutani Haku'un Roshi used to say, "It is probably possible to control the brain so that no thoughts arise, but that would be an inner state in which no creativity is possible."[4] Wu-men's point is that if you try to cut off thoughts and feelings you might be able to reach a dead space as Yasutani Roshi suggests. Or, more likely, thoughts and feelings will defeat your efforts and come flooding through, and you'll be desperately trying to plug the dike. Such an endeavor brings only despair. Inevitably you notice that you are thinking something as you sit there on your cushions in zazen. Remember Mu at such a time. Notice and remember; notice and remember—a very simple, yet very exacting, practice.

Of course, this practice is not intended as a denial of thoughts and feelings. Even anger can be positive and instructive if it is simply a wave that washes through. Thoughts and feelings have a positive role in zazen, too, for they serve as reminders, just like bird song. Quoting Tung-shan Liang-chieh (Tozan Ryokai):

> *The songs of the cuckoo*
> *urges me to come home.*[5]

And you begin again. Noticing and remembering, noticing and remembering, gradually you become big with Mu—all things become big with Mu. Fantasies, plans, and sensations become absorbed in Mu. Mu breathes Mu. The whole universe breathes Mu.

Thoughts will come back. But no matter how important and instructive they may seem, ignore their content and significance, and persevere with your Mu. Let thoughts or sounds or sensations remind you to come back to Mu. Pay attention to Mu the way you would to a loved one, letting everything else go.

The barrier is Mu, but it always has a personal frame. For some the barrier is "Who am I really?" and that question is resolved through Mu. For others it is "What is death?" and that question too is resolved through Mu. For me it was "What am I doing here?" For many students it is Shakyamuni's question, "Why should there be suffering in the world?" The discursive words in such questions just take the inquirer around and around in the brain. With Mu—the single word of a single syllable—the agonizing interrogatives "who?" "why?" and "what?" are not answered in any literal sense, but they are certainly resolved.

"If you do not pass the barrier of the ancestors," says Wu-men, "if you do not cut off the mind road, then you are a ghost clinging to bushes and grasses." The ghost is one who can't let go. "Bushes" and "grasses" are shorthand for the many fixations that provide the ghost with identity—such as money and possessions, old resentments, and persistent habits of thought. We are all ghosts after all!

"What is the barrier of the Ancestral Teachers? It is just this one word 'Mu'—the barrier of our faith. We call it the Gateless Barrier of the Zen tradition." Beyond the Zen tradition, a single word of a single syllable is a perennial theme of focused meditation. The author of *The Cloud of Unknowing*, a fourteenth-century manual of Christian mysticism, declares, "Short prayer pierces Heaven." Cry out "Mu" in your heart the way you would cry "Fire!" if you awakened with your house ablaze. In *The Cloud of Unknowing* we find:

> And just as this little word "fire" stirs and pierces the Heavens more quickly, so does a little word of one syllable do the same when it is not only spoken or thought, but secretly intended in the depths of the spirit. The depth is height, for spiritually all is one, height and depth, length and breadth. It pierces the ears of Almighty God more than does any psalter thoughtlessly muttered in one's teeth. This is the reason it is said that *short prayer pierces Heaven.*[6]

Buddhists might not resonate with "Almighty God" as a useful metaphor. One of my students complained to me that his Alcoholics Anonymous program required him to place his trust in a higher power. "As a Buddhist, how can I do that?" he asked. We were standing at the window of the Castle Memorial Hospital in rural O'ahu where he was undergoing treatment. I pointed out the window at the Ko'olau Mountains towering above the hospital. Mountains have stupendous power, the power of things-as-they-are. The one who cried out "Fire!" in a burning house is gathered and all of a piece—like a mountain, like the cardinal that celebrates itself from the telephone wires, or the gecko who calls from the rafters, or the Zen student who breathes "Mu" with skin, flesh, bones, and marrow.

"When you pass through this barrier," Wu-men continues, "you will not only interview Chao-chou intimately. You will walk hand in hand with all the Ancestral Teachers in the successive generations of our lineage—the hair of your eyebrows entangled with theirs, seeing with the same eyes, hearing with the same ears." In this experience, we discover the original realms where we not only practice with our Dharma ancestors, we practice with all beings.

When people write to me from a place where there are no Zen centers and where it is impossible to find even a single Zen friend, I advise them, "Just sit with the awareness that you are sitting with us in the Diamond Sangha. Just sit with the awareness that you are sitting with everyone and every being in the whole universe, past, present, and future." We may not realize it, but we are all of us dwelling together in the original realm—sitting here in the Koko An Zendo, flitting around in the mango-tree branches, blowing and spawning in Lahaina Roads, and so on out through a vast multidimensional net of unknown magnitude.

This multidimensional net is not static but exquisitely dynamic—the mutual interdependence of all things and their mutual intersupport, the nature of our world. As philosophy this net forms a beautiful coherence. As experience it is the containment of all beings by me, by the *me* of you, and there are countless numbers of us. This experience is called "realization," and it is also called "intimacy"—the two words are synonyms in our lineage and you find that you yourself are their mind, the mind which Dogen said is "the mountains, rivers, the earth, the sun, the moon, and the stars."[7] You find that you include them or that they contain you. There is no barrier!

The word "intimate" is *ch'in-ch'ien* in Chinese, pronounced *shin-setsu* in Japanese. Its primary meaning is "apposite" or "to the point." But "having intimate connections" is the significance, and in everyday usage the term means "kind" or "generous" or "warmhearted." If you are invited to someone's home in Japan and you take along a little gift, your hostess will say that you are very *shinsetsu*—you are very kind and your conduct is just right. But implicit in that word is the message that you are intimate. So you can see, through etymology, how the

Buddhadharma of Interbeing is manifested in daily life. Wisdom and intimacy are actually the same thing.

As a Zen student you are challenged to find this intimacy in the ordinary, workaday, confrontive society you live in. How can you see with another's eyes, or hear with another's ears, across space and time or even face to face at the post office? If you steadfastly breathe "Mu" right through all feelings of anxiety when you are on your cushions, and if you ignore distractions and devote yourself to the matter at hand on other occasions, you will be like Pu-tang (Fudo) holding fast in the flames of hell.[8] Those flames are the distressing aspects of your life, and in persevering you will surely enter the original realm.

"Won't that be fulfilling? Is there anyone who would not want to pass this barrier?" Wu-men is inviting his ponies with a carrot. Be careful. Mu is only the first of the koans, and passing all the koans is only a good beginning. One peep into essential nature is a great release and a great encouragement, but if you take it as be-all and end-all, you'll drop straight to hell.

"So, then, make your whole body a mass of doubt, and with your three hundred and sixty bones and joints and your eighty-four thousand hair follicles concentrate on this one word 'Mu.'" When students asked Yamada Koun Roshi, "What is the 'great doubt' that Zen teachers are always urging upon us?" he said, "Great doubt is the condition of being one with Mu." Very simple. There's no need to manufacture doubt or to create it from outside. It's right here: What is Mu?

Wu-men uses Sung dynasty terms to convey this point. "Three hundred and sixty bones and joints and eighty-four thousand hair follicles" may not be accurate modern physiology, but as metaphors they illumine the Tao of complete physical and mental absorption in Mu. This Tao is a perennial human process found here in Zen—a path to understanding that is sought one direction or another in all world religions.

"Day and night, keep digging into it." Wu-men was speaking to monks in a monastery who can carry Mu with them day and night throughout they year—at least theoretically. We lay people can do the same during retreats. And like the accountant monk and the cook, we can find ways to keep digging into it in our daily life as well. I suggest that you commit yourself at home and in your workshop or office to practice Mu for single breaths at a time—at intervals between one task and another, when you are waiting for an appointment or for your children to fall asleep. You can do this without attracting undue attention to yourself. When your other responsibilities permit, you can practice on your cushions.

"Don't consider it to be nothingness. Don't think in terms of 'has' or 'has not.'" Mu is not nothingness or somethingness. Fixed notions of "nothing" bar you from true intimacy. After all, there's very little to be intimate with there! "Has" and "has not," like self and other, arise with the concept of the human skin as some kind of armor. Actually your skin is as porous as the universe. Each particle of its substance is vastly separate from the next, and all beings pass through.

"It is like swallowing a red-hot iron ball. You try to vomit it out, but you can't." Sitting there, big with Mu, letting Mu breathe Mu, you are completely caught up in your zazen. This is the red-hot iron ball that you can neither swallow nor spit out—a metaphor that can be precise at times and inexact at others. You might feel the heat, or you might just feel a great lump. Your whole abdomen might seem to be a great basketball. Whatever it seems, let it breathe Mu.

"Gradually you purify yourself, eliminating mistaken knowledge and attitudes you have held from the past. Inside and outside become one. You're like a mute person who has had a dream—you know it for yourself alone." Focusing on this single word "Mu," you become its intimate and all things become its intimate. You are no longer self-centered. The thrush calls "Mu," the fly buzzes "Mu," the crisp crack of the monitor's staff is Mu. These are not separate from your own breath and your own heartbeat. The self-centered preoccupations that kept you separate all these years simply fall away. You are like a fish in the water or a bird in the air—completely harmonized with your habitat. But you are not yet awakened in your habitat, for you are unable to express who or where you are.

"Suddenly Mu breaks open. The heavens are astonished, the earth is shaken." Well, first experiences of the original realm certainly differ. Some are full of emotion; some are mild. Kensho, the term used for this experience, simply means "seeing nature"—that is, seeing into essential nature. How you react is your peculiarity. But if your vision is genuine, you are hand in hand with all the ancestors.

"It is as though you have snatched the great sword of General Kuan."

General Kuan was a heroic warrior in years preceding the Han dynasty. Here he is Mañjushri, the incarnation of wisdom, who wields an exquisitely sharp sword that cuts off delusions and self-centered tendencies. Now at last the sword of Mañjushri is your own sword, and you are mounted on his lion.

"When you meet the Buddha, you kill the Buddha. When you meet Bodhidharma, you kill Bodhidharma." Of course, there is no need to kill the Buddha in one sense—he isn't around at all. Bodhidharma, our revered ancestor, is nowhere to be seen either. But Wu-men was not speaking so loftily. Swing Mañjushri's sword and cut off the mind road, he is saying, even if it is occupied with the Buddha himself. Cut off the Three Poisons of greed, hatred, and ignorance. What remains? Only the beautiful song of the thrush singing to the overcast sky.

"In the Six Worlds and the Four Modes of Birth, you enjoy a samadhi of frolic and play." These worlds and modes are Sung dynasty metaphors for all realms. The Six Worlds are those of devils, hungry ghosts, animals, titans, human beings, and angels—realms through which we migrate every metamorphosis. Samadhi means "absorption" or "oneness." In short, wherever you are and whatever you are, you are not just yourself anymore. You include all. This is the great life of the Sambhogakaya, the Body of Bliss. You are immersed in frolic and play because children, lambs, and birds are frolicking in your own blood.

"How, then, should you work with it? Exhaust all your life energy on this one word 'Mu.' If you do not falter, then it's done!" Wu-men recaps his comment with this line. Give yourself to Mu. Let Mu breathe Mu. Don't give energy to anything except Mu. Don't feel that you are faltering because you don't realize it. When you do falter, come back to Mu at your first chance. With all your faltering, don't falter.

"A single spark lights your Dharma candle." Those sparks are always going off. You are not floating alone in a sensory-deprivation bath. As you lose yourself in Mu, you are open. Your body is no other than the sounds of the world. As you focus on Mu, let it be open. Let the buzzing fly put an end to "has" and "has not." Let the cry of the gecko put an end to birth and death. Let somebody's cough put an end to ignorance and realization.

That's Wu-men's comment. Yamada Roshi used to say that he read it constantly, and each time found something new. This is a hint about Mu as well, for this koan is not a raft you discard when you finally make it your own. I am still working on Mu, a great mystery, though it is no longer alien.

Wu-men's verse is equally important in its own way: "Dog, buddha nature..." Moving on from Mu, the basic koan of our practice, Wu-men sets forth the first of subsequent koans and brings us back to the dog—and indeed to all beings.

"The full presentation of the whole." That's another arcanum. With Mu you gathered yourself. With Wu-men's verse you allow the world to gather itself. The world gathers you. You gather the world. The great gathering!

"With a bit of 'has' or 'has not' / body is lost, life is lost." Wu-men is very concerned about this point. In his comment he cautions us: "Don't consider it to be nothingness. Don't think in terms of 'has' or 'has not.'" Be diligent with your total being—don't let yourself be confined by your skull.

If, however, you are preoccupied with "has" and "has not," that is, if you cultivate thoughts about attaining something, you cut off your head, or rather you cut off your body. You cut off the whole world. Preoccupied with brooding, fantasy, memory, or whatever, you are unable to hear the thrush in the avocado tree or smell the *kahili ti* in the early evening. What a loss!

Notes

1. Koun Yamada, *Gateless Gate* (Boston: Wisdom Publications, 2004), p. 15.

2. See *Meditations on the Tarot* [anonymous] (New York: Amity House, 1985), pp. 3–4.

3. Hee-Jin Kim, trans., *Flowers of Emptiness: Selections from Dogen's Shobogenzo* (Lewiston, N.Y.: Edwin Mellon Press, 1985), p. 66.

4. Haku'un Yasutani, "Introductory Lectures on Zen Training," in *The Three Pillars of Zen*, ed. Philip Kapleau (Boston, Beacon Press, 1965): p. 32.

5. William F. Powell, trans., *The Record of Tung-shan* (Honolulu: University of Hawaii Press, 1986), p. 63.

6. Ira Progoff, trans., *The Cloud of Unknowing* (New York: Julian Press, 1957), p. 148.

7. Kazuaki Tanahashi, trans., *Shinjin Gakudo* ("Body-and-Mind Study of the Way") in *Moon in a Dewdrop: Writings of Zen Master Dogen* (San Francisco: North Point Press, 1985), p. 89.

8. D.T. Suzuki, *Sengai: The Zen Master* (Greenwich, Conn.: New York Graphic Society, 1971), pp. 46–47.

Working with Mu

Koryu Osaka

When you climb mountains, you can't climb a high one from the very beginning without preparation; rather you first climb lower mountains in preparation for taking on higher peaks. Similarly, in Japan, when we have a week-long sesshin, we first have a short sesshin, three or four days in length, to prepare for the Great Sesshin, as the longer one is called. It is rather difficult to work on a koan right away, after not having sat a sesshin for a while. Your body, breath, and mind should be ready. By adequately preparing your body, breath, and mind, you can then effectively work on your koan. Even though at first, it is very difficult to do good zazen, the proper posture, breathing, and focus are essential. Zazen improves and progresses almost endlessly.

In order to adjust your body and mind ideally, two or three days should be spent in either counting the breath or following the breath, by which both mind and body settle into a very harmonious, steady condition. For those who are sitting daily, it is advisable to practice by counting the breath or following the breath for the first few minutes of each sitting, then, having adjusted yourself well, start working on your koan. This is always a wise way to practice zazen.

[...] When Buddha Shakyamuni attained enlightenment he exclaimed: "How miraculously wonderful it is! All beings have the Tathagata's virtues and wisdom!" Mu literally means "negation, nothing." It's like the English prefix "un" or the word "no."

The Buddha's words definitely say that all beings have buddha nature. But we hear Joshu's answer; he says, "No." This is quite a contradiction to the Buddha's statement. We must find the answer to this contradiction, and we find it in "Mu." The point of this koan is not in whether the dog has buddha nature or not. This is not about the dog, or Joshu's answer: it is about you! You must resolve it yourself.

[...] Now let us appreciate Mumon's comment, "For the practice of Zen, you must pass the barriers set up by the masters of Zen." That is to say, in order to realize Zen, to understand what Zen is, you must pass through this koan, and realize it yourself. The very subtle dynamic state of enlightenment cannot be realized only by a psychological or philosophical interpretation. If you don't pass through this koan, you are like "a phantom among the undergrowth and weeds." Now what is this barrier? It is simply Mu, the barrier-gate of Zen, and this is why it is called "the Gateless Barrier of the Zen Sect."

Now what are the barriers set up by the masters? That is to say, what is the koan? It is this single syllable Mu. When you realize Mu, you will see the Buddha Shakyamuni, and all the great masters, such as Tozan, Rinzai, and Joshu. You will see things in the same way as they. Not only will you see them face to face and hear the same things as they hear, but also you will enjoy and go on the way hand in hand with them.

And so Mumon asks us, "Is not this a blessed condition? Wouldn't you like to pass this barrier?" And he continues, "Then concentrate your whole body, with its 360 bones and joints, and 84,000 hair follicles, into this question; day and night, without ceasing, hold it before you." That means with your whole might, with your whole concentration and effort and devotion, question this, day and night. Needless to say, this Mu doesn't mean "nothing"—but it is not "something" either.

When you work on this koan, try to knead it like dough when you make bread. Knead that Mu in your lower abdomen. And when you do it day after day, it will create strength, energy, and power within you, and with that strength you work on it still harder. When you work on this further, it is as though a red-hot iron ball is stuck in your throat that you can neither spit out nor swallow. And when you continue this state, that hot iron ball burns away all delusions and illusions, all miscellaneous thoughts and opinions, all unnecessary thinking that bothers you. Then eventually you come to the point where there is no distinction between inside yourself and outside yourself, between subjective and objective—and then you totally become One in the absolute state.

That is the state of mind in which there is no dog, there is no Joshu, there is no self; even the universe itself doesn't exist.

When you reach that point, to try to express that experience in words is like a mute man who dreams and wants to tell about what he has dreamt but can't. And when you have that experience, you really will "astonish the heavens above and shake the earth beneath."

In China, there once was a general by the name of Kan-u who was such a strong man that when he wielded his sword no one could stand before him. When you become One with the absolute, you can freely wield the sword of wisdom by which you are able to cut through delusions and illusions and desires. You will become a person who freely comes and goes in the six realms of existence—heaven, hell, human, fighting spirits, hungry ghosts, and animals—and can save beings in each of them according to necessity.

The whole essence of work on this koan can be summed up like this: You totally become Mu, from morning to night; even in dreams—even in sleep!—you are with Mu and Mu becomes yourself. That is the way to work on this koan.

When you work on this all the time, you will get very used to it, and without trying to put much effort into it, you will be in that state day and night. As you maintain such a state, you eventually totally become one with Mu, and you become Mu yourself, and Mu becomes your self, and you become the whole universe. And when you continue to maintain this state, ultimately an explosion will take place.

Mumon composed a poem on this koan: "Dog! buddha nature! The perfect manifestation, the absolute command. A little 'has' or 'has not,' and body is lost! Life is lost!" Mu itself is the buddha nature, and when you thoroughly make this your own, in that moment, you realize what you are. If you fall into the sphere of dualism, even just a little bit, then you lose sight of it, you completely lose the total of this koan, as Mumon says: "If you think in terms of duality, you lose both body and mind."

Mumon has explained it based on his own experience. However, this sort of experience is not easy to have, and I should like to offer a few more words that may make your practice more effective.

It is always helpful to adjust your breathing. When you inhale, try to push your lower abdomen forward slightly. When you exhale, as the lung volume decreases, the diaphragm goes up. That means that the lower abdomen will slightly contract too. Work on Mu in harmony with your breathing. Concentrating on Mu, try to hold it in your lower abdomen throughout your inhalation and exhalation.

This practice is not only good for penetrating a koan, but also it creates a very healthy physical condition. Your lower abdomen expands on the inhalation, and simultaneously your diaphragm moves downward. On the exhalation, the lower abdomen contracts while the diaphragm goes up. This vertical movement of the diaphragm and horizontal movement of the lower abdomen stimulates the internal organs so that your body starts to function better. In this way, not only can you improve your physical condition, but your mind becomes clearer as well.

When you start practicing this sort of breathing, deep in your lower abdomen, the initially slight movement of the diaphragm increases. Then according to the increased motion of the diaphragm, your breathing becomes slower. The average frequency of normal breathing is seventeen breaths per minute. As practice continues, the frequency starts to decrease. When you really improve your breathing, it becomes only a few breaths per minute. As you breathe like this you start feeling very comfortable; not only comfortable, it even becomes a delightful feeling, and the air also becomes tastier. This delightful feeling is created not only because of the mental condition, but even your blood, skin, internal organs, each functions in its best way, and these organs feel joy and delight.

This is how you will create a strong harmony within yourself.

Joshu's Dog

Nyogen Senzaki
Edited by Roko Sherry Chayat

Bodhisattvas: The first koan in the *Gateless Gate* is "Joshu's Dog." This koan is usually the first one given to the Zen student. Many masters in China and Japan entered Zen through this gate. Do not think that it is easy just because it is the first. A koan is the thesis of the postgraduate course in Buddhism. Those who have studied the teachings for twenty years may consider themselves scholars of Buddhism, but until they pass through this gate of Joshu's Dog, they will remain strangers outside the door of Buddhadharma. Each koan is the key of emancipation. Once you are freed from your fetters, you do not need the key any more.

A stanza from the Shodoka ("Song of Realization") goes:

> *The wonderful power of emancipation!*
> *It is applied in countless ways—in limitless ways!*
> *One should make four kinds of offerings for this power.*
> *If you want to pay for it,*
> *A million gold pieces are not enough.*
> *If you sacrifice everything you have, it cannot cover your debts.*
> *Only a few words from your realization are payment in full,*
> *Even for the debts of the remote past.*[1]

You can get this power of emancipation when you pass "Joshu's Dog." Your answer to this koan will be your payment in full, even for the debts of the remote past.

The great Chinese master Joshu always spoke his Zen, using a few choice words, instead of hitting or shaking his students as other teachers did. I know that students who cling to worldly sentiments do not like the rough manner of Zen. They should meet our Joshu first, and study his simplest word, "Mu."

Each sentient being has buddha nature. This dog must have one. But before you conceptualize about such nonsense, influenced by the idea of the soul in Christianity, Joshu will say "Mu." Get out! Then you may think of the idea of "manifestation." Fine word! So you think of the manifestation of buddha nature as a dog. Before you can express such nonsense, Joshu will say "Mu." You are clinging to a ghost of Brahman. Get out! Whatever you say is just the shadow of your conceptual thinking. Whatever you conceive of is a figment of your imagination. Now tell me, has a dog buddha nature or not? Why did Joshu say "Mu"?

Mumon's Comment

To realize Zen, one has to pass through the barrier set up by the patriarchs.
   Do not think that the barrier is in the book. It is right here in front of your nose.

Enlightenment is certain when the road of thinking is blocked.
   Meditation blocks the road of thinking.

If you do not pass the patriarchs' barrier, if your road of thinking is not blocked, whatever you think, whatever you do, will be like an entangling ghost. You are not an independent person if you do not pass this barrier. You cannot walk freely throughout heaven and earth. *You may ask, what is the barrier set up by the patriarchs? This one word, Mu, is it. This is the barrier of Zen. If you pass through it, you will see Joshu face to face. Then you can walk hand in hand with the whole line of patriarchs. Is this not a wondrous thing? If you want to pass this barrier, you must work so that every bone in your body, every pore of your skin, is filled through and through with this question, What is Mu? You must carry it day and night.*

   Didn't I tell you it is not an easy job? Don't be afraid, however. Just carry the koan, and ignore all contending thoughts. They will disappear soon, leaving you alone in samadhi. Do not believe Mu is the common negative. It is not nothingness as the opposite of existence. Joshu did not say the dog has buddha nature. He did not say the dog has no buddha nature. He only pointed directly to your own buddha nature! Listen to what he said: "Mu."

If you really want to pass this barrier, you should feel as though you have a hot iron ball in your throat that you can neither swallow nor spit up.

Don't be afraid; he means you should shut up, and cut off even the slightest movement of your intellectual faculty.

Then your previous conceptualizing disappears. Like a fruit ripening in season, subjectivity and objectivity are experienced as one.

There you are, in samadhi.

You are like a dumb person who has had a dream. You know it, but you cannot speak about it. When you enter this condition, your ego-shell is crushed, and you can shake the heavens and move the earth. You are like a great warrior with a sharp sword.

Neither Japan nor China has such a warrior; therefore they have to fight each other.[2]

Cut down the buddha who stands in your way.

What Mumon means here is complete unification.

Kill the patriarch who sets up obstacles.

This is an expression in Chinese rhetoric, meaning once you become a buddha, you have no more use for buddhas. Some Japanese blockhead could not understand such a peculiar expression, and many other quaint Chinese terms as well, and took them all as invitations to stir hatred. This is one of the causes of the conflict between China and Japan. Ignorance is not bliss, it is a terrible thing.

You will walk freely through birth and death. You can enter any place as if it were your own playground. I will tell you how to do this. Just concentrate all your energy into Mu, and do not allow any discontinuity.

When you enter Mu and there is no discontinuity, your attainment will be like a candle that illuminates the whole universe.

Discontinuity may be allowed at first while you are engaged in you everyday work, but when you are meditating in the zendo or in your home, you must carry on with this koan, minute after minute, bravely. Our seclusion week is an opportunity for you to engage in this sort of adventure. After you train yourselves well, then even in the midst of everyday work you will find your leisure moments filled with this koan.

Notes

1. "Shodoka," by Yokadiaishi (Ch. Yung-chia Hsuan-ch'e), an outstanding disciple of Huineng, the Sixth Ancestor, was translated by Senzaki and Ruth Strout McCandless, published in *Buddhism and Zen* by the Philosophical Library, New York, in 1953, and reissued in paperback by North Point Press in 1987.

2. Japan had invaded China and was seeking possession of Manchuria during Senzaki's work on the *Gateless Gate*.

COMMENTARY ON JOSHU'S MU

Yamamoto Gempo

Translated by Eido Shimano

THIS MU IS CALLED *Maka Shikan* in the Tendai Sect, and is beyond *Mu* and *U*, No and Yes. You must return to the source. In the practice of Zen, heaven and earth and I have completely the same root. All phenomena and I are exactly the same body. The purpose of Zen training is to clarify the truth, nothing else.

So the Sixth Ancestor said, "If you cannot clarify the truth, there is no advantage, you only suffer."

If you truly understand, you do not think, "I can't do it." You do not daydream. To clarify the truth, you must realize the basic wisdom. A person who thinks "I am a great man" cannot reply to a question about his true nature.

Therefore, Hakuin Zenji said, "hear the sound of one hand." Joshu said, "Mu." The old patriarchs said, "This Mu is like a sword to cut off delusion and fantasy."

If this is not so, then we cannot find our own master, and we will follow various paths, wandering here and there.

So Mumon said, "In the study of Zen, we must pass through the barrier of the ancient teachers. For pure enlightenment, we must block up and cut off our line of thought."

Our minds are continually running—sometimes liking, sometimes disliking. This is the road we must cut off. We must die to ourselves once.

If you do not cut off your mind road, 84,000 delusions spring up. Once you kill these delusions, they all become your friends and help you, and there is no delusion, fantasy, greed, and so on. They all become your family. If this is not done, you spend your life in a dream, like ghosts dependent on weeds in the forest.

All the ancestors felt very sorry for humanity, and they have acted as our guides. If you do not follow them and cut off your mind road, you are truly a ghost.

All of us have two eyes and a complete body. If our mind-eye opens we become doubly powerful.

What is the barrier of the ancestors? It is simply the one word *Mu*. Concentrate all your energy on this Mu. You will feel pleasure. Your body may seem to become very large. Your head will become clear.

The gateway to Zen is this one barrier. So we call it the gateless barrier of Zen. Those who pass through intimately interview Joshu himself, and moreover they walk hand in hand with all the successive patriarchs, the hair of their eyebrows tangled with one another, seeing with the same eyes, hearing with the same ears.

The patriarchs are Shakyamuni, Bodhidharma, and so on. Walking hand in hand, the hair of our eyebrows tangled together, is like two mirrors facing each other—there is no shadow between.

Our mind and the patriarchs' minds are completely one; we see and hear the past, present, and future with the same eyes and ears.

In the next world, Maitreya, the future buddha, will appear and speak on the doctrine, but even in the next world the truth is the same: to see with the same eyes, to hear with the same ears. How wonderful! Your face gradually becomes like Amida; your hands and eyes will have the strength of Kannon.

Rinzai said, "If you think about clothing, you will get clothing; if you think about food, then you will accumulate one hundred different-tasting foods."

Even when you awaken, if your action separates your from your enlightenment, then your enlightenment has no meaning. You must enjoy all your actions each day.

If you think, well, I am a salaried person, so I must work—well, I am a monk, so I must get up early and recite sutras—this won't do. If you do things according to your own situation with pleasure, there is no place for discontentment.

Here is the lotus land.

This very body is the Buddha.

So you must pass the barrier. Never sit sloppily. You must pass the barrier. For this purpose you arouse your entire body with its three hundred and sixty bones and its eighty-four thousand hair follicles to a single spirit of complete doubt. When you eat rice, think, "Who is eating? Who wants to eat? Who feels cold?"

"I am a man—Shakyamuni, Confucius, and Christ were men. I was born a man like them, so I must concentrate my three hundred and sixty bones and eighty-four thousand hair follicles on this one word Mu."

In the *Zen Kan Saku Shin*, the story of ancient teachers, we learn of one great student who had dysentery. He went to the toilet many times. His body became emaciated. Then he thought, "All right, I will die," and he decided not to go to the toilet any more, just to sit with Mu, and after a time he realized something and his illness completely disappeared and he recovered his health.

Hakuin Zenji all his life lived with this book, *Zen Kan Saku Shin*, and its inspiring stories. So, whether you feel cold or hot, just keep Mu. Carry it with you day and night. Don't form an image of empty Mu. Don't form an image of relative Mu.

It is truly beyond yes and no. Swallow this red-hot iron ball, and then even if you want to hear, you cannot hear; even if you want to swallow, you cannot swallow. Just Mu.

If you quibble about this or that it won't do. This is not quibbling or theory. If you read all of the sutras and hear all of the Buddha's lectures, you cannot understand them on the basis of theory. So we reject everything, and this one week we have sesshin. We cannot swallow; we cannot cough up. Dissipate all your bad learning and your bad knowledge and all your bad karma will disappear. At this point, you are limited to understanding for yourself alone, like a dumb man who has had a dream.

When you realize, "now I understand," at this important time, when you see other people, most of them will look drunk, but the few who have awakened to the truth will seem very steady. These few people who control themselves are quite different. The others are like dolls dangling from the rearview mirror of an automobile. We can see another's mind when we are awakened.

You may truly understand everything, but then you may feel that you do not understand anything—after that, a complete understanding of everything will come.

Then with the explosion of crossing-over, you will astonish the heavens and shake the earth. As though you have snatched away the great sword from the commander of the barrier, you will kill buddhas and ancestors if they confront you.

If you meet a buddha, you will kill him; if you meet a patriarch, you will kill him—but there is no buddha, no patriarch, for they and you are exactly the same.

You must be careful about this passage about killing. Our training is not only about realizing enlightenment; it is also about accumulating virtue. So be sure that you understand the meaning. You must not kill time; that is, you must not waste time. If you kill time, you lose your virtue.

At the very cliff-edge of birth and death, you will be completely free. In the six paths and four existences you will enjoy a samadhi of frolic and play.

Do you ask me how to carry on? Exhaust your daily energy in raising the one word Mu. If you allow no interruptions, you are doing well. You will light your own Dharma lamp at last.

This is true not only during sesshin. Always keep on. I have a camera. Its lens is very clear. Therefore I can take a good picture. If you keep your own mirror clear, you can understand any person immediately.

If you see one inch of a snake, you know its length. If a man says one word, you know whether he is good or bad. If this is not so, we cannot do effective work. The purpose of training is to realize the truth, to spend a life without error, to know our own nature and to resolve everything.

Always carry buddha nature and live beyond yes and no—just Mu. Sit as hard as you can—Mu Mu Mu. What joy! The great nature is like the sun. There is no light bigger than the sun in our world.

So if you are very intelligent, your intelligence is not enough. Man is a small heaven and earth. Heaven and earth and I have the same roots. Everything and I are completely the same. Where does that light come from?

Please awaken clearly!

COMMENTARY ON JOSHU'S MU

Harada Sogaku

Translated by Eido Shimano

ALL SUTRAS HAVE TITLES that give the spirit of their contents. In the same way, if you read the title of this book carefully, *Mumonkan* ("no-gate barrier" or "gateless gate"), you will graduate to the way of enlightenment.

The truth is, there is no gate; but a barrier-gate appears. From the point of view of the patriarchs, there is no gate. Heaven and earth stand alone, walk alone. Aren't all sentient beings fundamentally Buddha?

If you just hear the words, *Mumon* ("no gate"), you can attain pure enlightenment. But we are ordinary fellows, thinking, "I, you, he, she, we, they."

There is no one who cannot become Buddha. Though there is no gate, Shakyamuni said,

> *Oh! Wonderful, wonderful!*
> *All beings have the Tathagata's wisdom*
> *And the form of virtue!*

There is no one who cannot become Buddha. Though there is no gate, we dream and are like a snake in a stick of bamboo. We cannot move, and we suffer. Mumon has shown us forty-eight ways to break through this dream-gate.

In ancient times and now, in China and in Japan, 80 or 90 percent of all Zen students work on Mu. There is no difference between Mu and other koans, but with Mu it is easier to enter samadhi, and there is no space for delusion to appear.

Mumon broke through the bottom of the bucket with Mu, so he chose Mu as the number one koan in his book.

Many teachers may utter only one word to their many students. According to the depth of each teacher's understanding; according to his love for his students; according to his maturity of mind—this word is spoken differently on each occasion.

This Mu is not yes or no. If you think yes or no, this is relativistic or dualistic. I always say to you, heaven and earth are the same.

So, what is Mu? Joshu pointed to the fact itself and said Mu. In Zen, we have no fixed symbolism to save people, so we cannot imagine what will appear as the answer to a question.

Joshu's symbolism is the one Mu of heaven and earth. This is "willow is green; flower is red." True buddha nature is shown without any covering. Joshu chewed food for his baby students.

There is absolutely no meaning—this absolute no-meaning is the meaning of the patriarchs. There is no shadow, no depth. There are no ifs, ands, or buts, just Mu. We may compare Mu to buddha nature or to the original face, but this is just intellectual understanding.

In the practice of Zen we must pass through the barrier of the ancient teachers. The barrier of ancient teachers is actually my barrier. But even if ancestors make many barriers, there is no barrier for the person who passes one of them once. The ancestors kindly made barriers for students so they could go beyond life and death. You must pass freely and proudly through these barriers.

For pure enlightenment, we must block up and cut off our line of thought. What is our line of thought? It is acquired ideas, measurement, imagination of this or that, and confused imagery. This is our line of thought. If you have something in your head, it won't do at all.

If we do not pass the barrier of the ancestors, if we do not cut off our thoughts, then we are ghosts dependent on weeds in the forest. Belief, enlightenment, and dignity: all are weeds in the forest. If you hold something, you are dependent on those weeds, and there is no freedom.

What is the barrier of the patriarchs? It is simply the one word Mu, and the gateway to Zen is this one barrier.

The doctrine of Zen is truly the gateless gate: therefore, if you pass this barrier, you intimately interview Joshu himself, and, moreover, those who pass through walk hand in hand with all the successive patriarchs, the hair of their eyebrows tangled with one another's, seeing with the same eyes, hearing with the same ears. Isn't that joyous? Don't you want to pass through this barrier?

Dogen Zenji said about this:

> The color of the mountain,
> The sound of the valley,
> These are exactly the same
> As are Shakyamuni's voice and form.

Arouse your entire body with its three hundred and sixty bones and eighty-four thousand hair follicles to a single spirit of complete doubt.

What is this doubt? Ten people will have ten opinions, but just Mu. There is no other way but just Mu.

All of us surely will awaken, but if your Mu is not yet pure, you can't yet awaken. Mu Mu Mu Mu—this is doubt.

The old patriarchs said, under great doubt there is great awakening; under small doubt there is small awakening.

If your samadhi of doubt is great your enlightenment is great. Therefore, you must have great doubt that is as deep as possible.

Concentrate on this one word Mu. Carry it with you day and night. What is "carry"? It does not mean that something "is carried," for this is dualistic: just carry and make it your own. In short, you must become Mu.

Don't form an image of empty Mu. Don't form an image of relative Mu. Relative Mu is yes and no. This is merely an explanation of Buddhism, as for example, "form is emptiness, emptiness is form," but Joshu's Mu is not an explanation of Buddhism. It is truly beyond ideas. So Mumon said, don't use this kind of thinking, just Mu, just Mu, just Mu.

Gradually the koan and the self become completely one. Even if you want to reject it, you cannot. Confucius, when he learned music, forgot the taste of meat for three days. It is like this.

Not only during your waking hours, but also during sleep, don't forget. Don't separate from Mu.

Our work is universal. From the time you get up until you go to bed;

from the time you go to bed until you get up, don't stop. Carry on! Carry on! If you do not exert yourself, what can you get?

If you continue with this work, finally you will not be able to reject or separate from Mu. Then your acquired bad knowledge and bad feeling will disappear. At this point you are limited to knowing, like the dumb man who has a dream. You cannot tell others about it, but you yourself know. However, this is not enlightenment. Some people think it is awakening, so be careful.

If you continue with just Mu after Mu, gradually your self-belief will become stronger and you will feel, "I am sure I can do it." Gradually, gradually your faith in the Dharma will develop. But this is not yet the truth. You are just looking at an illusory world. Continue carrying your Mu as if your life depended on it.

Then suddenly we jump into the broad daylight of heaven and earth. This is called enlightenment, or passing the barrier. If you truly arrive here, "above the heaven and below the earth, I alone am the world-honored one."

In killing circumstances, kill Shakyamuni, Amida, and Maitreya. In saving circumstances, save even a maggot. As though you have snatched away the great sword from the commander of the barrier, you will kill buddhas and patriarchs if they confront you. Of course life and death are disregarded.

In the six paths and the four existences you will enjoy a samadhi of frolic and play. If you go to heaven or hell according to the laws of cause and effect, in both places it will be like playing a part. There is no liking or disliking.

I suppose you want enlightenment. The way is very simple. Exhaust your daily energy in raising the one word Mu, and do your best. If you allow no interruptions, you are doing well. This interruption is dreadful, and on ordinary days it is very difficult to keep on, so we have a seven-day sesshin. Let us work together. If we allow the egg to get cold, it will spoil.

If you want to awaken in a short period, you must be consistent. If you are consistent you will light your own Dharma lamp at last.

By training like this for five years or thirty years, enlightenment will illumine the dark world of beginningless beginning and endless end. So we must bend our bones in this training.

COMMENTARY ON THE KOAN MU

Haku'un Yasutani

Translated by Philip Kapleau

HERE I WILL TAKE UP the first case in *Mumonkan*, entitled "Joshu [on the inherent nature of a] dog." [...] The protagonist of this koan is Joshu, a renowned Chinese Zen master. I think it would be better to refer to him as the Patriarch Joshu. Inasmuch as my commentary on today's koan will be quite long, I shall omit telling you the facts of Joshu's life. Suffice it to say he was, as you all know, a great patriarch of Zen. While there are numerous koans centering around him, without a doubt this is one of the best known. Master Mumon worked zealously on it for six years and finally came to self-realization. Evidently it made a deep impression on him, for he placed it first in the collection of his forty-eight koans. Actually there is no particular reason why this koan should be first—any of the others could have been placed at the head just as well—but Mumon's feeling for it was so intimate that he naturally put it at the very beginning.

The first line reads: "A monk in *all seriousness* asked Joshu..." That is, his question was neither frivolous nor casual but deeply considered.

The next portion, "Has a dog buddha nature or not?" raises the question: What is buddha nature? A well-known passage in the *Nirvana Sutra* states that every sentient being has buddha nature. The expression "every sentient being" means all existence. Not alone human beings, but animals, even plants, are sentient beings. Accordingly, a dog, a monkey, a dragonfly, a worm equally have buddha nature according to the *Nirvana Sutra*. In the context of this koan, however, you may consider the term as referring only to animals.

What then is buddha nature? Briefly, the nature of everything is such

71

that it can become Buddha. Now, some of you, thinking there is something called *the* buddha nature hidden within us, may inquire as to the whereabouts of this buddha nature. You may tend to equate it with conscience, which everyone, even the wicked, is presumed to possess. You will never understand the truth of buddha nature so long as you harbor such a specious view. The Patriarch Dogen interpreted this expression in the *Nirvana Sutra* to mean that what is intrinsic to all sentient beings is buddha nature, and not that all sentient beings have something called *the* buddha nature. Thus in Dogen's view there is only buddha nature, nothing else.

In Buddhism, "buddha nature" is an intimate expression and "Dharma nature" an impersonal one. But whether we say buddha nature or Dharma nature, the substance is the same. One who has become enlightened to the Dharma is a buddha; hence Buddha arises from Dharma. The *Diamond Sutra* says that all buddhas and their enlightenment issue from this Dharma. Dharma, it follows, is the mother of buddhahood. Actually there is neither mother nor son, for as I have said, it is the same whether you say Buddha or Dharma.

What is the Dharma of Dharma nature? Dharma means phenomena. What we ordinarily term phenomena—that is, what is evident to the senses—in Buddhism is called Dharma. The word "phenomena," since it relates only to the observable features without implying what causes them to appear, has a limited connotation. These phenomena are termed Dharma (or Law) simply because they appear neither by accident nor through the will of some special agency superintending the universe. All phenomena are the result of the operation of the law of cause and effect. They arise when causes and conditions governing them mature. When one of these causes or conditions becomes altered, these phenomena change correspondingly. When the combination of causes and conditions completely disintegrates, the form itself disappears. All existence being the expression of the law of cause and effect, all phenomena are equally this Law, this Dharma. Now, as there are multiple modes of existence, so there are multiple dharmas corresponding to these existences. The substance of these manifold dharmas we call Dharma nature. Whether we say Dharma nature or use the more personal term buddha nature, these expressions refer to one reality. Stated differently, all phenomena are transformations of buddha or Dharma nature. Everything by its very nature is subject to the process of infinite transformation—this is its buddha or Dharma nature.

What is the substance of this buddha or Dharma nature? In Buddhism it is called *ku* [*shunyata*]. Now, ku is not mere emptiness. It is that which is living, dynamic, devoid of mass, unfixed, beyond individuality or personality—the matrix of all phenomena. Here we have the fundamental principle or doctrine or philosophy of Buddhism.

For the Buddha Shakyamuni this was not mere theory but truth which he directly realized. With the experience of enlightenment, which is the source of all Buddhist doctrine, you grasp the world of ku. This world—unfixed, devoid of mass, beyond individuality or personality—is outside the realm of imagination. Accordingly, the true substance of things, that is, their buddha or Dharma nature, is inconceivable and inscrutable. Since everything imaginable partakes of form or color, whatever one imagines to be buddha nature must of necessity be unreal. Indeed, that which can be conceived is but a picture of buddha nature, not buddha nature itself. But while buddha nature is beyond all conception and imagination, because we ourselves are intrinsically buddha nature, it is possible for us to awaken to it. Only through the experience of enlightenment, however, can we affirm it in the Heart. Enlightenment therefore is all.

Once you realize the world of ku you will readily comprehend the nature of the phenomenal world and cease clinging to it. What we see is illusory, without substance, like the antics of puppets in a film. Are you afraid to die? You need not be. For whether you are killed or die naturally, death has no more substantiality than the movements of these puppets. Or to put it another way, it is no more real than the cutting of air with a knife, or the bursting of bubbles, which reappear no matter how often they are broken.

Having once perceived the world of buddha nature, we are indifferent to death since we know we will be reborn through affinity with a father and a mother. We are reborn when our karmic relations impel us to be reborn. We die when our karmic relations decree that we die. And we are killed when our karmic relations lead us to be killed. We are the manifestation of our karmic relations at any given moment, and upon their modification we change accordingly. What we call life is no more than a procession of transformations. If we do not change, we are lifeless. We grow and age because we are alive. The evidence of our having lived is the fact that we die. We die because we are alive. Living means birth and death. Creation and destruction signify life.

When you truly understand this fundamental principle you will not be anxious about your life or your death. You will then attain a steadfast mind and be happy in your daily life. Even though heaven and earth were turned upside down, you would have no fear. And if an atomic or hydrogen bomb were exploded, you would not quake in terror. So long as you become one with the bomb, what would there be to fear? "Impossible!" you say. But whether you wanted to or not, you would perforce become one with it, would you not? By the same token, if you were caught in a holocaust, inevitably you would be burnt. Therefore become one with fire when there is no escaping it! If you fall into poverty, live that way without grumbling—then your poverty will not be a burden to you. Likewise, if you are rich, live with your riches. All this is the functioning of buddha nature. In short, buddha nature has the quality of infinite adaptability.

Coming back to the koan, we must approach the question, "Has a dog buddha nature or not?" with caution, since we do not know whether the monk is ignorant or is feigning ignorance in order to test Joshu. Should Joshu answer either "It has" or "It has not," he would be cut down. Do you see why? Because what is involved is not a matter of "has" or "has not." Everything being buddha nature, either answer would be absurd. But this is "Dharma dueling." Joshu must parry the thrust. He does so by sharply retorting, "Mu!" Here the dialogue ends.

In other versions of the dialogue between Joshu and the monk the latter continues by inquiring: "Why hasn't a dog buddha nature when the *Nirvana Sutra* says all sentient beings do have it?" Joshu countered with: "Because it has ignorance and attachment." What this means is that the dog's buddha nature is not other than karma. Acts performed with a delusive mind produce painful results. This is karma. In plainer words, a dog is a dog as a result of its past karma's conditioning it to become a dog. This is the functioning of buddha nature. So do not talk as though there were a particular thing called "buddha nature." This is the implication of

Joshu's Mu. It is clear, then, that Mu has nothing to do with the existence or non-existence of buddha nature but is itself buddha nature. The retort "Mu!" exposes and at the same time fully thrusts buddha nature before us. Now while you may be unable to fully understand what I am saying, you will not go astray if you construe buddha nature in this manner.

Buddha nature cannot be grasped by the intellect. To experience it directly you must search your mind with the utmost devotion until you are absolutely convinced of its existence, for, after all, you yourself are this buddha nature. When I told you earlier that buddha nature was ku—impersonal, devoid of mass, unfixed, and capable of endless transformation—I merely offered you a portrait of it. It is possible to *think* of buddha nature in these terms, but you must understand that whatever you can conceive or imagine must necessarily be unreal. Hence there is no other way than to experience the truth in your own mind. This way has been shown, with the greatest kindness, by Mumon.

Let us now consider Mumon's comment. He begins by saying: "In the practice of Zen..." Zazen, receiving dokusan [that is, private instructions], hearing teisho—these are all Zen practice. Being attentive in the details of your daily life is also training in Zen. When your life and Zen are one you are truly living Zen. Unless it accords with your everyday activities Zen is merely an embellishment. You must be careful not to flaunt Zen but to blend it unpretentiously into your life. To give a concrete example of attentiveness: when you step out of the clogs at the porch or the kitchen or out of the slippers of the toilet room, you must be careful to arrange them neatly so that the next person can use them readily even in the dark. Such mindfulness is a practical demonstration of Zen. If you put your clogs or shoes on absentmindedly you are not attentive. When you walk you must step watchfully so that you do not stumble or fall. Do not become remiss!

But I am digressing. To continue: "...you must pass through the barrier gate set up by the patriarchs." Mu is just such a barrier. I have already indicated to you that, from the first, there is no barrier. Everything being buddha nature, there is no gate through which to go in or out. But in order to awaken us to the truth that everything is buddha nature, the patriarchs reluctantly set up barriers and goad us into passing through them. They condemn our faulty practice and reject our incomplete answers. As you steadily grow in sincerity you will one day suddenly come to self-realization. When this happens you will be able to pass through the barrier gate easily. The *Mumonkan* is a book containing forty-eight such barriers.

The next line begins: "To realize this wondrous thing called enlightenment..." Observe the word "wondrous." Because enlightenment is unexplainable and inconceivable it is described as wondrous. "...you must cut off all [discriminating] thoughts." This means that it is useless to approach Zen from the standpoint of supposition or logic. You can never come to enlightenment through inference, cognition, or conceptualization. Cease clinging to all thought-forms! I stress this, because it is the central point of Zen practice. And particularly do not make the mistake of thinking enlightenment must be this or that.

"If you cannot pass through the barrier and exhaust the arising of thoughts, you are like a ghost clinging to the trees and grass." Ghosts do not appear openly in the daytime, but come out furtively after dark, it is said, hugging the earth or clinging to willow trees. They are dependent upon these supports for their very existence. In a sense human beings are also ghostlike, since most of us cannot function independent of money, social standing, honor, companionship, authority; or else we feel the need to identify ourselves with an organization or an ideology. If you would be a man of true worth and not a phantom, you must be able to walk upright by yourself, dependent on nothing. When you harbor philosophical concepts or religious beliefs or ideas or theories of one kind or another, you too are a phantom, for inevitably you become bound to them. Only when your mind is empty of such abstractions are you truly free and independent.

The next two sentences read: "What, then, is this barrier set by the patriarchs? It is Mu, the one barrier of the supreme teaching." The supreme teaching is not a system of morality but that which lies at the root of all such systems, namely, Zen. Only that which is of unalloyed purity, free from the superstitious or the supernatural, can be called the root of all teachings and therefore supreme. In Buddhism Zen is the only teaching which is not to one degree or another tainted with elements of the supernatural—thus Zen alone can truly be called the supreme teaching and Mu the one barrier of this supreme teaching. You can understand "one barrier" to mean the sole barrier or one out of many. Ultimately there is no barrier.

"One who has passed through it cannot only see Joshu face to face...." Since we are living in another age, of course we cannot actually see the physical Joshu. To "see Joshu face to face" means to understand his Mind. "...can walk hand in hand with the whole line of patriarchs." The line of patriarchs begins with Maha Kashyapa, who succeeded the Buddha, it goes on to Bodhidharma, the twenty-eighth, and continues right up to the present. "...eyebrow to eyebrow..." is a figure of speech implying great intimacy. "...hear with the same ears and see with the same eyes" connotes the ability to look at things from the same viewpoint as the Buddha and Bodhidharma. It implies, of course, that we have clearly grasped the world of enlightenment.

"How marvelous!" Marvelous indeed! Only those who recognize the preciousness of the Buddha, the Dharma, and the patriarchs can appreciate such an exclamation. Yes, how truly marvelous! Those who do not care for the Buddha and the Dharma may feel anything but marvel, but that cannot be helped.

"Who would not want to pass through this barrier?"—this phrase aims at enticing you to search for the truth within yourself. "For this you must concentrate day and night, questioning yourself [about Mu] through every one of your 360 bones and 84,000 pores." These figures reflect the thinking of the ancients, who believed that the body was constructed in this fashion. In any case, what this refers to is your entire being. Let all of you become one mass of doubt and questioning. Concentrate on and penetrate fully into Mu. To penetrate into Mu means to achieve absolute unity with it. How can you achieve this unity? By holding to Mu tenaciously day and night! Do not separate yourself from it under any circumstances! Focus your mind on it constantly. "Do not construe Mu as nothingness and do not conceive it in terms of existence or non-existence." You must not, in other words, think of Mu as a problem involving the existence or non-existence of buddha nature. Then what do you do? You stop speculating and concentrate wholly on Mu—just Mu!

Do not dawdle, practice with every ounce of energy. "[You must reach the point where you feel] as though you had swallowed a red-hot iron ball...." It is hyperbole, of course, to speak of swallowing a red-hot iron ball. However, we often carelessly swallow a hot rice-cake which, lodging in the throat, causes considerable discomfort. Once you swallow Mu up you will likewise feel intensely uncomfortable and try desperately to dislodge it. "...that you cannot disgorge despite your every effort"—this describes the state of those who work on this koan. Because self-realization is so tantalizing a prospect they cannot quit; neither can they grasp Mu's significance readily. So there is no other way for them but to concentrate on Mu until they "turn blue in the face."

The comparison with a red-hot iron ball is apt. You must melt down your illusions with the red-hot iron ball of Mu stuck in your throat. The opinions you hold and your worldly knowledge are your illusions. Included also are philosophical and moral concepts, no matter how lofty, as well as religious beliefs and dogmas, not to mention innocent, commonplace thoughts. In short, all conceivable ideas are embraced within the term "illusions" and as such are a hindrance to the realization of your Essential nature. So dissolve them with the fireball of Mu!

You must not practice fitfully. You will never succeed if you do zazen only when you have the whim to, and give up easily. You must carry on steadfastly for one, two, three, or even five years without remissions, constantly vigilant. Thus you will gradually gain in purity. At first you will not be able to pour yourself wholeheartedly into Mu. It will escape you quickly because your mind will start to wander. You will have to concentrate harder—just "Mu! Mu! Mu!" Again it will elude you. Once more you attempt to focus on it and again you fail. This is the usual pattern in the early stages of practice. Even when Mu does not slip away, your concentration becomes disrupted because of various mind defilements. These defilements disappear in time, yet since you have not achieved oneness with Mu you are still far from ripe. Absolute unity with Mu, unthinking absorption in Mu—this is ripeness. Upon your attainment to this stage of purity, both inside and outside naturally fuse. "Inside and outside" has various shades of meaning. It may be understood as meaning subjectivity and objectivity or mind and body. When you fully absorb yourself in Mu, the eternal and internal merge into a single unity. But, unable to speak about it, you will be like "a mute who has had a dream." One who is dumb is unable to talk about his dream of the night before.

In the same way, you will relish the taste of samadhi yourself but be unable to tell others about it.

At this stage self-realization will abruptly take place. Instantaneously! "Bursting into enlightenment" requires but an instant. It is as though an explosion had occurred. When this happens you will experience so much! "You will astound the heavens and shake the earth." Everything will appear so changed that you will think heaven and earth have been overturned. Of course there is not literal toppling over. With enlightenment you see the world as buddha nature, but this does not mean that all becomes as radiant as a halo. Rather, each thing *just as it is* takes on an entirely new significance or worth. Miraculously, everything is radically transformed though remaining as it is.

This is how Mumon describes it: "As though having captured the great sword of General Kuan..." General Kuan was a courageous general who was invincible in combat with his "blue-dragon" sword. So Mumon says you will become as powerful as he who captures the "blue-dragon" sword of General Kuan. Which is to say that nothing untoward can happen to you. Through self-realization one acquires self-confidence and an imposing bearing. When one comes before the roshi his manner implies, "Test me in any way you wish," and such is his assurance that he could even thrash the master.

"...you will be able to slay the Buddha should you meet him and dispatch all the patriarchs you encounter." The timid will be flabbergasted when they hear this and denounce Zen as an instrument of the devil. Others, less squeamish yet equally unable to understand the spirit of these words, will feel uneasy. To be sure, Buddhism inspires in us the utmost respect for all buddhas. But at the same time it admonishes us that eventually we must free ourselves from that attachment to them. When we have experienced the Mind of Shakyamuni Buddha and cultivated his incomparable virtues, we have realized the highest aim of Buddhism. Then we bid him farewell, shouldering the task of propagating his teachings. I have never heard of such an attitude in religions teaching belief in God. While the aim of the Buddhist is to become a buddha, nevertheless, to put it bluntly, you can slay the Buddha and all the patriarchs. You who realize enlightenment will be able to say: "Were the honored Shakyamuni and the great Bodhidharma to appear, I would cut them down instantly, demanding: 'Why do you totter forth? You are no longer needed!'" Such will be your resoluteness.

"Facing life and death, you are utterly free; in the Six Realms of Existence and the Four Modes of Birth you move about in a samadhi of innocent delight." You will be able to face death and rebirth without anxiety. The Six Realms are the realms of maya, namely, hell, the worlds of pretas [hungry ghosts], beasts, asuras [fighting demons], human beings, and devas [heavenly beings]. The Four Modes of Birth are birth through the womb, birth through eggs hatched outside the body, birth through moisture, and birth through metamorphosis. To be born in heaven and hell, since it requires no physical progenitors, is birth through metamorphosis. Who ever heard of a heavenly being that had to undergo the trauma of being born? There are neither midwives nor obstetricians in heaven or hell.

Wherever you may be born, and by whatever means, you will be able to live with the spontaneity and joy of children at play—this is what is meant by a "samadhi of innocent delight." Samadhi is complete absorption. Once you are enlightened you can descend to the deepest hell or rise to the highest heaven with freedom and rapture.

"How, then, do you achieve this?" Through zazen. "Devote yourself to Mu energetically and wholeheartedly." Persevere with all the force of your body and spirit. "If you continue this way without intermission..." You must not start and then quit. You must carry on to the very end, like a hen sitting on an egg until she hatches it. You must concentrate on Mu unflinchingly, determined not to give up until you attain kensho. "...your mind will, like a lamp flashed on in the dark, suddenly become bright. Wonderful indeed!" With enlightenment the mind, released from the darkness of its infinite past, will brighten immediately. "Wonderful indeed!" is added since nothing could be more wonderful.

The first line of Mumon's verse reads: "A dog, buddha nature"—there is no need for "nature." "A dog *is* Buddha"—is superfluous. "A dog, Buddha"—still redundant. "Dog!"—that's enough! Or just "Buddha!" You have said too much when you say "A dog is Buddha." "Dog!"—that is all. It is completely Buddha.

"This is the...whole, the absolute imperative!" That is to say, it is the authentic decree of Shakyamuni Buddha—it is the correct Dharma. You are this Dharma to perfection! It is not being begrudged—it is fully revealed!

"Once you begin to think 'has' or 'has not' you are as good as dead." What does "you are as good as dead" mean? Simply that your precious buddha life [of Oneness] will vanish.

JOSHU'S MU

Zenkei Shibayama

Translated by Sumiko Kudo

TEISHO ON THE KOAN

THIS KOAN is extremely short and simple. Because of this simplicity, it is uniquely valuable and is an excellent koan.

[...] In the biography of Joshu a series of mondo are recorded, from which his koan is extracted. There have been many attempts to interpret these mondo and to explain the koan in relation to them. We do not have to worry about such attempts here but should directly grip the koan itself. Knowing well its context, Master Mumon presents a simple, direct, and clear koan. Its simplicity plays an important role.

"A monk once asked Master Joshu, 'Has a dog the buddha nature or not?'" This monk was well aware that all sentient beings have the buddha nature without exception. This is therefore a piercingly effective and unapproachable question which would not be answered if the master were to say yes or no. The monk is demanding that Joshu show him the real buddha nature, and he is not asking for its interpretation or conceptual understanding. What a cutting question!

Joshu, like the genuine capable master that he was, answered "Mu!" without the least hesitation. He threw himself—the whole universe—out as "Mu" in front of the questioner. Here is no Joshu, no world, but just "Mu." This is the koan of Joshu's "Mu."

The experience of the buddha nature itself is creatively expressed here by "Mu." Although literally "Mu" means No, in this case it points to the incomparable satori which transcends both yes and no, to the religious experience of the truth one can attain when he casts away his discriminating mind. It has nothing to do with the dualistic interpretation of yes and no, being and nonbeing. It is truth itself, the Absolute itself.

Joshu, the questioning monk, and the dog are however only incidental to the story, and they do not have any vital significance in themselves. Unless one grasps the koan within himself as he lives here and now, it ceases to be a real koan. We should not read it as an old story; you yourselves have to *be* directly "Mu" and make not only the monk, but Joshu as well, show the white feather. Then the buddha nature is "Mu"; Joshu is "Mu." Not only that, you yourself and the whole universe are nothing but "Mu." Further, "Mu" itself falls far short, it is ever the unnamable "it."

Master Daie says, "Joshu's 'Mu'—work directly at it. Be just it." He is telling us to be straightforwardly no-self, be "Mu," and present it right here. This is a very inviting instruction, indeed.

Once my own teacher, Master Bukai, threw his *nyoi* (a stick about fifty centimeters long which a Zen master always carries with him) in front of me and demanded, "Now, transcend the yes-and-no of this nyoi!" and he did not allow me a moment's hesitation. Training in Zen aims at the direct experience of breaking through to concrete Reality. That breaking through to Reality has to be personally attained by oneself. Zen can never be an idea or knowledge, which are only shadows of Reality. You may reason out that "Mu" transcends both yes and no, that it is the Absolute Oneness where all the dualistic discrimination is exhausted. While you are thus conceptualizing, real "Mu" is lost forever.

My teacher asked me once, "Show me the form of 'Mu'!" When I said, "It has no form whatsoever, " he pressed me, saying, "I want to see that form which has no-form." How cutting and drastic! Unless one can freely and clearly present the form of "Mu," it turns out to be a meaningless corpse.

In the biography of Master Hakuin we read the following moving story of his first encounter with his teacher, Master Shoju. Shoju asked Hakuin, "Tell me, what is Joshu's 'Mu'?" Hakuin elatedly replied, "Pervading the universe! Not a spot whatsoever to take hold of!" As soon as he had given that answer, Shoju took hold of Hakuin's nose and gave it a twist. "I am quite at ease to take hold of it," said Shoju, laughing aloud. The next moment he released it and abused Hakuin, "You! Dead monk in a cave! Are you self-satisfied with such 'Mu'?" This completely put Hakuin out of countenance.

We have to realize that this one word "Mu" has such exhaustive depth and lucidity that once one has really grasped it as his own he has the ability to penetrate all Zen koans.

Often people remark that "Mu" is an initial koan for beginners, which is a great mistake. A koan in Zen is fundamentally different from questions and problems in general. Etymologically the term *koan* means "the place where the truth is." In actual training its role is to smash up our dualistic consciousness and open our inner spiritual eye to a new vista. In actual cases there may be differences in the depth of the spirituality and ability of Zen students who break through a koan. This is inevitable for human beings living in this world. For any koan, however, there should be no discrimination or gradation as an initial koan for beginners or difficult ones for the advanced. An old Zen master said, "If you break through one koan, hundred and thousands of koans have all been penetrated at once." Another master said, "It is like cutting a reel of thread: one cut, and all is cut."

The use of a koan in Zen training developed spontaneously in the southern Sung dynasty in China when a reminiscent, traditionalist tendency began to prevail in Zen circles. In the early period of the southern Sung, Joshu's "Mu" was already being widely used as a koan. Mumon himself was driven into the abyss of Great Doubt by this koan and finally had the experience of breaking through it. Out of his own training and experience, he must have extracted the most essential part from several mondo and presented it to his disciples as a simple, direct koan.

This koan is taken from a mondo between Joshu and a monk, and *Joshu Zenji Goroku* ("Sayings of Master Joshu") and a few other books record similar mondo. In the chapter "Joshu Junen" in *Goto Egen*, volume 4, we read, "A monk asked Joshu, 'Has a dog the buddha nature or not?' The master said 'Mu.' The monk asked, "From buddhas above down to creeping creatures like ants, all have the buddha nature. Why is it that a dog has not?' 'Because he has ignorance and attachment,' the master replied."

Joshu Zenji Goroku has the following mondo: "A monk asked, 'Has a dog the buddha nature or not?' The master said 'Mu.' Monk: 'Even creeping creatures all have the buddha nature. Why is it that the dog has not?' Master: 'Because he has ignorance and attachment.'"

Another monk asked Joshu, "Has a dog the buddha nature or not?" The master said, "U" ("Yes"). The monk asked, "Having the buddha nature, why is he in such a dog-body?" Master: "Knowingly he dared to be so."

Although generally Joshu is supposed to have originated this mondo on the buddha nature, we read the following mondo in the biography of Master Ikan (775–817) of Kozenji at Keicho: Monk: "Has a dog the buddha nature or not?" Master: "Yes" (U). Monk: "Have you, O master, the buddha nature or not?" Master: "I have not." Monk: "All sentient beings have the buddha nature. Why is it that you alone, master, have not?" Master: "I am not among all sentient beings." Monk: "If you are not among sentient beings, are you then a buddha or not?" Master: "I am not a buddha." Monk: "What kind of thing are you after all?" Master: "I am not a thing either." Monk: "Can it be seen and thought of?" Master: "Even if you try to think about it and know it, you are unable to do so. It is therefore called 'unknowable.'"

Let us put aside for the time being historical studies of the koan. "Mu" as a koan is to open our spiritual eye to Reality, to "Mu," that is, Joshu's Zen—this is the sole task of this koan, and everything else is just complimentary and not of primary importance. We may simply read about it for our information.

All sentient beings without exception have the buddha nature. This is the fundamental truth of nondualism and equality. On the other hand, this actual world of ours is dualistic and full of discriminations. The above mondo presents to us the basic contradiction between the fundamental truth of nondualism and actual phenomena. The ancient masters made us face the fact that we human beings from the very beginning have been living in this fundamental contradiction. It was the compassion of the masters that led them to try this to intensify their disciples' Great Doubt, their spiritual quest, and finally lead them to satori by breaking through it. If here one really breaks through this koan, which uniquely presents before him the core of human contradiction, he can clearly see for himself with his genuine Zen eye what these mondo are trying to tell us.

Teisho on Mumon's Commentary

First Mumon tells us what must be the right attitude for a Zen student, that is, what is fundamentally required of him in studying Zen. As Master Daiye says, "Satori is the fundamental experience in Zen." One has to cast his ordinary self away and be reborn in a new Self in a different dimension. In other words, the student must personally have the inner experience called satori, by which he is reborn as the True Self. This fundamental experience of awakening is essential in Zen. Although various different expressions are used when talking about the fact of this religious awakening, it cannot be real Zen without it. Mumon therefore declares at the very beginning that "in studying Zen one must pass the barriers set up by the ancient Zen masters." The barrier of the ancient Zen masters is the barrier to Zen, and the obstacle to transcend is the dualism of yes and no, subject and object. Practically, the sayings of ancient masters, which are called koans, are such barriers.

The phrase "incomparable satori" indicates the eternal emancipation or absolute freedom that is attained by directly breaking through the Zen barrier. In order to break through it, Mumon stresses that one must once and for all cast away his discriminating mind completely. "Discriminating mind" is our ordinary consciousness, which is dualistic, discriminating, and the cause of all sorts of illusions. Mumon asks us to cast this away. To get rid of it requires that one's whole being must be the koan. There should be nothing left, and the secret of Zen lies in this really throwing oneself away. One does not have that naturally and automatically come about without seeking for it. What is important here is for him to actually do it himself.

"Those who have not passed the barrier and have not cast away the discriminating mind are all phantoms haunting trees and plants."

There is a superstition that the phantoms of those who after death are not in peace haunt trees and plants and cast evil spells on people. Here it means those people who do not have a fundamental spiritual basis, those who cling to words and logic and are enslaved by dualistic views, without grasping the subjective point of view.

Mumon says that anyone who is unable to pass the barrier of the old masters or to wipe out his discriminating mind—that is, if his Zen mind is not awakened—is like a phantom, without reality. There is no significance in such an existence. Thus, by using extreme and abusive language Mumon tries to make us ashamed of our unenlightened existence and to arouse in us the great spiritual quest.

"Now, tell me," Mumon demands, "what is the barrier of the Zen masters?" Having aroused our interest, he answers himself that this "Mu" is the ultimate barrier of Zen. If once one has broken through it, he is the master of all the barriers and the forty-eight koans and commentaries of the *Mumonkan* are all his tools. This is therefore called "The Gateless Barrier of Zen," Mumon remarks. We should remember however that it is not only the first koan, but that any of the forty-eight koans of the *Mumonkan* is the barrier of Zen.

"Those who have passed the barrier will not only see Joshu clearly, but will go hand in hand with all the masters in the past, see them face to face. You will see with the same eye that they see with and hear with the same ear. Wouldn't it be wonderful?"

Mumon tells us how wonderful it is to experience breaking through the barrier and to live the life of satori. Once the gate is broken through, ultimate peace is attained. You can get hold of old Joshu alive. Further, you will live in the same spirituality with all the Zen masters, see them face to face, and enjoy the truth of Oneness. How wonderful, how splendid! He praises the life of satori in the highest terms. There are no ages in satori; no distinctions of I and you, space and time. Wherever it may be and whenever it may be, just here and now you see and hear—it is Joshu, it is your Self, and "Mu." There can be no greater joy. To experience this is to attain eternal peace.

"Don't you want to pass the barrier? Then concentrate yourself into this 'Mu' with your 360 bones and 84,000 pores, making your whole body one great inquiry."

Having described the great joy of satori, Mumon now turns to his disciples and speaks directly to them, "Are there any among you who want to pass this barrier of the ancient masters?" He then goes on to give practical instructions as to how they should carry on their training in order to break through the barrier—how to attain satori. He tells them to inquire, with their heart and soul, what it is to transcend yes and no, you and I. They are to cast their whole being, from head to foot, into this inquiry and carry on with it. There will be no world, no self, but just one Great Doubt. This is "Mu." "Just be Mu!" Mumon urges the disciples.

"To concentrate" is to be unified and identified. "To concentrate oneself into 'Mu'" is for "Mu" and the self to be one—to be one and then to transcend both "Mu" and the self.

"Day and night work intently at it; do not attempt nihilistic or dualistic interpretations."

Mumon's instructions continue; never be negligent, even for a short while, but do zazen and devote yourself to the koan day and night. An old master used to describe this training process, saying, "Work like a mother hen trying to hatch her eggs." Do not misunderstand "Mu" as nihilistic emptiness. Never in the world take it as a dualistic no in opposition to yes. Needless to say, it has nothing to do with intellectual discrimination or dualistic reasoning. It is utterly beyond all description.

"It is like having swallowed a red hot iron ball; you try to vomit it but cannot. Cast away your illusory discriminating knowledge and consciousness accumulated up to now, and keep on working harder. After a while, when your efforts come to fruition, all the oppositions (such as in and out) will naturally be identified. You will then be like a dumb person who has had a wonderful dream: he only knows it personally, within himself."

"Like having swallowed a red hot iron ball" describes the one who, with his whole being, body and soul, has plunged into the Great Doubt, the spiritual quest. All the emotions are exhausted, all the intellect has come to its extremity; there is not an inch for the discrimination to enter. This is the state of utmost spiritual intensification. When it is hot, the whole universe is nothing but the heat; when you see, it is just one pure act of seeing—there is no room there for any thought to come in. In such a state, Mumon warns us, never give up but straightforwardly carry on with your striving. In such a state no thought of discrimination can be present. "Illusory discriminating knowledge and consciousness accumulated up to now" refers to our dualistically working mind we have had before. No trace of it is now left. You are thoroughly lucid and transparent like a crystal. Subject and object, in and out, being and nonbeing are just one, and this very one ceases to be one any longer. Rinzai said, describing this state, "The whole universe is sheer darkness." Hakuin said "It was like sitting in an ice cave a million miles thick." This is the moment when the I and the world are both altogether gone. This is exactly the moment when one's discriminating mind is emptied and cast away. When one is in the abyss of absolute "Mu" in actual training, the inexpressible moment comes upon him—the moment when "Mu" is awakened to "Mu," that is, when he is revived as the self of no-self. At this mysterious moment, he is like a dumb person who has had a wonderful dream, for he is fully aware of it, but is unable to use words to express it. The Absolute Nothingness ("Mu") is awakened to itself. This is the moment of realization when subject-object opposition is altogether transcended. To describe it we have to use such words as inexpressible or mysterious. "You will then be like a dumb person who has had a wonderful dream: he only knows it personally, within himself."

Then Mumon tries again to describe the experience of the one who has just broken through the barrier: "Suddenly you break through the barrier; you will astonish heaven and shake the earth." I myself, however, should like to reverse the order of these two sentences and say, "Suddenly you break through the barrier; you will astonish heaven and shake the earth. You will then be like a dumb person who has had a wonderful dream: he only knows it personally, within himself." This would be more faithful to actual experience. Zen calls this experience "incomparable satori," or "to die a Great Death once and to revive from death." Mumon described his experience of attaining satori by saying that "all beings on earth have opened their eyes." This is the most important and essential process one has to go through in Zen training.

"It is as if you have snatched the great sword of General Kan. You kill the Buddha if you meet him; you kill the ancient masters if you meet them. On the brink of life and death, you are utterly free, and in the six realms and the four modes of life you live, with great joy, a genuine life in complete freedom."

General Kan was a brave general famous in ancient China. With his great sword he used to freely cut and conquer his enemies. Once one attains the satori of this "Mu," his absolute inner freedom can be compared to the man who has the great sword of that famous strong general in his own hand.

Having experienced this exquisite moment of breaking through the barrier, one's self, the world, and everything change. It is just like one who was born blind getting his sight. Here Mumon tells us how absolutely free he now is. He sees, he hears, and everything, as it is, is given new life. Mumon in his own poem speaks of this wonder, "Mount Sumeru jumps up and dances." Only those who have actually experienced it themselves can really appreciate what Mumon sings here.

"You kill the Buddha if you meet him; you kill the ancient masters if you meet them."

This expression is often misunderstood. Zen postulates absolute freedom in which all attachments and restraints are completely wiped away. The Buddha therefore is to be cast away and so are the Patriarchs. Any restraints whatsoever in the mind are to be cast away. For the one who has passed through the abyss of Great Doubt, transcending subject and object, you and I, and has been revived as the True Self, can there be anything to disturb him? The term "to kill" should not be interpreted in our ordinary ethical sense. "To kill" is to transcend names and ideas. If you meet the Buddha, the Buddha is "Mu." If you meet ancient masters, they are "Mu." Therefore he says that if you pass the barrier you will "not only see Joshu clearly, but go hand in hand with all the masters in the past, see them face to face. You will see with the same eye that they see with and hear with the same ear."

To live is an aspect of "Mu"; to die is also an aspect of "Mu." If you stand, your standing is "Mu." If you sit, your sitting is "Mu." The six realms refer to the six stages of existence, i.e., the celestial world, human world, fighting world, beasts, hungry beings, and hell. The four modes are four different forms of life, i.e., viviparous, oviparous, from moisture, and metamorphic. Originally the phrase referred to various stages of life in transmigration, depending on the law of causation. The reference to the six realms and the four modes of life means, "under whatever circumstances you may live, in whatever situation you may find yourself." Both favorable conditions and adverse situations are "Mu," working differently as you live, at any time, at any place. How wonderful it is to live such a serene life with perfect freedom, the spiritual freedom of the one who has attained religious peace!

"Now, how should one strive? With might and main work at this 'Mu,' and *be* 'Mu.'"

Mumon once again gives his direct instruction on how one should carry out his Zen training in order to break through the barrier of the Zen masters to attain incomparable satori and his Zen personality. How should he work at "Mu"? All that can be said is: "Be just 'Mu' with might and main." To be "Mu" is to cast everything—yourself and the universe—into it.

"If you do not stop or waver in your striving, then behold, when the Dharma candle is lighted, the darkness is at once enlightened."

This can be simply taken as a candle on the altar. Once one's mind bursts open to the truth of "Mu," the ignorance is at once enlightened, just as all darkness is gone when a candle is lighted.

Mumon warns his disciples that they should not stop or waver in their striving. In other words, he says that with might and main you must be "Mu" through and through, and never stop striving to maintain that. An old Japanese Zen master has a waka poem:

> *When your bow is broken and your arrows are exhausted,*
> *There, shoot!*
> *Shoot with your whole being!*

A Western philosopher has said, "Man's extremity is God's opportunity." When man is at his very extremity and still goes on striving with his whole being, without stopping, the moment to break through suddenly comes to him. This is the moment of fundamental change when one is reborn as a True Self. It is as if a candle were lighted in darkness. Darkness is at once illumined.

Master Engo has a poem in the *Hekigan-roku*:

> *It is like cutting a reel of thread:*
> *One cut, and all is cut.*
> *It is like dyeing a reel of thread:*
> *One dip and all is dyed.*

I join Mumon in saying, "Wouldn't it be wonderful!" In his commentary Mumon has tried his best to tell us how exquisite and wonderful true Zen attainment is, and pointed out the way to experience it.

TEISHO ON MUMON'S POEM

[...] Following his detailed commentary on Joshu's "Mu," Mumon wrote this poem to comment on it once more, so that he might clearly and simply present the essence of satori.

He first presents the koan itself directly to us: "The dog! the buddha nature!" What else is needed here? As it is, it is "Mu." As they are, they are "Mu." Those who really know it will fully understand it all by this.

The second line says, "The truth is manifested in full." The original Chinese term used for truth literally means "True Law," that is, the Buddha's fundamental command. It is nothing but "Mu" itself. Look, it is right in front of you, Mumon says. A blind person fails to see the sunlight, but it is not the fault of the sun.

"A moment of yes-and-no: lost are your body and soul." Out of his compassion Mumon adds the last two lines, which say that even if a thought of discrimination comes, the truth of "Mu" is altogether gone. When one is really "Mu" through and through, to call it "Mu" is already incorrect, for that belongs to the dualistic world of letters. "Mu" here is just temporarily used in order to transcend U (yes) and Mu (no). If one is afraid of losing his body and soul, what can be accomplished? The secret here can be communicated only to those who have once died the Great Death.

ENCOURAGEMENT TALK

Philip Kapleau

LISTEN TO THESE WORDS of an ancient Zen master: "Zen work does not consist merely in reciting a koan. The main thing is to arouse the 'doubt-sensation.' But even this is not enough. You must break right through it. If you cannot seem to do so you must put forth all your strength, strain every nerve, and keep on trying."

What is this doubt-sensation? It is a burning perplexity, a fundamental question that gives you no rest. For example: If all beings are inherently flawless and endowed with virtue and compassion, as the Buddha declared, why is there so much hatred and selfishness, violence and suffering everywhere? This basic question can be pondered whenever you find yourself free to do so—at home, at work, anytime. But when you are sitting in the formal zazen posture and using the body-mind in a more focused manner, questioning a koan like "What is Mu?" or an inquiry like "Who am I?—strictly speaking, "*What* am I?"—is a way of bringing to keener intensity this same basic doubt. The koan assigned you does not *replace* the underlying doubt-sensation; it simply sharpens it by raising it to consciousness. The basic doubt-sensation may be likened to a drill of which the bit is, "What is Mu?"

At first the Mu may seem artificial and outside you, but as you become more deeply involved with it, it will grow into your own most urgent life question, for Mu is but another name for Mind—this undefiled, all-embracing Mind common to everyone. You may wonder, "Why, if I already possess this pure Mind as a birthright, don't I know it?" The answer is, "Because your defilements, your deluded notions about yourself and your relation to what you conceive as the world outside you, obscure the light of this Mind." To raise the doubt-sensation, which grinds away these impurities, you must carry on your questioning at all times until the solution comes to you, for only then can you see into your fundamental nature, make real in yourself this Mind, and be reborn into a life that is truly alive.

Remind yourselves: Mu is my cushion, my mat, my body. And it is also what is *not* my cushion, what is *not* my mat, what is *not* my body. Mu seems to be a thing and a no-thing at the same time. Logically, this is a contradiction, so here, too, doubt arises. Or if you prefer, you may revert to the full koan, asking yourselves, "Why did Joshu answer 'Mu!' [...] when asked, 'Does even a dog possess the buddha nature?'" [...] Since the sutras say the buddha nature is intrinsic to all existence, Joshu's response is a contradiction, and doubt arises. How do you dispel this doubt? When you reach the point where there's not even a hair's-breadth separation between you and Mu, the "answer" will reveal itself and the contradiction will be resolved, for the question and the answer are not two; they only appear so to your dualistically ensnared mind, which discriminates self from not-self, this from that.

In the beginning, working on Mu is like bobbing for apples. You try to bite into one and it slips away. You try again and the same thing happens. But just as you cannot begin chewing and eating the apple until you get your teeth into it, in the same way, before you can ask, "What is Mu?" you need to have the Mu firmly in your mind. After a while, having gone deeper into the question, you no longer need to ask the whole question: just concentrate fully on the word "Mu," or "who" if you are working on "Who am I?" The echo in your subconscious will be "What is Mu?" or "Who am I?" for the question has already been planted there. Remember, Mu is not a *mantra*, it is a penetrating probe, an intense questioning. But even at this point the question will only scratch the surface if the Mu or Who is merely repeated mechanically. Just "Mu," asked as a perplexing question, is enough if you really need to *know* what Mu is; this keeps the questioning alive, and it is the questioning, fueled by the doubt and the conviction that you can find out, that gives strength to the Mu.

Consider a man sitting in his office who suddenly notices that his watch is missing. He looks about, expecting to find it nearby, but it is nowhere in sight. If he had left his office momentarily, or was not certain he had been wearing the watch there, he would search lackadaisically or soon stop searching and assume the watch was elsewhere. But if he had not left the office and no one else had come in, and furthermore was certain he had been wearing the watch there, he would become more perplexed and begin searching the office thoroughly. Knowing the watch must be there, his determination to find it, and the energy he puts into the search, would grow stronger every moment until he had forgotten everything else. This is raising the doubt-sensation. This is how you must question Mu.

But to do this there must be the deeper conviction that you can see through the koan in this fashion. And there must be faith that by resolving the koan you will realize your True-mind. As one master put it, "Where there is great doubt there will be great awakening: small doubt, small awakening: no doubt, no awakening."

People often wonder when they hear "to strain every nerve" whether it means they are supposed to huff and puff and gnash their teeth and bellow "Mu." They may even try this, and soon find themselves tense and overwrought. But what it means to strain every nerve is that all of yourself is involved in the practice, whether it is Mu or something else. It means not to sit blankly, or "Mu" yourself to sleep. Look at a cat sitting absolutely still as it watches a mouse emerge from its hole. The cat looks frozen but actually is almost quivering with concentration. Here there is no wild or frantic activity—just intense, one-pointed attention. You also see this in a hungry dog that has a meat bone held up before it. At that moment the dog's whole world is the color and size of that bone. And there are also people who, while sitting completely motionless and silent in zazen, have broken out in a sweat during the dead of winter, so intense was their concentration. This same samadhi-like state each of you can experience yourself through single-minded absorption in your koan.

One final word: Remember that while these hints are meant to help you—the roshi and monitors try in every way to stimulate and encourage, to pry and nudge—what works for one person may not work for another. If what is said applies to you, use it; if it does not, discard it. There is no one way, no should's or ought's. But do not resort to techniques; they are always from the outside. Techniques belong to the world of technology, not to spiritual practice. To apply yourselves fully some of you need to huff and puff, and this is all right for you because if you didn't work in this way you could never mobilize the energy necessary to break out of a certain level. The point is, you must find your own way.

JOSHU'S DOG

Koun Yamada

ON THE CASE

THE STORY is as you read it: Once a monk asked Joshu, "Does a dog have buddha nature?" Joshu answered, "Mu!" The Chinese character means "nothing," or "nonbeing," or "to have nothing." Therefore, if we take this answer literally, it means, "No, a dog does not have buddha nature."

But that is not right. Why not? Because Shakyamuni Buddha declared that all living beings have buddha nature. According to the sutras, when Shakyamuni Buddha attained his great enlightenment, he was astonished by the magnificence of the essential universe and, quite beside himself, exclaimed, "All living beings have buddha nature! But owing to their delusions, they cannot recognize this."

The monk in the story could not believe these words. To him buddha nature was the most venerable, most highly developed personality, and a buddha was one who had achieved this perfect personality. How then could a dog have buddha nature? How could a dog be as perfect as Buddha? He could not believe that such a thing was possible, so he asked Joshu sincerely, "Does a dog have buddha nature?" And Joshu answered, "Mu!"

Joshu, great as he was, could not deny Shakyamuni's affirmation. Therefore his answer does not mean that a dog lacks buddha nature.

Then what does Mu mean?

This is the point of the koan. If you try to find any special meaning in Mu, you miss Joshu and you'll never meet him. You'll never be able to pass through the barrier of Mu. So what should be done? That is the question! Zen practitioners must try to find the answer by themselves and present it to the roshi. In almost all Japanese zendo, the explanation of

Mu will stop at this point. However, I'll tell you this: Mu has no meaning whatsoever. If you want to solve the problem of Mu, you must become one with it! You must forget yourself in working on it. Your consciousness must be completely absorbed in your practice of Mu.

ON MUMON'S COMMENTARY

Mumon teaches us very forcefully but very kindly how to practice Mu. He himself attained great enlightenment after practicing Mu heart and soul for six years. This commentary is his *teisho* on the koan Mu and is a vivid account of his own experience. Read it many times and you will learn the true way to practice Mu.

Mumon says, "For the practice of Zen, you must pass the barrier set up by the patriarchs of Zen."

The barriers set up by Zen patriarchs are called koans. Among them, the Mu koan is exemplary. It may, indeed, be one of the best, for it is very simple and leaves no room for concepts to enter. That is the most desirable requisite for a koan.

Mumon continues: "To attain to marvelous enlightenment, you must completely extinguish all thoughts of the ordinary mind. If you have not passed the barrier and have not extinguished all thoughts, you are a phantom haunting the weeds and trees."

"A phantom haunting the weeds and trees" means a person who has no firmly established view of life and the world. In China, as well as in Japan, phantoms or ghosts are thought to have no legs. They are unable to stand by themselves and are always floating about among the undergrowth or among trees such as willows.

Since the time of Joshu, innumerable Zen students, in both China and Japan, have come to enlightenment by practicing Mu. In Japanese, practicing Mu is called *tantei* or *nentei*, which means, "solely taking hold of." Do it totally to the very end. And what is the end? It is, of course, nothing other than enlightenment itself. You must persevere until you attain it. Concentrate your whole energy on Mu. By "energy" I do not mean physical energy but the spiritual energy necessary to keep from letting go of Mu. While you are practicing the *nentei* of Mu you must be constantly and clearly conscious of Mu. Identify yourself with it. Become truly one with Mu. Melt yourself into Mu. To do this, you must forget everything, even yourself, in Mu.

Referring to this stage, Mumon says, "Concentrate your whole self into this Mu, making your whole body with its 360 bones and joints and 84,000 pores into a solid lump of doubt." In old Chinese physiology, the human body was thought to have 360 bones and 84,000 pores, but in the present day the numbers are simply taken to mean the whole human body. Being absorbed in Mu, you should extinguish the awareness of "I." All concepts and dualistic ideas, such as subject and object, you and I, inside and out, good and bad, the Buddha and living beings—all these must completely disappear from your consciousness. When absorption in Mu has become pure and complete, your body and soul will become like one solid iron ball of Mu. Referring to this state, Mumon says, "It [Mu] must be like a red-hot iron ball which you have gulped down and which you try to vomit up but cannot."

When this happens, don't stop! Don't be concerned! Press on! Then suddenly the ball of Mu will break open and your true self will spring forth instantly, in a flash!

Mumon says, "It will astonish the heavens and shake the earth."

You will feel as though the whole universe has totally collapsed. Strange as it may seem, this experience has the power to free you from the agonies of the world. It emancipates you from anxiety over all worldly suffering. You feel as though the heavy burdens you have been carrying in mind and body have suddenly fallen away. It is a great surprise. The joy and happiness at that time are beyond all words, and there are no philosophies or theories attached to it. This is the enlightenment, the satori of Zen. Once you have attained this experience, you will become perfectly free.

Mumon says, "It will be just as if you had snatched the great sword of General Kan: If you meet a buddha, you will kill him. If you meet a patriarch, you will kill him. Though you may stand on the brink of life and death, you will enjoy great freedom. In the six realms and the four modes of birth, you will live in the samadhi of innocent play."

General Kan was a celebrated warrior under Emperor Ryuho, founder of the Han dynasty. He brandished a great sword, cutting down numerous enemies. He is still worshipped as a deity of war in China. The wonderfully free state of mind of someone who attains deep realization through practicing Mu is here compared to the mind of one who deprives General Kan of his sword.

It is hardly necessary to add that when Mumon says, "If you meet a buddha, you will kill him. If you meet a patriarch, you will kill him," he is not talking about killing buddhas and patriarchs bodily. His words refer to eradicating all concepts about buddhas and patriarchs.

The six realms mentioned by Mumon are the six different stages of existence according to ancient Buddhist philosophy. There are: hell, the world of hungry ghosts, the world of beasts, the world of fighting spirits, the world of human beings, and the world of gods and devas. As for the four modes of birth, it was once thought in Indian physiology that the modes of birth of all living beings could be classified into four types: viviparous, oviparous, from moisture, and metamorphic. So the phrase "In the six realms and four modes of birth" means all the circumstances of one's life, whatever they may be.

ON THE VERSE

[...] "Dog—buddha nature!" The main case is condensed into one phrase. It is nothing other than Mu. Dog, buddha nature, and Mu are totally one. It is the perfect manifestation, the absolute command. By this, our true self is perfectly manifested with absolute authority to cut off all delusions. If you think that Joshu's answer means that the dog does not have buddha nature, you are quite wrong. For when Joshu answered "Mu!" he was far removed from the world of dualistic concepts. Therefore the verse says, "A little 'has' or 'has not,' and body is lost! Life is lost!" If you have the slightest thought about the dog having or not having buddha nature, your essential life will be killed by that thought. Now, just show me: Dog—buddha nature!

First Gate: JoJu's Dog

Seung Sahn

THE FIRST QUESTION IS: Buddha said all things have buddha nature. Nature means substance. All things have this substance. But JoJu said the dog had no buddha nature. Which one is correct?

The second question is: JoJu said "Mu." What does "Mu" mean?

The third question is: Does a dog have buddha nature? What can you do? Many students understand this, but understanding cannot help. You must attain the correct function of freedom from life and death—only understanding freedom from life and death cannot help you.

[Consider these correspondences between the author—Seung Sahn, also called Soen Sa Nim—and some of his students.]

> Dear Soen Sa Nim,
> Thanks for the *kong-an*, "JoJu's Dog."
> I have played (wrestled) with this kong-an for days, but I feel ready to reply to you:
> You ask who is correct, JoJu or Buddha? Buddha's finger points to moon. JoJu's finger points to moon. Same moon, different finger.
> You ask what "Mu!" means. Mu! is JoJu's bark, "Mu!"
> You ask if a dog has buddha nature. Dogs and men are just like this. When hungry they must eat, when tired, they must sleep.
> AAGH!
> *Ned*

Dear Ned,

About your kong-an: Your work is not good, not bad. But first, Buddha and JoJu: Which one is correct? You say, "Buddha's finger points at moon. JoJu's finger points at moon. Same moon, different fingers." You make many fingers. Also, you are attached to fingers. How do you see the moon? So I say to you, your answer is like hitting the moon with a stick.

Next, you say JoJu's Mu means JoJu's bark, Mu! Why make JoJu's bark? I want *your* bark. I say to you, you are scratching your right foot when your left foot itches.

Next you say, "Dogs and men are just like this. When hungry they must eat; when tired they must sleep." You say "just like this." But your speech is "only like this." "Just like this" and "only like this" are very different. Example: Here is a bell. If you say it is a bell, you are attached to name and form. If you say it is not a bell, you are attached to emptiness. At that time, if you say, "When hungry, eat; when tired, sleep," or "The sky is blue, the tree is green," these are "only like this." They are only the truth, but they are not correct answers. At that time, you must pick up the bell and ring it. That is "just like this." So "just like this" and "only like this" are different. Again, I ask you: Does a dog have buddha nature? Tell me! Tell me! If you don't understand, only go straight. Don't be attached to your understanding. Only go straight—don't know. Then, your opinion, your condition, and your situation will disappear, and the correct opinion, correct condition, and correct situation will appear. Then you are complete. O.K.?

I hope you only go straight—don't know, which is clear like space, soon finish the Great Work of life and death, get Enlightenment, and save all people from suffering.

Yours in the Dharma,

S.S.

Dear Soen Sa Nim,

You say I make "gates" [...] and "fingers" and "hindrances." I think this is so. I must make many things. I feel like I am attached to my thoughts and chase them (like a dog after its own tail). You say my work is "not good, not bad." Thanks, I needed that!

About my dog kong-an: Does a dog have buddha nature? My answer is, "I think so."

You say you hope I will only go straight and don't know. I will try. [...]

Respectfully yours,
Ned

Dear Ned,

Your mind is very smooth. Your only problem is that you are holding your understanding. Don't check your understanding. When your understanding disappears, then your mind is clear like space. If it is clear like space, it is clear like a clear mirror. Red comes, red; white comes, white. If somebody is sad, I am sad; if somebody is happy; I am happy. You can see; you can hear; you can smell; all, just like this, is truth.

You answer to the dog kong-an was, "I think so!" So I hit you thirty times. Why think? Zen is cutting off all thinking and becoming empty mind. Then this empty mind shines to everything; then, everything is clear. The sky is blue; the trees are green.

The questions are:

1. Buddha said all things have buddha nature. JoJu said the dog has no buddha nature. Which one is correct?

2. Next, JoJu said, "Mu!" What does that mean?

3. I ask you: Does a dog have buddha nature?

Three questions. If you don't understand, only go straight ahead. Don't check your understanding. If you are attached to understanding, you have a problem. Put it all down. Only don't know—always, everywhere. Don't worry about thoughts coming and going. Let it be. Try, try, don't know for 10,000 years, non-stop. O.K.?

I hope you will only keep don't know, which is clear like space, soon finish the Great Work of life and death, get Enlightenment, and save all people from suffering.

Yours in the Dharma,
S.S.

Dear Soen Sa Nim,

[...] In this letter, you asked me about JoJu's dog. If I were JoJu, I could have considered cutting that monk up into little pieces—although he's hardly worth the effort. Some people mistake JoJu's answer and say, "JoJu said that a dog does not have buddha nature." This, as Yuan Wu says, is like adding frost to the snow. Just by opening his mouth, that poor monk has already dropped into Hell; JoJu just didn't want to follow him there. So using his mind-sword, JoJu said, "Mu!" and stopped that Hell-bound train before it was too late.

Now, if you ask me this question: "Does a dog have buddha nature?" I might chase around and around my tail looking for an answer—but you know a dog chasing its tail has motion, but no direction.

Yours in the Dharma,
Mark

Dear Mark,

Your dog letter is not good, not bad, but much thinking, thinking, thinking. I hit you thirty times!! Again, I ask you:

A monk once asked JoJu, "Does a dog have buddha nature?"

JoJu answered, "Mu!"

1. Buddha said everything has buddha nature. JoJu said a dog has no buddha nature. Which is correct?

2. JoJu said, "Mu!" What does this mean?

3. Does a dog have buddha nature?

You must answer these three questions. Much thinking is no good; you must believe in yourself 100%. Many words are not necessary, just one point, O.K.? If you don't understand, only go straight—don't know. Don't make anything; don't hold anything; don't check anything.

I hope you only go straight—don't know, which is clear like space, soon finish the Great Work of life and death, get Enlightenment, and save all people from suffering.

Yours in the Dharma,
S.S.

Mu

Taizan Maezumi
Edited by Anton Tenkei Coppens

WHAT IS DHARMA? Incomparably profound and infinitely subtle, it is rarely encountered. For millions of aeons, see, it is hard to meet, hard to encounter. How come? You see it, hear it, receive and maintain it. What does that mean?

What we just chanted is the *Gatha on Opening the Sutra*. What is the sutra? Sutra is the equivalent of the Dharma.

You asked me to talk about koans. That's what I have been doing. Still I have one more day to sum it up what koan is and how to practice.

As a matter of fact some of you are working on case koans, some of you on Mu-ji. But all of us in one way or another are working on Mu-ji, see.

In a way you know the answer and that is the problem. One of you came to *dokusan* complaining, Roshi, you are tricking us. Mu-ji, what is Mu-ji? There is no such thing!

If there was no such thing, we wouldn't ask you to work on it. What is Mu? Is it some crazy stuff we deal with? Can't be, is it?

A monk asks Joshu whether a dog has buddha nature or not. Joshu said, No! You shouldn't get too involved with yourself but you should get more involved with the dog! No? Why not? Does a dog have buddha nature or not? What would you answer? Ask Sensei next time to talk about this. Mumonkan, the first case, that's Joshu's dog, see. And it's in the *Shoyoroku* too, the *Book of Equanimity*. The same koan, see, but slightly different.

One time Joshu says, No. Another time, Joshu says, Yes. He doesn't always say, Mu Mu Mu! We are not making any trouble for you, but you are making trouble for yourself. Mu-ji, what is it? And if you say, I am Mu—No! You're not Mu! Are you? Answer me!

What I am talking about is the most meaty part of koan practice. Am I right?

Dogen Zenji said all kinds of things. Like this, fish and water and bird and air. "The bird is life and the fish is life. Life is the bird and life is the fish. Beyond these there are further implications and ramifications. Now if a bird or a fish tries to reach the limit of its element before moving in it, this bird or this fish will not find its way or its place. Realizing this place, one's daily life is the realization of the ultimate reality, genjokoan. Realizing this way, one's daily life is the realization of ultimate reality, realization of koan."

What is this place and this way? That's what Joshu is talking about, see, this place and this way. And when you understand that, the realization of koan, koan manifests by itself. A nice passage.

"Since the place and the way are neither large, neither subject or object, neither existing previously not just arising now, they therefore exist thus." That's echoless, isn't it? That's what Nangaku and the Sixth Patriarch talk about. Who are you? Who is that in front of me? Where did you come from? What is your life? You can't say it is big or small, this or that, past, future, or even the present. It's a famous koan, see, the three times, past, present, future. All together it's ungraspable.

If it's ungraspable how can you see that this is it? I'm asking you! What is Mu? And definitely, Dogen Zenji doesn't say it doesn't exist. See, it just does exist. What is that? You can't even ask, see? What else can you do? What else should we do? Best answer? Shikantaza.

You do all kinds of side business; that's what makes you confused. You're supposed to do shikantaza and you're not at all doing shikantaza, but doing something else. You come to tell me, "I'm doing shikantaza, I'm counting to ten, and working on koans." In a way it makes sense, and in a way, it's outrageous! Indeed, you are inviting the problem yourself. Yesterday Sensei told me, "I gave one talk here about Mu-ji. And it was totally echoless! They didn't understand what I said." Yes, in a way it's a kind of understanding.

Mu-ji. What is it, see? These are so many instructions about how to work on that koan. All you should do is just do it! That is what you are told to do. That's the easiest, surest way. But if you just do it, it works. That's how it has been practiced. Now of course, everything has pros and cons. That's why we have different ways to practice. So I think Sensei is doing very nicely, sometimes emphasizing case koans, sometimes just letting you sit.

And in one way or another your life is the echoless valley. Regardless how you take it, it is a complete thing. Acting, reacting, responding, not responding. Rising and falling. All in itself it happens echolessly.

Maybe an important thing to mention here is that Buddha guarantees us, our life is no exception, the life of each of us is nothing but the wisdom and compassion of Tathagata Buddhas. It doesn't matter whether you deny it or not. Whether you accept it or not, that's what it is, see?

Hakuin Zenji says in his famous *Song of Zazen*: All beings are intrinsically buddhas. He has an interesting analogy—it is like water and ice. Without water there is no ice. And without sentient beings, no buddhas. What's the difference there? Ice and water. Ice bangs into things, it's hard. So, we should make it melt if we want to be flexible. So, how to make it melt? That is to be our practice, to actually experience that state of liquidity. Not solidness. Of course solidness is nice, but better to be flexible. So, how to make it liquid? Dogen Zenji says, "Forget the self." Mu-ji, the same, see? Dissolve yourself into Mu-ji! Don't hold on to yourself when you are dealing with Mu. Someone told me, "I put Mu in my stomach!" It doesn't work that way, you get stomachache. Then sometimes it goes up to your head and you become crazy!

So either way is okay—let Mu-ji occupy yourself completely or you give yourself away all together to Mu-ji. Either way it works. But no half way. It's the same with shikantaza. If you really do shikantaza you understand what Dogen Zenji is talking about. But if there is a split, you don't understand the absoluteness completeness of your life, of your zazen, of your breathing, of your practice. But when you really do it, you appreciate. Then the koan manifests as your life.

That is what Dogen Zenji says in the *Bendowa*. *Bendowa* is a beautiful fascicle. I want you to memorize all of it. And take any passage as a koan. Any passage is a beautiful koan. Even in just the first sentence I see dozens of koans. Even each word.

"All buddhas and tathagatas together transmitting *myoho*, subtle

Dharma." For what? In order to verify, confirm *anuttara-samyak-sambodhi*. To confirm that is the best way, unsurpassable way. That's what shikantaza is.

But how come shikantaza is so good? It is *jijuyu-zanmai*, self-sustained, self-contained, self-fulfilled, self-fulfilling samadhi! It's autonomous. It all works by itself, see? Jijuyu-zanmai, that's the key! So working on Mu-ji you can't be messed up with Mu. But you are the one to take care of it, whether it's Mu or yes or no, yin and yang. Doesn't matter, just take care of it.

It's an interesting thing, see, Dogen Zenji says the main gate to get in that jijuyu-zanmai is *tanza*, "straight sitting" and *sanzen*, "penetrating Zen." These two are the keys to get into that main gate. In a way he talks about zazen as a means to get into that house—whatever is inside, whomever is inside—right through the front gate. So we shouldn't stick too much to any particular idea, then we freeze ourselves. So we make ourselves to be quite flexible. The really important thing is to confirm your life as the *Hannya Shingyo* says and as Dogen Zenji says—no object, no subject, no this or that, no *yin* and *yang*. And be rootless! Don't stick to anyplace! In one way or another, that's what we do. No place to stick to, then what's the problem? That's in a way what Mu-ji is. If you say, "This is it," you got stuck to it, see. That's not it.

Then what would you say? Anything? Everything? Right there you got stuck. Your very life itself, nothing to do with it! Isn't it? What does your life have to do with all of this, anything, everything? So it shouldn't be ideas; that's what Dogen Zenji talks about here.

Just exist as thus!

What's that?

In the *Diamond Sutra* it says "ungraspable." Is it ungraspable? Sure it's graspable. Pinch your nose! I'm not kidding. Then how come it's ungraspable? Grabbing it and yet not grabbing it. What's that? See, there is pain, joy, and generally we believe that something exists as me. It doesn't matter if that's ego, survival, consciousness or subconsciousness, big or small, deluded or enlightened. We think something is here. And what does the *Heart Sutra* say? No gain, no loss, nothing, no wisdom. Not even no wisdom, that's funny. There is not even no wisdom. No wisdom, no gain, that's what that means!

We say there is ego, there is no ego. But we exist as thus, as oneself. And Avalokiteshvara Bodhisattva is the one who sees oneself who exists as oneself, by itself, of itself, for itself, it's very democratic!

I mention this because, being so, you can be the Kanzeon Bosatsu! Being so, you can really see what's going on and what you can do. I like that passage in the *Lotus Sutra* where Kanzeon expounds the Dharma to the buddhas. He appears to the buddhas as a buddha. To the shravaka and pratyekabuddhas he appears as a shravaka and pratyekabuddha. What does that mean? To expound the Dharma Kanzeon goes through thirty-three transformations: women, children, monks, laymen, laywomen, even animals. What does that mean?

It's a marvelous genjokoan! All of you practicing, really be Kanzeon. Live the life of Kanzeon Bodhisattva. What life could be better than that?

When you receive jukai, what is that? The most important part of jukai is to realize your life as Mu! That's what jukai means!

Of course, whether you realize it or not, that's what it is. No choice. I'm not kidding.

How can anybody say the practice of Mu is fake? If it is fake we make it fake. Actually it is not. Your life can't be fake!

To receive jukai is to take refuge in the Three Treasures, Buddha, Dharma, and Sangha. That's the important thing. What is the Buddha Treasure? Anuttara-samyak-sambodhi. What is that? Rootless tree. Supreme, unsurpassable, the very best way! Where no hindrance is found. Nothing is held on to.

And what is Dharma Treasure? Dogen Zenji simply defines it as pure, clean and undefiled. How do we make things defiled, good, bad, right, wrong, clean, dirty? Even to say *pure* and *genuine* in a way is defilement too. But we have to say something. Genuine, apart from defilement, see that's the Dharma. No yin and yang, no subject, object. No separation. If there is no separation how can you compare anything as if one thing is better or worse than the other?

This infinitely subtle Dharma is nothing but our life. Even calling it pure and genuine, that much is extra! Such a genuine, solid, nice, unified thing as our life which exists as thus, is the echoless valley that Dogen Zenji talks about.

One lady asked the sisters, "The corpse is here, where did the man go?"

What's left? Buddha nature is left. Isn't it a nice way to say it? If you don't believe it, I can't help it. If buddha nature is gone, what is left? You're left as you are. What's wrong with that?

I'm trying to put this together, see—what case koan means, what genjokoan means, what our life means, what taking jukai means. And who is Kanzeon Bodhisattva? What to do with your life?

All together, it's nothing but koan. How to solve it? In a way, such an attitude is already a little bit out of place. What is there to solve? It's already solved. And saying it's already solved is not quite right either. It has never been a problem! I'm glad you laugh!

Many koans are like that. "My mind is uneasy, it is not at peace. Please pacify it." Isn't that what you ask? Bring me your uneasy mind! There is no such mind! "I am not liberated, please liberate me." Who binds you?

Isn't it obvious?

This koan "yes" "no." Doesn't matter whether it's yes or no. What is buddha nature? That's what Dogen Zenji says: instead of thinking about where is Mu or what is Mu, consider what buddha nature is. That's what Bodhidharma says too. To realize your own buddha nature is to receive jukai, to receive *kai* to transmit kai. Actually kai, that's what buddha nature is.

What is the koan? It's really nothing but *my* life. Not your life or their lives—always *my* life. And when I really make my life the life of the Three Treasures, then everything becomes my life. That's truly what Buddha is. Since we are baby buddhas we try to grow up. So all together, in one way or another, it's a wonderful genjokoan. So please appreciate your life.

METHOD OF PRACTICE

Thich Thien-An

MU CAN BE USED as a meditation technique. This method is practiced primarily in the Rinzai Zen tradition, where the koan "Mu" is especially emphasized. The body is kept straight, the hands together on the lap, with the thumbs touching each other on top so as to make a circle. This circle represents Mu, the moon and emptiness. During meditation the mind is kept in a state of emptiness. The meditator meditates that he is Mu, that all beings are Mu, that everything is Mu. Because all is Mu there is no separate identity. All men are interrelated and interdependent, all extensions of each other. Through this method of meditation we can realize the oneness of all things. In this oneness we can discover our true Self and learn to live in harmony with others and in unity with the whole universe. Let us be with Mu, meditate on Mu, and feel Mu—nothing more or nothing less.

THE EXPERIENCE OF WU

Sheng Yen

THE DOOR OF CHAN is entered by Wu. When we meditate on Wu we ask, "What is Wu?" On entering Wu, we experience emptiness; we are not aware of existence, either of ours or the world's. This is an elementary level of Wu; if it is enlightenment, it is shallow enlightenment. When we go deeper, everything exists again. We discover that the mind reflects everything. This is a deep level of Wu.

Into enlightenment, there is emptiness. Out of enlightenment, there is existence. These phrases are not easy to understand. When we enter Wu, what are we seeking? Nothing. Nothing can be pursued or sought. Thus it is Wu, "nothing" or "there is not." But when one is deeply enlightened, what happens? At that time, there is nothing in life that confuses, misleads, or poses any problem. One is as expansive as time and space. Thus we say that entering the realm of Wu, there is emptiness; going deeper into Wu, one returns to existence. Emptiness and existence are not separate things; they are just one thing. Fundamentally Wu is the same as existence. If there is existence in deep enlightenment, is there also self? Yes. If you didn't have a self, you wouldn't be able to do anything. In truth, it is the attachment to self that has vanished.

Therefore, you should not think that the self ceases to exist with enlightenment. The enlightened self exists on behalf of all things. However, at the deepest levels of enlightenment one does not exist on behalf of anything; one just exists.

In Buddhism we often speak of the enlightened state as "no-self" because we have no better words for it. What this phrase says is that, at this stage, existence does not rely on self, others, or anything. It is a spontaneous, natural existence. Accordingly, one helps sentient beings. Not for the sake of self, not for the sake of others; one just naturally helps sentient beings.

Deeply enlightened persons need not maintain any particular identity; they have no need for position or place. Nor is it necessary for them to adopt an identity in accordance with the sentient beings they are helping. Bodhisattvas have no particular point of view. Like a mirror, they are only a reflection of sentient beings. They do not say, "I will behave in this or that way to help people." They reflect the problems and attitudes of sentient beings, but fundamentally these problems don't exist for them. Otherwise, they would need a point of view. When one exists neither for oneself nor for others, but just naturally helps sentient beings, this is called "no-function." If you were to have a particular point of view, then it would not be no-function. When you think of function, you are still thinking in terms of "in order to…" So we say 'no-function.' This is Wu, emptiness.

MODERN COMMENTARIES

"Mu" by Taizan Maezumi

THREE COMMENTARIES

Shodo Harada

Translated by Daichi Priscilla Storandt

Edited by Jane Shotaku Lago,
Tim Jundo Williams, and Mitra Bishop

1.

WE HAVE TO DO ZAZEN in *complete* dedication to it with every single one of our 360 thousand smallest pores and all of our joints, from the top of our head to the bottoms of our feet. With every single bit of our body, mind, and being we burn with this deep desire to know!

[...] We have to burn completely, from the top of our heads to the bottoms of our feet. We have to burn with this Mu, we have to burn with this question, this investigation! We have to do it to where our hands are Mu and our feet are Mu and our body and mind and everything are burning with this Mu and we don't get caught on any nihilistic *or* confirmative idea about anything. That Mu is burning! It's as if we have swallowed a brightly burning, shining, hot iron ball that is in our mouth. We can't swallow it down completely nor can we spit it out—to do the Mu with this state of mind! And because we do that we are able to continue in all of the twenty-four hours of the day. From morning to night, from night to morning we continue to let go of every single bit of our mental understanding. All of our conditioning, all of our habits—they are loosened and ripped away. Any idea that we have understood this previously, any idea of a previous experience we may have ever had—that all has to go. It all has to be let go of totally; we are directly becoming and perceiving this life energy, exactly as it is. We just use this Mu as its expression. That which has no form, that which has no substance—to realize that directly, we do this Mu.

We do this Mu on and on and on, and that life energy is continuing without any gap, without any pause. We ripen and we ripen and we ripen as we continue until eventually we can't even tell what is going on, what we're doing, what is going on around us. *This* has no shape and cannot be found anywhere as something particular, but only in a state of mind that pierces through it all and overflows in every single direction. A truly serene state of mind, it pours through everything. There are no longer any small-minded ideas possible. We can't have a thought in this state of mind, only the actuality of that full tautness surging through us beyond any possibility of verbal expression. And then we become just like a person who cannot speak, a person who is mute, unable to talk, trying to tell their dream. We cannot express this with words.

We can only continue—and we continue until we realize that place. We pass through here to—what will it be? What will it be that will bring this into rebirth? For the Buddha it was becoming the morning star; for Hakuin it was the ringing of the morning bell. But it is not that idea that we are hearing something or that we are seeing something with our eyes. It is not a small and divided-up matter like that; it is filling our ears, it is filling our eyes, it extends throughout the heavens and earth. What is it that made Master Tozan sweat so profusely when that question was asked? That state of mind is what has to be realized with our whole experience, not left up to some idea about a God or a buddha, but to realize this experience totally, or it is not living Zen.

2.

Twice the terrorists have attacked London, and even now the horror of those attacks has not allowed life to return to normal. The fear continues. Those who were killed were written about in the paper, while those who survived are filled with the possibility of their own deaths. It is said that humans can become buddhas, but they can also become devils. Those possibilities seem apparent when something like this happens.

When people, through no fault of their own, are killed by those who are so dissatisfied and discontent, the entire world becomes a battlefield. When people are under severe pressure, their dissatisfaction can explode. Then hate gives birth to hate, anger gives birth to anger. There is no solution to this. When someone wants to kill people in great numbers, there's no way to prevent it or to prepare for it.

People all over the world become more insecure and full of fear. Buddhism says that human beings have five types of eyes: physical eyes, heavenly eyes, eternal eyes, Dharma eyes, and buddha eyes.

If we look at human beings with our physical eyes, there is no question that we are animals. The heavenly eyes see things that are far away; they have no perception of a physical body. Eternal eyes see humans as they really are, in true emptiness; these are the eyes of wisdom. Dharma eyes are those that see the emptiness and see this world and humans as beautiful; these are the eyes of the artist. The Buddha eyes see all beings as our own children, to be loved from pure compassion. To see everything as empty and every person as our own child is to love everything dearly. To open the eye of compassion is enlightenment or satori.

Our transient naked eye sees humans in their animal form. If there is any way to stop the idiocy of people today it is through Buddhism, which sees and knows all people as buddhas.

[...] Once a monk asked Joshu, "Does a dog have buddha nature?" The monk wanted to know if even a dog has buddha nature.

The Buddha taught that all things—even plants, trees, and grasses— are without exception endowed with buddha nature. Does this hungry, greedy dog, who goes searching from garbage pail to garbage can, also have buddha nature? This mind that is always looking for something, wishing for something to be thankful for and always getting caught on everything that happens, this unawakened person like me, is there really buddha nature there? This is what the monk was asking.

This type of question makes use of the commonplace things among which we live. In making use of those things, we find the true mastery of Zen.

Without hesitating, Joshu replied, "Mu."

This answer of Joshu has become an enormous challenge used by all people of training to realize truth. New people of training have to pass this barrier before going further with their training. It's basic that all beings are from the origin buddhas; this is a given, a bottom-line understanding. Joshu did not negate this. If we look at it in a different way, he is saying that the substance of buddha nature is Mu. Joshu is presenting this from his own experience, and it's from there that this Mu is born and has profound meaning. To realize this we have to know the same experience; an intellectual explanation won't do. If we don't go beyond that, we can't realize the true experience of all existence.

Buddha nature is that with which we all are endowed prior to our personality and our character. It's the same in everyone and unites all beings. It is pure human nature.

It can also be called the true Dharma, that law which is true for the original mind of all beings. Because it is a law of mind, it has no form and no substance. It has no color, yet it has light and a life energy that brings wonder. It is energy that has no form yet has the ability to make all things happen, to move everything. This is why none of the dualistic opposites of the world—such as male versus female, political power versus powerlessness—have anything to do with true wisdom. The energy of this is the same in every era, forever, without change.

This energy is shared by all people. Even if we die, it doesn't die. It's beyond birth and death, embracing everything while going beyond space. It transcends all time. That which is unlimited and unable to be described is buddha nature. Because we don't realize this we are confused and deluded from dusk to dawn. To this question Joshu answered succinctly, "Mu."

The person who compiled the *Mumonkan*, Mumon Ekai Roshi, took six years to realize this koan. He wrote that all day, every day, he carried this Mu, forgetting everything else until he even forgot to keep his feet moving. Then, when he heard the drum signaling a ceremony he suddenly broke through completely. In the first chapter of the *Mumonkan*, Joshu's Mu, he writes, "With all of the 360 smallest joints, the 84,000 pores, we bring forth this great doubt and day and night work intently at it. Do not attempt nihilistic or dualistic interpretations. It is like having gulped a red hot iron ball. You try to spit it out but can't."

Your whole body, your whole mind, has to go into this from the top of your head to the bottoms of your feet. With your whole body and mind you have to throw yourself completely into this, giving rise to this great doubt. You must bring the actuality of your concentration into full view. You have to melt into oneness with Mu.

Your whole body and mind are thrown into that Mu as you become it. Day and night, work intently at it. Do not attempt conceptual interpretations. From morning until night and from night until morning, become a complete fool: *muuuuumuuuu*. Bring your awareness into one word, focus your attention into one point, and come to know this place where it is as if you have a burning red hot iron ball in your throat that you can neither swallow nor spit out. Entering this place, you are aware of nothing but Mu. This is what is most important; this is samadhi. Samadhi is the central point of Buddhism, the fulcrum. To understand the truth of any religion there has to be this pure concentration.

Continue with not a second of laxness—*muu muu muu*—keeping it going until you enter samadhi. Cut away all of the illusory discriminating knowledge and consciousness you have accumulated, and keep on working harder. All of that muddy past awareness and ideas, all of that gathered previous knowledge you thought was necessary, all of it obscures your clear awareness. With *muuumuuumuu*, concentrate and let go of all of that extra thinking. Then you return to the state of mind you had at birth and continue for one week, two weeks, one year, two years, until your efforts come to fruition and there's no longer any sense of a difference between inside and outside, self and other. You become one layer of mu—no more self, no more heavens and earth, only one layer of Mu. Then it's as if you have seen a dream but are unable to speak of it. Yet no matter how fantastic this state of mind is, you can't tell other people about it. No one can understand. You are like a mute seeing a dream and laughing, but no one else can get it. You are certain that this is the place the Buddha was talking about and smile.

But this is not yet enlightenment. Suddenly you smash the barrier. You astonish heaven and shake the earth. You kill the Buddha if you meet the Buddha, and you kill the ancient masters if you meet them. On the brink of life and death you are utterly free. In the six realms and the four modes of life you live, with great joy, a genuine life in complete freedom.

The actual experience of that place of no more inside or outside, just one layer of Mu, is truly wonderful, but this is still not the complete picture. There is no you there, so the ability to create is negated. That which creates the heavens and earth, that true self, has to be realized. It must be manifested. This place of no inside and no outside is what the ancients called the Great Death. From there, from that absolute Mu, you have to come back to life, exploding into the place that startles the heavens and the earth.

Within each person's actual truth we die and die and die, and then with one touch from the outside our mind is reborn completely with vivid life energy. Startling the heavens and the earth, we are suddenly reborn. It can be only this way, as if the skies are falling. Everything we ever held on to is let go of, and we can then realize this world of nothing at all in one instant of experience. If you know this experience, it is as if you have snatched the sword of the great General Kan. You kill the Buddha if you meet him, and you kill the ancients if you meet them. A totally free and infinite functioning is born. In this whole world there is nothing to be thankful to, nothing to enter your awareness in any way. This is because even an idea of something to be thankful for is already dualistic. In clear awareness there is nowhere for even the tiniest bit of shadow to enter.

On the brink of life and death we are utterly free. There is no way for even birth and death to remain. Even that great problem is no longer something to be attached to. In all the modes of life we know great joy. We become all life-forms—we know this world, the animals' world, or any world. We have nothing to be deluded by. We are attached to nothing and moved around by nothing. As Rinzai puts it, to be in hell is like being at the amusement park. Even if we are right smack in the middle of the worst hell, it's as if we are in the best amusement park.

In telling us how to do Mu, Mumon says to put it all aside and look at Mu with everything you have; all of your concentration, every bit of your body and mind. If from morning until night you continue your attentive focus with no gap, then it is as it was described in the old days: from a flavorless stone, a spark will rise. But most important of all is to allow no gaps for thoughts. This is the only way it works. Mumon Ekai teaches us from his own experience and kindly explains in greatest detail. This is the true teaching for this koan, not Joshu's one word of "Mu." We are not looking at anything extra or holding anything else in our mind when we do that Mu. Our practice ends with that, but the actual case continues: "It is said that there is buddha nature in a dog. So why does the master say Mu?"

The Buddha said that all beings have buddha nature, so why do you say Mu about this dog? Why do you say there is nothing there?

Joshu replies that it is because of the karma of our five desires. Joshu makes the truth of the matter clear. He acknowledges those desires and the various conflicts in society. But then why does the Buddha say we are all buddhas? If we have buddha nature, why do we argue and why are we deluded? If we are honest, we will always come up against this problem.

Joshu's answer is succinct: "Look! Or have you lost the buddha nature? Don't think anything extraneous!"

Here Joshu says it clearly. It's not about analyzing the six realms; that kind of mentality is mistaken from the bottom up. Joshu is not thinking about those various realms but is saying not to double your awareness. This is why his teacher, Nansen, said, "The three thousand buddhas don't know it but the raccoon and the bear-cat do—why?" What is being said here is that this karma has to be seen. Our eyes and ears and nose and mouth and body and feelings, all of our six roots, have to encounter that sword of Mu. Everything we touch with our eyes, ears, nose, mouth, and awareness, all of it, every attachment, has to be cut away to become that one Mu, or else it is impossible.

A different monk asked, "Does a dog have buddha nature or not?"

This was the same question, but Joshu saw what this monk needed and said, "U."

The monk said then, as if grabbing Joshu's tail, "If we have buddha nature, why did we dive into this shit bag?"

Joshu answered, "Knowingly we transgressed."

In the records of Joshu a high official asks Joshu if even he, Joshu, one of such profound wisdom, will still fall into hell? Joshu replies, "Me? I am going straight in ahead of everyone!"

The official was amazed and asked, "How can you say that?"

"Because if I don't go there, how will I be able to meet you?"

In the *Vimalakirti Sutra* it also says that the sicknesses of the Bodhisattva come because of the sicknesses of all people. "In the six realms and the four modes of life you live with great joy, a genuine life in complete freedom."

Joshu said only "Mu," but the greatest truth of the whole of the heavens and earth is manifested there. All of the roots of the six realms and four modes of life are ripped away. All of it is extinguished and let go of, and all of the roots of delusion and attachment are obliterated. This is the great Wisdom. All of our conditioned thinking forms the great doubt, and there is no person of training without this doubt. When our eyes are opened, we awaken to great faith. Here is the foundation of all religion.

And so Mumon Ekai Zenji says in his poem:

> *The dog! the buddha nature!*
> *The truth is manifested in full!*
> *A moment of yes and no*
> *Lost are your body and soul!*

3.

The great and well-known Master Joshu (778–897) lived a truly long life, dying at the age of 120. When his state of mind was deeply cultivated and he was at a ripe old age, a monk asked him, "I am yet unable to awaken to the truth. I have knocked on this door and tried at the next, reading this book and that, like a roaming wild dog, full of desires and attachments. In someone so ignorant as I am, where could there be anything like a buddha nature?"

The monk was humble, straightforward, and sincere, with that actual question and confusion that monks must face. Elderly Master Joshu replied, "Mu."

Since the time of Joshu, people of training have used his words for shaving our flesh and crying tears of blood. Putting our life on the line and scraping away our life energy we become tools of attack. Now, even one thousand years later, he is a monster we can't touch. With this word "Mu," Joshu was not negating the Buddha's teaching of the truth of our quality of buddha nature.

One sharp layperson who saw through this clearly has said that delusion or confusion is a division in awareness. Shortly after we are born we begin gathering all kinds of information, experiences, and ideas. We cannot live without being in dualism, yet this is a source of delusion, the actual substance of our suffering. With this Mu, Joshu cut through all of that awareness completely.

[...] Master Mumon Ekai had abundant experience and struggling, and he wrote of this Mu koan subtly and profoundly. Those who are putting their lives on the line with this koan can see how kindly and from what actual experience he was writing. Mumon Ekai Zenji wrote that to experience this state of mind of Mu one must become completely one with this Mu. With our whole body and with our whole mind, we concentrate everything into this one word of "Mu" and melt completely into that Mu. We become that Mu completely, all day long, from morning until night and from night until morning, becoming totally that breath which is Mu, making our awareness into a sword of Mu and with it cutting everything that we encounter. We cut everything that comes into our awareness through our eyes, our ears, our nose, our mouth. If for one week, one month, one year we cut away everything that sways our awareness, continually deepening, we will naturally enter into the samadhi of Mu. He teaches kindly in this way. He knows exactly what he is talking about because he has experienced it directly.

We then become at one with the heavens and the earth. Any space between the subjective that sees and the objective that is seen disappears completely. We are settled smack into the full tautness of Mu. Only right here can we know that truth prior to our separation. We return to this, and for the first time we know the very source of our pain.

The people of old called this the state of mind of no division between outside and inside the place of only one bar of iron for ten thousand miles. This is also called the Great Death. Without this experience we cannot talk about the Buddhadharma.

This transparent, full, and taut state of mind of Mu is very serene, but it does not yet have any creative functioning. After six years of meditation and training the Buddha entered right into this deep samadhi, and at the sight of the morning star on the morning of the eighth of December, he suddenly was deeply awakened and experienced a whole new life energy.

All of the Buddhadharma is based on this deep awakening of the Buddha. The base of the ego, all of life energy, all of existence, the true master of all was realized here, and with this experience everything was transformed and the true awakening occurred. To awaken, to realize satori, is to understand the deepest meaning and value of all living things. It is not just to praise the God in the heavens, or to think of things conceptually and as a matter of destiny, or to naturally throw everything away. It is to realize that the bright source of all things is our awareness. We must see this clearly.

Is this very mind moment a moment of purity or a moment of attach-ment? On this depends the meaning and value of all existence in the world. This is truly that one solid bar of iron that reaches for ten thou-sand miles. With this state of mind the entire world is purified, and from here comes all of world peace as well.

Joshu's Mu

Eido Shimano

About Joshu, no introduction is necessary. But, about Mumon Ekai, he was the compiler of "Gateless Gate," and according to the record, he lived from the late twelfth century to the middle of the thirteenth century—a rather important period of Zen history.

While he was a traveling monk, he met Getsurin Shikan Zenji, and it was he who gave Mumon Ekai the koan known as Joshu's Mu.

So Mumon Ekai, as a traveling monk, stayed at Shikan Zenji's temple, and really dedicated himself to the practice of this koan.

As you heard today, the striking of the hoku drum—today's first *dong!*—was good.

In those days evidently the lunch was informed by that signal, the drum, instead of the *umpan*. After six years of Mu samadhi, day and night, one day he heard this *dong!* And it was that sound that opened his eyes. He composed a verse, which goes as follows:

> *A thunderclap under the clear blue sky;*
> *All things on the good Earth have opened their eyes at once.*
> *Myriad things under the sun bow simultaneously;*
> *Mount Sumeru jumps and dances.*

Evidently, it was so great, that not only he jumped and danced, not only he was bowing; together with all things simultaneously, he couldn't help but bow. He realized that all existence on this Earth opened its Dharma eyes at once. In short, all existence had kensho with him. *With* him, is quite important.

He presented this verse to his teacher, Getsurin Zenji, and there was a short dialogue between them. Master Getsurin acknowledged the clear insight of Mumon Ekai. As all of you know, "Gateless Gate" has forty-eight cases, but case number one is the only one where he speaks on "what is Mu?" and how to practice.

[...] Mumon's comment—"In order to practice Zen," which you are doing, "you must pass the barrier set up by the ancient teachers." Actually, ask yourself: who has set up this barrier? Did the ancient teachers set it up? Did you set it up? A tenth of an inch's difference, and Heaven and Earth are set apart. "To attain this incomparably profound and minutely subtle realization, you must..."—*must* is a very strong word—"you must completely cast away the discriminating mind," which you have set up. It's your judgmental mind, your opinionated mind...that you set up. When you judge, and when you form opinions, you confine the world and your experience to something knowable, and then you are convinced you understand, and this is when you are furthest from true understanding. These are the greatest barriers. "If you do not pass the barriers," plural, "and do not cast away your discriminating mind"—your opinionated, judgmental mind—"you will be like a ghost clinging to the bushes and weeds." That's your life. The hungry ghost is not someplace else. If you open your heart, and introspect yourself, all of us would agree that we are hungry ghosts, pretending as if we were human beings.

Then Master Mumon asks, "Now tell me—what is the barrier of the ancient teachers?" This is quite misleading. What is the barrier *you* set up by yourself? You bind yourself. Looking at your faces, half of your faces say, "Oh I didn't do that." And *that is* a barrier! You say, "I won't accept that statement. It has nothing to do with me. Maybe ancient teachers, ancient students." But if so, *why* are we here to do Rohatsu Sesshin? Dogen Zenji severely criticized koan Zen, saying that unless it becomes your blood and your flesh, a koan may end up just becoming a game, a game of interpretation or an expression game..."Tell me, what is the barrier—it is this single word, Mu. This is the front gate of Zen." Not only front, but rear, too; right-hand side, left-hand side gates, above, below. We often quote a saying by Daio Kokoshi, *"There is a reality even prior to Heaven and Earth; indeed it has no form much less a name."* That is a poetic way to say Mu. But a quotation is after all a quotation. It's not your blood. Therefore it has been called the "gateless barrier of the Zen school." No gate in the front, no gate in the back, no gate east or west, south, north, above Heaven, below—*we* are the ones who set it up and push ourselves into a cage, and then scream for freedom. He's saying gateless *cages*.

If you pass through it you will not only see Joshu Jushin Zenji face-to-face, but you will also go hand-in-hand with successive teachers, Rinzai Gigen Zenji, Daito Kokoshi Kanzan Egen Zenji, Hakuin Ekaku Zenji, Ryoga Kutsu Soen Zenji, Hannya Kutsu Gempo Zenji, etc.... "Entangling your eyebrows with theirs, seeing with the same eyes, hearing with the same ears. Isn't that delightful? Would you like to pass this barrier?" Yes!!

Then, his kind, truly *kind* instruction starts...it is quite logical, not an enigma: "Arouse your entire body with it, three-hundred sixty bones and joints! And its eight-four thousand pores of the skin." Everybody understands this English, but to understand it is one thing. To *do* it, to truly *arouse your ENTIRE body and mind*—that is quite a different matter, than simply knowing it conceptually. Especially during sesshin, and particularly in the case of each one of you, and your practice: *knowing* is not as important as *doing*. Or better: allow yourself to be *done*.

"Summon a spirit of great question, and concentrate on this Mu." What is it? Is he talking about a dog? Is he talking about buddha nature? Obviously, at one level he was talking about buddha nature, which includes dogs, cats, and all. But, most importantly for *us*, as spiritual slaves awaiting an emancipation proclamation...Even if it was proclaimed, what's needed is *actualization*. One hundred years after Abraham Lincoln proclaimed emancipation, Martin Luther King said that nothing is changed!

Summon a spirit of great question, great doubt: Why is this? Truly, what is *this*?

"Carry it continuously day and night." One thing everybody does day and night is breathe. This ceaseless exhaling and inhaling. Each organ has its own particular functions: eyes to see, ears to hear, nose to smell. Hands to grasp. Feet to walk. Tongue to taste and talk. None of these has the exclusive function of sustaining the breath. This function belongs to the lungs and diaphragm. Between the lungs we have the heart, and beneath the diaphragm we have such organs as the stomach, liver, kidneys, gallbladder, small and large intestines, etc....Unlike these involuntary organs and muscles, the diaphragm is partially voluntary. It is the only one that we can influence with our will, breath and relaxation. You cannot tell your kidneys to slow down, you cannot compel your stomach to digest faster or convince your heart to beat at a different pace. But you are born with the ability to influence the expansion and contraction of your diaphragm. In other words, *breathing* is partially within the range of our control, biologically speaking. If we are constructed in this way, there may be some purpose or benefit to it. What we discover as we relax in our practice, loosen the diaphragm with our elongated exhalations, allowing inner organs to be massaged and receive plenty of oxygen, we find it gets easier to carry our breath-awareness day and night, to carry Mu day and night. When our diaphragm is too tight, even if we want to carry Mu constantly, without interruption, it is impossible. Even with all our sincerity, it cannot be done. Flexibility is required; depth of breath.

For this reason, going out to shout Mu is quite important. If you can train your exhalation it will become naturally long and calm. In the Zendo, when we sit quietly, our breath is naturally slower than when we are doing something else. When the *ki* (energy) circulates without impediments, essential concerns increase, while trivial matters naturally drop out. So, know the simple structure of the body-mind and its functions. As my friend Dr. Iwahara often said, "the human body is a masterpiece, created by god." Truly a masterpiece! What I have said is not at all a difficult thing, and you already know it. However, to train your diaphragm is the first step. The more you deeply relax, the more your center of gravity becomes low. The Japanese called it *kikai tanden* ("energy ocean, cultivated field"), informally known as *hara*, and it is considered the center of all practices of the Way: The way of the sword, the way of archery, the way of tea, etc....and of course the way of the Way, zazen.

It's not mere pushing, nor forcing—but gently guiding your energy down. Tenderly give attention to your belly, together with the diaphragm. Soften your belly, loosen the diaphragm, so that the lungs can work at their maximum capacity. Because the diaphragm's movement sends blood back to the heart, it is often called a "second heart." Our *second heart* is something we can guide, we can encourage.

So, we should know our own body-mind mechanism. "Arouse your entire body with its three hundred-sixty bones and joints, and its eighty-four thousand pores of the skin. Summon up the spirit of great question and concentrate on Mu. Carry it continuously day and night." To bring your total being, body-mind into a single question, "What is Mu?"

We can do it. In the meantime, "do not form a nihilistic conception of nothingness. Or relative conception of 'has' or 'has not,'" of yes and no. "It will be just as if you swallowed a red-hot iron ball, which you cannot spit out, even if you try. All the illusory ideas and delusive thoughts," which we unconsciously accumulated, life after life up to the present, "will be extinguished," in his case upon hearing the sound of the drum, *dong!* He realized that things he thought were real were in fact illusion. At least let us accept this much—that we are living in an illusory world and think it is real.

There is great resistance to accepting what I have just said. This too will become a barrier, set up by you. It's fear, really fear. More so than ignorance, it's really fear. You can somehow deal with loneliness. But fear! In Japan, more than thirty-five thousand people commit suicide in a year. Thirty-five thousand people successfully kill themselves. And the unsuccessful ones, those who tried to commit suicide but were somehow saved, are about five times more than this—so one hundred-seventy thousand people attempt to kill themselves a year. Perhaps one million people think about it but lack the guts to do it. The reason why I mention this in connection with *fear* is that everyone is afraid to die, yet they think that physical death is the answer to becoming free from fear! Really what they fear is living, so they run right toward death. And it's not only in Japan. I don't know the exact number, but it's a serious sociological problem all around the world.

"All the illusory ideas and delusive thoughts accumulated up to the present will be extinguished," in his case, *has been extinguished.* "In the readiness of time,"...this is my favorite expression, *the readiness of time.* When time is ready, everything is ready. Be patient! Not only in Mu practice, but also in everything else. "In the readiness of time, both internal and external will spontaneously merge." With the readiness of time you realize that internal and external are from the beginning *merged;* you only thought that they were two different matters, that one is *in* while the other is *out.* "You will know this"—in fact, you do *know* this already—and yet we search Mu someplace else. "You cannot convey it, like a dumb man who has had a dream. Then, all of a sudden, an explosive conversion will occur." This is available to everybody. But whether or not you can have faith in this sort of happening, that is the tenth of an inch's difference, which sets apart Heaven from Earth.

"All of a sudden an explosive conversion will occur," *undoubtedly*. It is the moment you have even the slightest suspicion that delays the occurrence. Don't doubt. Don't have fixed opinions, but believe in what Buddha said, in what Mumon is saying, in what Joshu says, "You will astonish the Heavens and shake the Earth." The Earth won't be shaken, and Heaven won't be astonished—*you* will be astonished, at how wonderful you are. How wonderful we are! "Sentient beings are originally buddhas," the *Song of Zazen's* first line. You will clap your hands and say, "Thank you, Master Hakuin, and I'm sorry for all these years that I did not believe you!"

"It will be as if you snatched the great sword of valiant general Kwan, when you meet a buddha you'll kill him." Not to kill the Buddha...you are the Buddha, so—you kill your self, your suspicious *mind*. "When you meet the ancient teachers, you will kill them."

We are not talking about the ancient patriarchs but about all kinds of delusive, illusory, opinionated, judgmental ideas, which we *all* have. They are our greatest enemies. You may think they are your greatest allies, protecting you; this is the typical upside-down view.

Heaven *helps* you when you become truly nothing: all right—I give myself to Heaven, or to the Dharma, or by whatever name you want to name it. Until that moment...you have to keep killing, killing, killing. You have to shout Mu. Don't use an ordinary way of thinking: how long will it take, how deep is my samadhi...in a way, that's none of your business. It will be sort of *given*, so to speak, if you have faith in the Dharma; if you work diligently, honestly; if you carry it continuously day and night, the readiness of time will naturally come. When? Don't ask that question.

"On the brink of life and death, you command perfect freedom. Among the six-fold world and four modes of existence, you enjoy deep samadhi."

Even though you may transmigrate into the sixfold world (the world of hell, the world of hungry spirit, the world of animals, of ashuras or angry demons, humans, and heaven) and the four modes of existence (birth from egg, from womb, from moisture, or by transformation) wherever you may be, you enjoy deep samadhi.

"Now, let me ask you again—*how will you strive?*"

"Employ every ounce of your energy to work on this Mu. If you hold on ceaselessly, behold—a single spark and the holy candle is lit."

Isn't this the greatest thing to happen, to experience in our human life? There's nothing better than this! However let us remember that there is no formula.

The verse says: "The dog, the buddha nature, *the truth is manifested in full*"—nothing is concealed. "The moment you say 'has' or 'has not'...," *yes* or *no*, *this* and *that*, the *moment* you say or think *this* or *that*, "you have lost your body and life."

Without judgment or opinion, without doubt or hesitation, be done with yourself.

On the Utter, Complete, Total Ordinariness of Mu

James Ishmael Ford

I LOVE WUMEN'S LITTLE SERMON on Mu. He evokes a lively practice and calls us to the importance of finding our own way into the Great Matter. And there should be no doubt, this project is as important as can be. This practice really is about life and death—and it's not some abstract idea of life and death. It is about our lived lives, our actual deaths, yours and mine. The old master gets it right down to his bones and marrow and he conveys it eloquently.

However, his very enthusiasm and passion can itself become a snare. For instance, there is no doubt that many of us encounter the koan as a red-hot iron ball. Particularly within the context of retreat where there are few other distractions, the question, the word, the noise Mu can become the holder for all the burning questions of life, rendered into this one thing. Mu. And hot is surely how that is encountered.

And it is also true that, for many of us, that red-hot iron ball isn't *at all* how it's encountered. Mu can be confusion itself. Neither burning hot nor freezing cold, just confusion. Mu can be a nagging something in the back of your head. Mu can be a small pebble in your shoe. Mu can become the longing inhabiting your dreams, emerging in so many unlikely ways. And Mu can be encountered like a blueberry found on a bush. You just reach out, pick it, and throw it into your mouth.

It can be any of these things. And more.

I have one friend who, many years before she took up the Zen way, was canoeing alone in Maine's far northern wilderness. Let's call her Rebecca. Out there in the wilderness in a moment as her paddle dipped into the water she was caught, first by the sound of a small splash, then by the feel of resistance as the paddle slipped deeper into the water, then by the smells of water and air and canoe all so clean they had little connection to the experiences of her life back in Boston. Rebecca was startled into silence. In that silence all that was left was the flow of life itself, a flock of geese, the clouds overhead, the splash of some fish, and that crisp smell.

The moment passed quickly enough, but some part of her never forgot. It seemed as if it were some small secret she and the universe shared. Time passed and things happened. There was a divorce. There were changes in work. Rebecca felt dissatisfaction with her life and who she had become, and wanted to find her way again. She thought what she needed was a spiritual discipline, and for whatever reason came to sit in the Zen style and ended up in one of our sanghas.

Early on she came in for an interview. We talked about life and practice and her hopes and we agreed that settling down and just noticing might be good for her. Rebecca took up the practice of breath-counting. After she had been sitting a while counting her breath, perhaps for seven or eight months, she had the thought that the koan way might be a right next step for her. And so, as is our usual practice in Boundless Way, she was presented with Mu. She made her bows and left.

Some months later Rebecca came to sesshin. A day or so into it she came into dokusan and said to me, "You know, James. I'm not sure why, but Mu for me is that moment of silence I experienced all those years ago, but made fresh. Instead of honking geese and the smell of forest air, it's the roar of that car which just drove down the road and that funny off-white color of the wall."

And she said one other thing. All of this caught my attention. We pursued the matter further. I asked her one of the usual checking questions. And she knew the answer. I asked another, and another, and she kept meeting them fully.

Here's the point. Rebecca never had the red-hot iron ball experience. She didn't need it. For her Mu was found like a flower opening, as gentle as gentle can be.

And if you think about it, that should be one of the options. What we're promised by the teachers of our way is that we and all things, we, you and I, and every blessed thing, share the same root. Mu is just a noise.

It is a placeholder. But what it holds for us is a way of being in the world, that in fact we're always experiencing. It's always here. We just don't notice it.

The catch is that the other way of being in the world, of slicing and dicing, of separating and weighing and judging, well, it's important, it's useful. In fact seeing into our shared place isn't particularly useful. It doesn't pay the bills. It doesn't get us a girlfriend or a boyfriend. It's in fact the most countercultural thing we can be about. And so, even though we are surrounded by it, often, usually, its very existence slips into the back of our human consciousness. And even though it is the background of our lives, we come to forget it.

But rarely do we forget it completely, it is our common heritage, our birthright as we enter into this universe. It peeks out at us in our dreams. It whispers to us in the dark. It beckons in the playing of children and the touch of a kiss. And it appears even in some very rough patches of our lives, sometimes the roughest. You never know when it will present.

Now I want to be clear here. Each of these phrases I've just used are metaphors, pointers. Don't look for a *thing* here. Just open your heart and mind.

Also, and this is important: there is a pernicious oneness, experienced in many ways, although most often as a projection of our egos. Here we come to think our sense of self, our ego, is the great One itself. And while there is a truth in that observation, the lie of it becomes obvious in the violence subtle or otherwise that arises out of our mounting defenses of this false one against the assaults of the world, all those endlessly arising other aspects of the One that are denied.

That said, back to the matter of Mu and its utter uselessness. If you've presented yourself to a Zen hall, if you've come for an interview with a Zen teacher, you're probably looking for an answer to some question about your life. There's been some nagging thing at the back of your heart or your head. Something, perhaps only the smallest thing, hints that the life lived up to this point isn't enough. Or even that phrase "not enough" doesn't quite express it; we find, those of us who come to Zen, often, some sense of dis-ease haunts us.

So, perhaps you're ready to let the call of gain, of success one way or another, fall down a notch or two. Perhaps you're ready for something that has no value. And so you take up our disciplines of sitting down, shutting up, and paying attention. Sitting is a good thing. Lots of sitting sometimes is a very good thing. And taking up the hard way is sometimes very necessary. Throwing our hearts and bodies into the practice, sometimes, can be the most important thing we can choose to do. There is a place for that red-hot iron ball.

But, actually, here's the secret: All you need do is step out of your own way. That's the only problem. We stand in our own way. It's already here. It's always here. Perhaps you first noticed it as a child, maybe as an adolescent. It's taught in Buddhism, and Taoism, and Judaism, and Islam, and Christianity. It's found somewhere in all religions. And, it's found in the hearts of people who claim no religion. It is as close as the throbbing in your jugular vein. It is proclaimed in the next breath you draw. It's found canoeing in Maine and it's found changing a diaper.

The pointers are everywhere. In that most Zen-like of Western spiritual testaments, the Gospel of Thomas, the sage Jesus declares that if you want to see him, cut a board in two, or pick up a stone. Saying you can find it when you cleave a board or pick up a stone doesn't mean there's some magical board out there waiting to be found or one rock is more precious than all others. Rather it is just this piece of wood.

It is just this pebble.

It is just this breath.

It is just this Mu.

Breathing.

Mu.

Presenting.

Mu.

Nowhere else.

Mu.

Easy as falling off a log.

No Is Not the Opposite of Anything: Using Zhaozhou's "Mu" in Zen Practice

Melissa Myozen Blacker

Wumen's Comments

THE KOAN MU contains within it the seeds of awareness that are cultivated throughout Zen practice, and Wumen's own commentary on the koan is an illuminating set of instructions on how to practice zazen, and specifically koan Zen, and how to find freedom from the constructions of the mind.

According to the teachings of Zen, everyone and everything has buddha nature, or the nature of being inherently awake. There are no exceptions to this. All sentient beings have the capacity to realize their own nature, and even nonsentient beings express it. Why, then, does the monk in this koan ask his question? And why does Zhaozhou answer him in the negative?

These questions point to the koan quality of the interchange. There is something here that disturbs, that provides a sense of not knowing, of being unsure. The ordinary cognitive mind struggles with understanding. Wumen's commentary that follows this koan in the Gateless Gate collection is a step-by-step guide to understanding not only the koan, but also how to proceed in the actual moment-by-moment practice of Zen. Let's look at it line by line.

For the practice of Zen, it is imperative that you pass through the barrier set up by the ancestral teachers.

The practice of Zen is not simply the practice of zazen, or sitting meditation. The true practice, and the only way we can really "pass through the barrier," is to learn to integrate what we experience while we practice zazen into every moment of our lives. This is not casual or intellectual study, but requires every fiber of our being. In each moment, our practice of Zen is actualized and made available to us. The barrier is something we encounter when we imagine that the life we're presently living is somehow lacking—that this life is not a life of practice. Passing through means seeing through a construction of our own making. The ancestral teachers are our ancestors in Zen, and they are also the embodiments of the living, breathing truth of this moment, who accompany us on our way through the barrier. They are rocks, stones, grass, birds, people, cars, you and me.

For subtle realization, it is of the utmost importance that you cut off the mind road.

It is easy to misunderstand the phrase "cut off the mind road." Wumen is not asking us to stop having thoughts, but to stop *following* them. To stop following thoughts resembles Dogen's advice: "to study the self is to forget the self." When we forget the self we stop putting a construction we call the self at the center of our lives. Similarly, when we watch the pattern of thoughts that arise moment after moment we can follow them to their origins, which turn out to be nothing more than fantasies, constructions of the mind. Seeing through these fantasies and constructions, we discover a world beyond thought, in which rain is only rain, not words or stories about rain. We come back to our true life, our true self. The "subtle realization" that Wumen mentions here is nothing more than this recognition of our naked, unborn self, alive to this moment, alive to the world as it is, not as we think or construct it to be. This smell, this taste, this touch, sight, sound (with no description in the way), this life, in this moment, and we along with it—perfect and complete.

If you do not pass through the barrier of the ancestors; if you do not cut off the mind road—then you are a ghost clinging to bushes and grasses.

If we are honest with ourselves, we can see how our usual life of the mind can resemble the condition of ghosts, helplessly floating and unable to engage with the world, clinging to what is useless, attached to objects everywhere. How can we avoid this attaching, this floating like a ghost and clinging? First of all we must recognize and even embrace this ghost-like nature in ourselves—how our minds wander "west of river, south of the lake" and how we cling to whatever presents itself to us as a temporary resting-place. The bushes and grasses are our habitual thoughts, our empty entertainments, anything that distracts us from this moment unobstructed by opinions and constructions. Even our relationships with those we love can take on the quality of uselessness or distractions if we fall into taking people for granted, unable to see them as they are, but as we want them to be. We cling to what cannot serve us, to what is fundamentally unable to nourish us. We are blind to the life that surrounds us, the life that, as the Tibetans say, is "kindly bent to ease us."

What is the barrier of the ancestral teachers? It is just this one word, Mu, the one barrier of our faith.

This one word Mu cuts through all of the many knots of thinking that make up the working of our minds. Everything that can be conceptualized is, at the least, somewhat removed from reality, and at the most, complete delusion. "People these days," says Zhaozhou in another story, "see this flower as though in a dream." To wake up, to recognize one's own buddha nature, and the awakened nature of all things, even dogs, demands direct perception, direct seeing, direct intimacy. Just No, just Mu, as a temporary skillful means, leads us to a moment, and to a life, where we exist in the world without commentary, without interpretation. This is the skill of Zhaozhou, who kindly and directly points out the deluded monk's confusion, as he cuts through what may be, at root, the heartfelt question: "Do even I have buddha nature?" In asking, the monk reveals his folly, but also his tender heart, brave enough to ask, ready to be cut through.

When you pass through this barrier, you will not only interview Chao-chou intimately, you will walk hand in hand with all the ancestral teachers in the successive generations of our lineage, the hair of your eyebrows entangled with theirs, seeing with the same eyes, hearing with the same ears. Won't that be joyous?

Wumen here describes one of the most tempting aspects of practice—the opportunity to find true, intimate companionship, in the company of people living and dead who have penetrated into this great matter. On one level, he's tempting us with a dualistic notion—that there are "special" people—whereas in reality, once we have touched the real nature of things, everything and everyone becomes our best friend. What's the difference between that cloud, the sound of that bird, Mahakashyapa smiling? And this is the very closest intimacy—seeing with their eyes, hearing with their ears—closer than tangled eyebrows. As the Sufis say, we long for the Friend, and even this longing is a trace of the Friend's constant presence.

Is there anyone who would not want to pass this barrier?

Wumen is enticing us again here: Enticing us with a promise of entry into a new world, a new way of being. This way is unimaginable until we actually experience it, live in it, and yet we tend to create expectations surrounding "passing through the barrier," waking up to reality. What will it be like? Will we be happy all the time, peaceful, content, serene? What will it feel like to heal the separation that has become so familiar to us, that seems so real—the separation of our opinion of ourselves from our true self. To live as a "true person of no rank" in Linji's phrase, to blend in with and ride the flow and current of our lives, is something everyone has tasted at some point—perhaps briefly and therefore unremembered and certainly unintegrated, or maybe profoundly and life-shatteringly, but then abandoned in the demands of consensual reality. "Isn't there anyone who wants to?" Wumen asks. "Don't you want to experience your wholeness, your birthright?"

So then, make your whole body a mass of doubt, and with your 360 bones and joints and your 84,000 hair follicles, concentrate on this one word Mu.

Here we have even clearer instructions, but how do we accomplish this? Wumen is talking here about complete concentration, but not in the way we are used to. Working with Mu or No takes not only our mind but also our entire body to accomplish itself. He is pointing to something beyond idle or even serious contemplation. We must merge completely with the question physically as well as mentally. We must breathe, touch, smell, see and taste No. There can be no cracks in this seamless work of cultivating a great doubt, a huge curiosity. What is No? Only No, only Mu. The body and mind become the bodymind and there is nothing but the question.

Day and night, keep digging into it.

Every moment devoted to this practice—this is what Wumen asks of us. What kind of a life can we lead if we are truly digging into our practice day and night? This is the life of one fabric, perhaps not yet realized, but enacted. We are instructed to do what we can't yet experience. Like St. Paul's "pray without ceasing," our devotion to practice prepares the ground for a seamless life. We are truly cultivating an empty field in which seeds of reality, through hearing teachings and experiencing life as directly as we can, begin to take root at the deepest place, eventually to blossom into wakefulness—into the opening of the mind's eye. Nothing but Mu, at every moment, filling our conscious and then our unconscious minds—every thought accompanied by this one word, which functions as a stand-in for a reality that is essentially nameless. Temporarily, everything becomes Mu, everything becomes No, every smell, sight, taste, and sound, everything we touch and think. There is no time off—there is only this one thing, called, for the time-being, No.

Don't consider it to be nothingness. Don't think in terms of "has" or "has not."

In fact, it is the nothingness that fills the universe. Mu or No reveals the essential nature of things, if we persist in using No constantly, faithfully, at every turn of the mind. How are we to understand something that is not the opposite of anything? The mind is forever making this and that, good and bad, has and has not. No is a single response to this dualism. It is the sound of the single hand, the original face. It is alone and has no quality of singleness. It accompanies, defines, and is one with everything.

Can we find a place where this one thing doesn't exist? In No everything comes alive, a voidness full of possibilities, and a fullness that is completely empty. The mind keeps trying to understand, and with each attempt, we must relentlessly answer with this single word, which means everything and has no meaning. This wonderful companion, dear No, dear Mu, leads us away from the suffering implicit in duality.

It is like swallowing a red-hot iron ball. You try to vomit it out, but you cannot.

Obsessing on some thought or series of thoughts, something that torments us and sticks to us like glue or Velcro, is a common experience for many of us. Here Wumen is inviting us to substitute something more helpful for these useless constructions. We must relate to No as we relate to something that completely preoccupies us. As strange as it may seem, we must become obsessed on purpose. This unusual instruction is a skillful means that directs us toward freedom. Just as the obsessive thought eventually unwinds itself, unsticks itself, often in a moment of sudden clarity, so No opens up, and what was foggy and muddy becomes lucid and apparent. This opening is only possible because of our mind's devotion to this one thing. Working with No is a discipline that trains our mind to be centered and one-pointed. It can feel painful or annoying because we must actually feel the stuckness, which is nothing more than the impossibility of understanding what is real with the dualistic mind.

Gradually you purify yourself, eliminating mistaken knowledge and attitudes you have held from the past.

All of the mind's constructions of reality have been acquired through a lifetime of learning how the world seems to work. These learnings are extremely useful in navigating the world of consensual reality, and without them we would be fairly helpless and would find it difficult to function. But they tend to obscure the actual workings of reality, especially if we trust them as real, rather than know them for what they truly are. To know that these constructions are representations of what is real but are not actually real is to be emancipated, to be freed to lead a life of bare attention to what is so. This freedom is the promise of No, and it is what is realized in the moment of the mind's awakening. Here it is, with nothing extra—just this, just this. No lights or heavenly choirs or even blissful states of mind compare to this feeling of rejoining our original mind, the mind that has always been present but has been obscured by our acquiring of seemingly helpful delusions.

Inside and outside become one, and you are like a dumb person who has had a dream. You know it for yourself alone.

The natural ripening of a person on this path may be so gradual as to be unnoticed, or so sudden as to feel like an explosion. Trusting this process of awakening, we begin to taste the experience of oneness, which is frankly indescribable. No matter how hard we try, we can't communicate this feeling, which is so unlike our previous life, our familiar construction of reality, that we may liken it to dreaming. But we have actually woken up to our true life, and we are struck dumb, wordless, in an experience that can't be described by the ordinary words we have used all our lives. It feels impossible to talk about this new, freshly felt life of realization, which is so amazing in its simplicity and ordinariness. The subtlety of this part of the path is misleading because it is actually not at all subtle. The profundity of the shift in consciousness, when outer and inner become one, must simply be lived, not described—but recognized, of course, by others on the same path.

Suddenly Mu breaks open. The heavens are astonished; the earth is shaken.

In another translation, Wumen describes this breaking open as the disintegration of the ego-shell. How could this cause such a powerful surge in personal energy, enough to shake the heavens and the earth? This shell of ego is of course a false construction, and as it drops away or wears away, the true self emerges, vividly alive and strong. This is the freedom of oneness, as Shakyamuni Buddha meant when he said, "In heaven above and earth below, I alone am." This is not a oneness that is exclusive, because it can't be—it includes everything, without exception. It draws on, joins with, truly is everything, and therefore is inexhaustible. Sometimes the idea of breaking open can seem frightening—after all, what are we to make of a phrase describing the loss of an identity we have held dear for so long? We have been fooled into identifying with a small, limited self, and cannot imagine a sense of ourselves as bigger without more ego getting formulated. We do not become nothing in this disintegration process, this breaking open—we become what we truly are.

It is as though you snatch away the great sword of General Kuan.

This path leads us to a life where we can truly meet each event, each person, each thing intimately and directly. This intimate directness has no hesitation in it. We perceive clearly, and we move or stay still according to circumstances. Like this ancient warrior Kuan, we are firm and direct, but not violent or wild. We encounter any barrier with an embracing heartfulness. The great warrior is calm and centered, full of wisdom and compassion—a bodhisattva.

When you meet the Buddha, you kill the Buddha. When you meet Bodhidharma, you kill Bodhidharma.

Some of us pull away from this seemingly violent concept of killing, so it is important to understand that what is being killed is constructions and stories—false differentiation. What is the difference between you and a buddha? We cause so much harm to ourselves by separating ourselves, by making high and low! Buddha nature, the wisdom of Zen masters, is all here, now, present and available, but concealed. In the process or moment of awakening, this wisdom is clearly and undeniably revealed.

At the very cliff-edge of birth and death, you find the Great Freedom.

In the boundless freedom of awakening, there are no dualities. Life as opposed to death doesn't exist. Each moment contains both and neither, and thus they are transcended, and we attain independence from them. To be truly alive is to know this at the deepest level.

In the six worlds and in the four modes of birth, you can enjoy a samadhi of frolic and play.

What this life could be and what burdens us seem to promise something completely different. How can we roam freely in the midst of all conditions and states of being, the six worlds and four modes of birth, which include difficulties as well as pleasures, joy and delight as well as suffering? The six worlds in Buddhist mythology include heaven and hell, the realms of hungry ghosts, animals, fighting spirits, and human beings, and the four modes of birth are from the womb, the egg, moisture, and metamorphosis. Wumen is telling us that we can now enjoy every circumstance, remaining fully present and focused wherever we go and with whatever we encounter. This is a life that encompasses and embraces everything. A life of ease and freedom, of frolic and play, is possible when everything is recognized as a part of everything else.

So, how should you work with it?

Here Wumen once again arouses our Way-seeking mind with his question, offering us the instructions that will lead us to freedom. It is important to realize that, until we awaken, we can't know what awakening is. And yet we desire this state we do not know—we yearn for it. Wumen knows this from his own experience. Here he is playing with our greed—beckoning us on into an unknown land. So much of initial practice is based on greed and desire, for enlightenment, happiness, power, serenity, or any one of a countless number of conceptualizations that are all we can imagine of the real thing. Wumen's use of our desire is truly compassionate, like in the Buddha's story of a father trying to get his children out of their burning house by laying out all their favorite toys on the grass. We come to his instructions eagerly, not really knowing where they will lead us. And we become grateful for everything that keeps us on this path, even our wanting mind.

Exhaust all your life-energy on this one word Mu.

The mind naturally wanders, and is filled with imaginary constructions of reality that bear some resemblance to the actual nature of reality but are never the thing itself. Wumen is giving us clear medicine for the ailment of being removed from the real. Teach the mind, relentlessly, to focus on one thing. He asks us to bring all of our energy, everything with nothing left over, to one point. Not letting the attention lapse allows us to make our mind a seamless fabric of this one thing. In a way, No is a substitute for something that is unnamable. In this practice, we give it a temporary designation, and we stay with this temporariness with all our might. Never letting the other constructions take root, we devote ourselves to this particular construction, simply returning to one thing, to No or Mu, again and again, until this practice of returning becomes one of abiding.

If you do not falter, then it's done! A single spark lights your Dharma candle.

You and the universe are not separate. In penetrating No, penetrating Mu, in realizing our part of the essential wholeness of reality, we free ourselves and the light of clarity that has been obscured and now is released. There is just this one thing, penetrating everywhere. "In heaven above and earth below, I alone am." This is not our personal light or our personal Dharma candle. It is the light that has always been present. We come alive to the fullness of our being, and everything else shines with its own light. Just Mu, just No—just this.

Practicing with Mu

On the surface, Zhaozhou's Mu is a simple dialogue between two human beings. When we first begin working with this koan, we must dive under the surface of its apparent meaning and possibly our own confusion about it. Our relationship with the koan begins when we start to deeply wonder, perhaps intellectually at first, what the monk was truly asking, and then to ponder Zhaozhou's answer.

As the wondering deepens, we may begin to relate to this dialogue emotionally, learning to identify with the underlying intentions of both the monk and Zhaozhou. We become both the questioner and the answering Zen master. And we recognize that the seemingly odd question of the monk is simply a way of putting into words our own deepest wondering and confusion, and that the loving, clear, and penetrating response of Zhaozhou is our most profound answer.

Eventually, question and answer both dissolve into the one word "Mu." When this dissolving occurs, Mu can become an integrated part of formal meditation practice and informal, daily-life practice. Wumen's suggestion to carry the practice with us day and night provides clear guidance in learning to take up Mu, not just as a meditation object, but also as a loving companion and teacher. Zhaozhou's one-word response to all of our longing and wonder at being human beings in the world can serve as a reminder of any small taste or great experience of nonduality. And eventually, our loving connection with Mu dissolves into simply becoming one with Mu. There is no longer any Mu, or any me. There's just this, over and over again, sometimes in the form of Mu and sometimes in the form of a cloud, a bird, a thought, a fire hydrant.

Those of us who have a firmly established breath practice can bring Mu to the breath, usually letting the word ride mentally on the physical sensation of the out breath. If we have felt grounded in shikantaza practice before we engaged in koan practice we can experiment with allowing Mu to be right here in the middle of whatever is arising, an accompaniment to the full presence of being in the present moment, something like the sound of a *basso continuo* in a piece of Baroque music.

Many of us find that the Japanese word Mu has a particular resonance because of the inspiration to our practice from reading Japanese-derived Zen texts and teachings. But we may also find that it is a challenge to focus on a word that has no meaning in English, and which can seem like a nonsense syllable. For some of us, there is a danger that the word Mu, because it has no meaning in English, can turn into a kind of mantra, creating a feeling of trance and a narrowing of awareness. While this may be useful temporarily to encourage concentration, we may become addicted to this feeling of deep absorption, and it can be more difficult for us to integrate our zazen practice into the hustle and bustle of the marketplace that we call modern life.

If this is happening in practice, I often encourage students to experiment

.with finding a word in their own language that carries a slight trace of meaning for them, just as a Japanese-speaker would resonate with the meaning of Mu in Japanese. Students with a familiarity with Chinese have settled in with "Wu." One student who is a non-native speaker of Japanese preferred to use the modern pronunciation of the character for Mu, which is *"nai."* An Indian student used "Neti," which helped her to connect with her Hindu heritage, and Spanish-speaking students have used "Nada," which can create a useful evocation of some Roman Catholic teachings, particularly the writings of San Juan de la Cruz, known to many as St. John of the Cross. And many native English-speaking students have begun to use the word "No."

There can be a risk in using No, or any word that carries meaning. Our ordinary dualistic mind can attach to the word as a reprimand or correction. The word No may carry a sense of negation, narrowness, and judgment. After all, this was the word that most of us learned when we first began using language to differentiate ourselves from others and form a unique identity. Anyone who has spent time with a toddler knows the power of "No!" However, continuing to practice with No on the breath or within the practice of shikantaza, this stage of feeling the negativity of the word is usually short-lived.

And with encouragement from a teacher, we can begin to open to a new meaning in this simple word, a discovery of the reminder of so much that can't be named in words. We may choose to add the word "dear" as a recollection of the generosity and clarity of Zhaozhou's original response, just as we might address a friend. "Dear Mu" or "dear No" can allow any harshness in the word to soften to a gentle, loving reminder not to become too attached to the mind's filters and concepts.

These filters can distort our perceptions, allowing the mind to create elaborate fantasies and thought-constructions about everything we encounter. Every time we say No to these thoughts and fantasies, we have an opportunity to see through them, to perception beyond thought, in which, for example, a flower is only a flower, not words, opinions, or stories about flowers. The compassionate practice of No allows us to see, hear, smell, taste, and feel, without any intermediary. By using No in this way, we become more alive to the vividness of this moment.

At this point in practice, Mu may take on a life of its own. As in Saint

Paul's admonition to "pray without ceasing" and the development of the practice of the Mercy prayer in the Russian Orthodox tradition as outlined in the book *The Way of the Pilgrim*, the effort and discipline of bringing the syllable to the breath or to the experience of the moment can begin to transform into ease. All thoughts, without any effort on our part, turn to Mu. Every time the mind attempts to describe, to remember, to put any kind of barrier in the way of nonarticulated reality, Mu arises as a reminder. It is as if Zhaozhou himself had taken residence in the mind, gently and firmly reminding us to lighten up and not take our thought-constructions and fantasies, or ourselves, too seriously.

When practicing with No, as No continues to arise naturally, the usually dualistic mind attempts to create a "yes" that is the opposite of this No. It is natural for the thinking mind to move into this kind of dualism and opposition. But with sincere and consistent practice, a freshness of attention is uncovered and revealed, and insight arises into a nondualistic relationship between No and Yes. This new kind of No always has "yes" embedded within it. We discover that Yes and No are one and the same. Any actual perception of the reality of the world and things, the senses and the mind, is found to always contain its opposite. Yes/No is one word, one understanding, and one reality. "Heaven and Earth and I are all of the same fabric"—another interpretation of what the Buddha proclaimed at the moment of his enlightenment.

This awareness of a world where there is nothing in opposition to anything else finds a visual example in the Taoist *Yin/Yang* symbol, where the dark space contains a dot of light, and the light space contains a dot of darkness. "No" deepens into something that is simply This, Mu, No, or whatever word has come to represent this understanding that has no name, and no opposite.

"No" becomes a way of talking about something that cannot be talked about, named or envisioned. It is like a stand-in for God, for the truth of the universe, for the Tathagata—"that which thus comes," which is what the Buddha called himself.

And perhaps eventually, but not ultimately, because there is no end to the deepening of this practice, we break through into the real meaning of No, and we experience the great joy of awakening that Wumen describes: "The heavens are astonished; the earth is shaken." There is no longer Mu, there is no longer me. Moment after moment unfolds as just this. This moment of opening to the source of everything allows us to begin to delve into the richness of koan practice, continuing to use No as a touchstone for that which cannot be named.

Even after many koans and years of practice, dear No, dear Mu remains with us, to keep us honest, to keep us present in the moment, and to gently remind us not to hold too tightly to anything that has something as its opposite.

Mu: Intimate and Simple

David Dae An Rynick

WOODY ALLEN put it succinctly in the joke that ends the movie *Annie Hall*: A man goes to a psychiatrist. When the psychiatrist asks what the problem is, the man says: "My brother thinks he is a chicken." The psychiatrist suggests the obvious: "Why don't you just tell him he's not a chicken?" To which the man replies: "We can't do that—we need the eggs."

This little story speaks of our essential attachment to the primary delusion of all human beings—that we are distinct and separate from the world in which we live. We perceive ourselves as discrete bodies moving in and among the other things of the world. We call this delusion "objective reality." The problem in cutting through this delusion is that the delusion is extremely useful. We need the eggs.

Seeing the world as a collection of objects allows us to make the predictions and plans necessary to live in our human world. We buy food at the grocery store for the meals we will cook in the coming week. We pay our bills and get ourselves to the meditation center in time for the teacher's talk. Through this amazing and unconscious illusion of the human brain, we are able to engage in the myriad complex social and physical transactions of our daily lives.

But this quality of human perception that is useful in so many ways is also the source of our great dissatisfaction and suffering. Having the capacity to plan is partly a function of imagining things could be different. We compare what we have to some image of what we might have, and this often makes us unhappy. We compare our bike to our friend's fancier bike or to the one in the advertisement and feel bad. We suffer because we wish we were thinner or thicker—or wiser or more loving. The Buddha's first teaching was pointing to this human condition of dissatisfaction, which he called *dukkha*. He said the cause of this dissatisfaction is our attachment, our wanting things to be different than they are. Wanting things to be different comes directly from the capacity to imagine that things *could* be different. All of Buddha's teachings and indeed the whole tradition of Buddhism can be seen as medicine for this condition of delusion.

This teaching, that our suffering comes from our attachment, may be easy to agree with, but to cut through the delusion of separateness is much more difficult. The koan tradition, and Mu in particular, is designed to assist in the journey of cutting through the stunning persistence of this human perception of separateness. It's not that perceiving objects is a bad thing—it's actually a necessary and wonderful capacity. The problem comes when this natural human perception obscures the other side of reality—that we are woven into the fabric of life. We are, at every moment, living our true life in the midst of this vast and amazing universe.

The point of Mu, and the point of Buddhism, is not to get rid of our capacity to think and plan, but rather to see through it so thoroughly that we are no longer held in its thrall. Mu is a tool to cut through.

In the Boundless Way Zen tradition of working with Mu, the student is first invited to reflect on the bare facts of the koan. What might have been behind this student's question: "Does a dog have buddha nature?" And if the teacher, Zhaozhou, were truly wise and kind, why would he say "Mu" or "No?" After these initial reflections, the student is instructed to become one with Mu—to become intimate with Mu. This is the essential work of Zen—to become intimate with our lives—to cut the gap between ourselves and ourselves, to move beyond this habitual perception of separation that is so effective and so painful.

Mu is what first brought me to Zen. Not Mu itself, because I had never heard of this enigmatic story about Zhaozhou, but this intention to cut through to the essence of life. In college, before Zen, I had a powerful experience of God's boundless love and the abundance of our lives just as they are. But the immediacy of this experience gradually faded over time—what was so vivid and unmistakable became just a memory. I could find no way back. It was then that I heard my first Zen teacher. He spoke clearly about the world of nonduality and nonseparation that I had experienced for myself. He presented Zen as a path of cultivating this experience of nonduality.

Most of us have had some experience of this world of nonseparation—some intimation that the world is more than a collection of objects, more than our to-do list that grows larger every day. Though we get continually swept away by the busyness of our lives, we have a sense that there is something else. We've read about it in Mary Oliver's poems and in Rumi's. We've had moments of great ease and immediacy walking in the woods or on the beach. Maybe we've read *Zen Mind, Beginner's Mind*—or the writings of other spiritual teachers. They make sense. Their words touch us. Some part of us knows the truth of this boundless world of freedom, yet our day-to-day experience is quite different.

The essential thrust of Zen is that intellectual understanding is not enough. Assenting to the idea that what we are is not separate from the world and knowing it for ourselves are two different things. Working with Mu is not an intellectual exercise. Mu is a tool to cut through the unconscious constructions of our mind. Mu is not a magical incantation or a mantra; it is a path that leads us toward our very own heart.

We can't stop our thinking, but through the working with Mu, we can break out of the habit force of our objective perception, which is so exceptionally strong. Mu provides the direction. Working with Mu, and indeed the whole Zen path, requires working with a teacher. Countless students have worked with Mu to find their way back to what they already knew—to the essential undivided nature of life. This experience has the possibility to change our lives at a fundamental level. Though, like every experience, it does not fixate in a particular place or feeling, once we have seen and known this for ourselves, we are forever changed.

There is no explaining the work of becoming intimate with Mu. It's not mystical and it's reached through thinking. The sound of the traffic is Mu. The feeling of the keys under my fingers as I type. This is Mu. Breathe in and breathe out. Now shallow and fast. Now deep and slow. Mu. The thought that I must unlock the back door for the repairman coming later today. Mu.

Of course the mind wanders away. But Mu is a guide, a direction toward this very moment. It makes no sense. This is beyond whatever idea we have about it. It points directly at the obvious that we set aside to get someplace else. Mu is the roadmap back to what we all know—the power and beauty of life as it is unfolding in every moment. As human beings we have the opportunity to live into this miracle that has already happened.

It's both ordinary and amazing. Nothing special, and what we've been looking for all our lives.

It's Not What You Think

Bodhin Kjolhede

What was Chao-chou conveying when he replied, "Mu"? He knew that the monk was really asking about Reality itself, and that he could only discover it through his own direct experience. Yet Chao-chou could no more remain silent than a bell when struck, and his response has gone on reverberating for the past 1,300 years: "Mu!"

What is Mu? The student could save himself a huge amount of time and trouble by laying down any hope of figuring it out. Because no one has ever figured it out. In fact, Mu's value is in silencing the figuring-out mind.

There seems to have been a time when students assigned to the koan Mu would grapple with the original story of the monk querying Chao-chou on the nature of a dog. But for the past century, at least, Zen teachers typically urge their students to focus simply on the word Mu. Thus the Japanese student who comes before his teacher will announce his practice as *Mu-ji*—"the word Mu."

What can be figured out about a single, two-letter word—which outside of Japan is not even of one's own language? The very foreignness of the word Mu to English speakers gives us an advantage: we're less likely to engage it on the level of linguistic meaning. If the question were "What is Reality?" it would stimulate thoughts. But when confronted by just "Mu," the mind is blocked. Thoughts gain no purchase. In *The Three Pillars of Zen* a frustrated student says to Yasutani Roshi in dokusan:

> How am I to entertain the question "What is Mu?" when I find it entirely meaningless? I can't even formulate the question for myself, much less resolve it. If I were to say to you "What is *baba*?" it would have no meaning for you. I find Mu equally meaningless.

To which Yasutani Roshi replies, "That is *precisely* why Mu is such an excellent koan!"

The linguistic meaning of Mu, then, is beside the point. It signifies negation, and is commonly defined as "no" or "not." But those of us actually practicing Zen would do best to understand Chao-chou's "Mu" as "It's not what you're thinking."

In Zen literature aimed at Western readers, the koan has often been likened to a "riddle" or "conundrum." But because our intellect is useless in resolving Mu, these comparisons are basically flawed. Coming to terms with Mu is both more difficult and simpler than solving any puzzle. Mu is more a solution than a problem. It's really another word for True Mind, and to the degree that we merge with it, we manifest this Essential Nature. The same could be true of any other word as well, but "Mu" works especially well as a meditation device in its sound—soft, open-voweled, simple. That, and the fact that at any given time thousands of Zen practitioners are mentally murmuring it, gives it a special status among words employed in meditation.

The basic instructions for actually working on the koan Mu couldn't be more simple: "Keep your mind, your attention, on the word Mu constantly. And whenever you notice your attention anywhere else, return it to Mu." Beyond this, it's all a matter of how *fully* the mind is absorbed in Mu. Even the newest beginner to Zen practice learns that our attention is usually divided; part of it can be aware of the breath or the koan while another part of it can be flitting around elsewhere. "Your mission, should you choose to accept it," is to become 100 percent absorbed in the practice. Thus, she who is working on Mu must *become* Mu.

To become fully absorbed in the word Mu is to be absorbed *into* it; no trace of self-consciousness remains. To reach this state—or no-state—is difficult in the extreme because of our mental habit forces. Until undertaking Zen practice each of us has spent almost every waking hour of our whole life engaged with our thoughts. These revolve around the notion at the core of our mental processes: "I." Ever since we learn this word and its sibling concepts, "me" and "my," they have occupied the center of our attention. Thus to become absolutely one with Mu, detaching from thoughts entirely, would be all but impossible save for one thing: we are already one with Mu. Mu is but another name for our own self-nature.

We *are* Mu, and always have been! Yet until we awaken to this fact through direct experience, Mu seems to stand before us as an object apart.

How, then, to reclaim our identity with Mu? There is no one way. In the beginning, when Mu seems especially apart from us, a common impulse is to try to mentally penetrate it. There it is, this *thing*, and we want in. Young men, especially, may apply themselves to Mu as they would a foreign territory to be conquered, a fortress to breach. They make one charge after another. Some may actually succeed, discovering once "inside" Mu that they were never outside it. Practitioners who go at Mu aggressively only do so out of a false sense of dichotomy between them as subject and Mu as object. But throwing your heart into Mu will dissolve even this most basic of human delusions—the self/other split.

For the first months or even years of Mu work, most students will periodically question whether they are doing it correctly. Even a more experienced student, when feeling frustrated, may imagine that if he could only get a more precise and finely-nuanced explanation of how to work on Mu, that would do the trick. Concern with right and wrong impedes the work. When introducing the student to Mu the teacher does offer practical advice to help him work effectively (though in ancient times monks would sometimes be left entirely on their own, and still find their way through Mu). But grappling with Mu is primarily a matter of heart. My teacher, Roshi Kapleau, used to say, "Technologies belong to the world of technology, not to koan work."

Applying oneself wholeheartedly to Mu, without calculations about method, is the surest way of discovering the essential spirit of it. Even he who feels compelled to mount an assault on Mu will see the apparent "otherness" of Mu soften, just as two boys can reach a closer friendship through a physical fight.

A more straightforward way to bond with Mu is to forego the battling stage and simply concentrate on becoming one with it from the outset. The teacher may suggest to the student that she endeavor to "embrace" Mu, "melt into" Mu, "sink into" Mu. "Love" is not a common word in Zen texts, largely because we are urged instead to experience the One Mind that is the very ground of genuine love. Yet the following words of the great botanist George Washington Carver capture the gist of resolving Mu: "If you love something enough, it will open its secrets to you."

Using Poison to Get Rid of Poison: The Book of Equanimity, Case 18

John Daido Loori

Prologue

A GOURD FLOATING on the water—push it down and it turns: a jewel in the sunlight—it has no definite shape. It cannot be attained by mindlessness, nor known by mindfulness. Immeasurably great people are turned about in the stream of words—is there anyone who can escape?

The Main Case

A monastic asked Chao-chou, "Does a dog have a buddha nature or not?" Chao-chou said, "Yes." The monastic said, "Since it has, why is it then in this skin-bag?" Chao-chou said, "Because he knows yet deliberately transgresses." Another monastic asked Chao-chou, "Does a dog have buddha nature or not?" Chao-chou said, "No." The monastic said, "All sentient beings have buddha nature—why does a dog have none, then?"

Chao-chou said, "Because he still has impulsive consciousness."

The Capping Verse

> *A dog's buddha nature exists, a dog's buddha nature does not exist;*
> *A straight hook basically seeks fish with abandon.*
> *Chasing the air, pursuing fragrance, cloud and water travelers—*
> *In noisy confusion they make excuses and explanations.*
> *Making an even presentation, he throws the shop wide open;*
> *Don't blame him for not being careful in the beginning—*

Pointing out the flaw, he takes away the jewel;
The king of Chin didn't know Lian Xiangru.

COMMENTARY

Every once in a while I like to present this koan and air it out for the benefit of the people working on Mu. In the Gateless Gate collection of koans, Wu-men deals with the bare-bones version of this case: A monastic asked Chao-chou, "Does a dog have buddha nature or not?" Chao-chou said, "Mu." *Mu* here means "no." That's the end of it.

That's all that Wu-men chose to introduce as the first koan.

The Book of Equanimity contains the above, expanded record of the exchanges between Chao-chou and the monastics. In fact, in the compilation of Chao-chou's writings, these two instances are not even listed together. They're two different encounters. Combining them into a single koan is a useful way of dealing with one of Chao-chou's teachings.

It is also vitally important to engage Wu-men's distilled version of the koan. Doing so serves as the cornerstone of the koan practice in our lineage. In the Korean lineage Mu is the koan students work with, studying its various permutations. Students working with a koan like Mu, or any koan for that matter, have to throw themselves totally into the koan, with the whole body and mind. They have to become the koan, losing themselves completely in this Mu. What is wonderful about Mu is that it's completely ungraspable.

When the teacher says to be Mu, the student has no idea what this Mu is. How can I be it? It's not tangible or accessible. The other formal introductory koans "the sound of one hand clapping" and "your original face before your parents were born" have the same attributes.

To really work with a koan and do it effectively means thoroughly immersing oneself in every aspect of the koan. I have a feeling that in the West "Chao-chou's Mu" has nowhere near the same impact that it had in China during Chao-chou's days, or even nowhere near the impact it would have had in Japan, with a Japanese Zen practitioner.

You have to appreciate the fact that the monastic in this koan did a lot of traveling to get to Chao-chou to ask this question. For him it was an incredibly important question. His very existence hinged on it. He risked his life journeying across China to reach this eminent authority and lay himself open in his doubt. Our way of dealing with authority in the West is very different from the way it is dealt with in the East.

When the Pope says something, some people believe it, some people don't, and some people argue about it. In the case of the great master Chao-chou, whose reputation was known all over China, when he said something it was taken quite seriously.

The monastic is asking a question that fills him with immense doubt. This is not an idle inquiry. The sutras say that every sentient and insentient being has buddha nature. He wants to know whether a dog has buddha nature. Chao-chou says "no." For many Americans, Mu is an important koan because it's the first koan, and usually it represents a breakthrough. The question seems not so significant. I don't think there are many people in the West who lose much sleep over whether a dog has buddha nature.

But this monastic did. And you have to put yourself in his body and mind, as well as that of Chao-chou to fully appreciate the monumental tension and the vitality of this koan. That's why Master Soen Sunim always tells his students, "I don't want to know about Mu. I want to know what Chao-chou was thinking before he said, 'Mu.'" How could you respond unless you're the body and mind of Chao-chou himself, the body and mind of the monastic?

There is a tendency among practitioners to turn koans into riddles or intellectual exercises, to deal with them on a very superficial level. For a koan to be fully engaged it has to become relevant to your life. You have to see the relevancy of the questions being brought up. If you see that, if you can switch places with the monastic or the teacher, or whomever or whatever is involved, then you'll see the importance of the koan in your own life. But if the koan remains an abstraction, a mental preoccupation, then its full impact doesn't touch you. It touches your mind, but it doesn't touch your life. You may develop a koan fluency and eloquence, but with no real depth, no real penetration to the heart of it.

The prologue says, "A gourd floating in the water—push it down and it turns." The prologue and the capping verse are speaking about the koan itself. They're telling you what it is about. A gourd floating on the water—push it down and it turns. That's the resiliency of the gourd.

When you poke at it, it just rolls over, slips away, and pops up again to the surface. You can't sink it. You can't fix it. It's free and has no abiding place. It doesn't attach to anything. That's Chao-chou, free and unhindered, like a dragon following the wind, riding the clouds.

"A jewel in the sunlight—it has no definite shape." Another translation says, "A diamond in the sunlight has no definite color." And it's true. If you look at a diamond as the sun passes by, as the light shifts, it changes. The sun changes, the diamond changes.

Is the cause the sun or is it the diamond, or is it both? Or perhaps it's neither.

What's the true color of the diamond?

"It cannot be attained by mindlessness, nor known by mindfulness."

No eye, ear, nose, tongue, body, or mind. Mindlessness is just blank consciousness. It doesn't function. Mindfulness practice is very conscious, very present, moment-to-moment awareness, but it still doesn't have the power to cut the roots of delusion. What's the reality of neither the yes-mind nor the no-mind, of neither affirmation nor denial?

The final line says, "Immeasurably great people are turned about in the stream of words—is there anyone who can escape?" The Hakuin system of koan study divides the koans into five groups. First are the *dharmakaya* koans, koans concerned with the absolute basis of reality. The second group contains the *kikan* koans on differentiation. Then there are *nanto* koans—koans that are difficult to pass through. There are also koans concerned with words and phrases, and how we get stuck in language. Finally there are the *goi* koans, pertaining to the Five Ranks of Master Tung-shan. In our lineage, the seven hundred koans taken up during the course of complete training are not broken up that way. They're all mixed together. But there is a lot of attention given to koans on the use of words and phrases. These are the places where we really stick. Examples abound. A monastic shows up, walks around his teacher's seat in a circle, rattles the rings on his staff, and the teacher says, "Right!" The monastic then goes to another teacher, does exactly the same thing, shakes the staff, and the teacher says, "Wrong!" "Why? The first teacher said I was right. Why do you say I'm wrong?" "He was right. You're wrong," the teacher responds. Why was he wrong? Why did one say "yes" and the other say "no"? Why did Master Fa-yen say, "One has it, one has not" when two monastics followed his instructions to the letter and did exactly the same thing, responding in precisely the same way? Why did Chao-chou say to one monastic that a dog has buddha nature, and to another monastic that he does not?

When we established Zen Mountain Monastery in 1980, there was an old man who used to hang out around the property. His name was Mr. Wilson. He had a dog, a big black Labrador mix that followed him every place he went. We couldn't find out much about Mr. Wilson from Mr. Wilson. He was somewhat incoherent, a bit eccentric. So I called up the property's previous owners and described him. They said, "Oh, he comes with the place." Mr. Wilson was always smiling. He had a beautiful smile—no teeth, but a smile that would light up his face. And he loved to walk. That's all he did from dawn until dusk.

He'd get up early in the morning and he would walk, just walk and walk and walk. We'd see him in Kingston or along the highways. We would always see him walking, with the dog close on his heels. We used to call the dog Ms. Wilson.

Mr. Wilson was a World War II veteran. What I gathered from the locals is that he evidently suffered some sort of injury in active combat. As a result he was "a little off." He would tell us incredible stories about gorillas and elephants that he saw in the field and chased back into the woods. He felt that was his job, to come around and make sure the wild animals didn't get into the building. That dedication created a problem. He would start his rounds at five o'clock in the morning, so during morning zazen we'd hear the door open and Mr. Wilson come into the kitchen to make himself coffee. He would turn on the gas but then forget to put a match to it. The smell of gas would drift up into the zendo. One morning I woke up in the parsonage, and he was in the living room.

We decided that since he wanted coffee, he could come in and have coffee, but he couldn't heat it. He would have to drink it cold, the way it was. (This was in the days before automatic coffee makers.) And he had to earn it. We would say, "Bring some wood for the fire," and he would come in carrying two sticks. When we gave him a hard time about it, he'd say, "Well, my job is to chase the gorillas away." So, there was something sensible about that.

As our relationship with Mr. Wilson deepened, a controversy arose in the sangha. One group of people didn't want him in the building. They were afraid of him. He looked like a Bowery bum. His clothes were bedraggled and his hair was unkempt. He had a home, but his veteran's checks were controlled by his brother and his brother's wife. He lived with them and they would give him only twenty-five cents a day, so he was always bumming.

He would go to Phoenicia, stop at different diners and get free cups of coffee. Besides walking, he loved coffee and cigarettes. The group in the sangha that didn't want him coming around was concerned that he was going to start a fire or hurt himself and we would be liable for him. There was another group that thought that he was just a poor derelict and we would show compassion and take care of him. And so the argument grew, becoming almost continuous and splitting the community.

I could not help but get involved. So to the group that didn't want him around I started selling Mr. Wilson as the Han-shan of Tremper Mountain. I said, "You know, they felt the same way about Han-shan. Everybody thought that he was a bum, but he was a deeply enlightened being. Mr. Wilson is a deeply enlightened being. If you don't believe it, talk to him." And they would ask him questions like, "Mr. Wilson, what's truth?" and he'd laugh and he'd say, "Got a light?" and they'd persist and he'd say, "Can I have a cup of coffee?" He would do Dharma combat with them. Word spread in the sangha that Mr. Wilson was very wise and special.

To the other group I would say, "This guy's a bum. He's dangerous. He should get a job. Why has he got to panhandle? Why can't he earn a living? He's strong enough. You ask him to bring in some wood and he brings in two sticks—he's lazy." The rift grew. The two groups went at each other, back and forth, for the first year and a half after the Monastery was founded. It was our first major sangha koan. And you should have heard the fighting over it! Just like in the famous koan in which Nan-chu'an's community fought over a cat, our sangha fought over Mr. Wilson. Nan-chu'an held up the cat and challenged his community: "Say a word of Zen or I will kill the cat!" Here, no one could kill the "cat" in a year-and-a-half, and no one could save it either. The "cat" just kept getting into everybody's craw—the "yes" people and the "no" people at each other's throats.

It all ended one afternoon during a February blizzard. Mr. Wilson was on one of his walks when a car hit and killed him. Then Ms. Wilson showed up at the monastery. She didn't know where to go. The family didn't want her. Actually, she wasn't even Mr. Wilson's dog. She just followed him. So she arrived and the controversy flared up again. It was as if the karma had been transmitted. There was a group that didn't want the dog hanging around here, and another group that wanted the dog. The second group would feed her on the sly, so the dog always kept coming back for food, of course. Then one day a bodhisattva from Maine showed up. He lived here for about six months, took consistent care of Ms. Wilson, and when he moved back to Maine he brought her with him.

She lived a long and happy life with him and died just last year.

Using poison to get rid of poison, seeing a cage he builds a cage. The first monastic in this koan says to Chao-chou, "Does a dog have buddha nature or not?" and Chao-chou answers, "Yes." "Since it has, why is it then in this skin bag?" You can tell by this second question what this monastic is thinking. "Because he knows, yet deliberately transgresses," Chao-chou replies. The second monastic: "Does a dog have buddha nature or not?" Chao-chou says, "No." The monastic continues, "All sentient beings have buddha nature—why does a dog have none, then?" Again, you can see where this monastic is coming from by the question that follows Chao-chou's "No." Chao-chou responds, "Because he still has impulsive consciousness." All dogs have buddha nature, all beings have buddha nature. Why doesn't a dog have it? Because of his karmic consciousness, because of his karma, because of the cause and effect of his dog nature.

What is going on? In both instances, Chao-chou reveals the truth. He doesn't lie. It's as if he were answering just to annoy the monastics. The verse says, "A dog's buddha nature exists, a dog's buddha nature does not exist." The two statements are obviously not the same, but both are true. How is it? Is there or isn't there buddha nature? Do humans have buddha nature?

The next line states, "A straight hook basically seeks fish with abandon." This refers to a story in another poem about a man who was fishing with a straight hook. When somebody asked him how he expected to catch anything with that, he answered, "I'm only interested in a fish with abandon." A fish that has no fixed place, a fish that's free to take a risk. In the great ocean of billions of fish, only a few have that degree of abandon. Here's my straight pin for you: there were really two dogs. One had the buddha nature and the other didn't. And the question is, which one had it and which one did not? This is not a riddle. It's a real, bottom-line question. Which one had it and which one did not have it? Only a fish with abandon can see it. Abandon words and ideas. Abandon eye, ear, nose, tongue, body, and mind. Abandon yes. Abandon no. Abandon body and mind. Abandon buddha nature. Abandon abandoning.

Every single thing that we hold on to, no matter how small, separates us from the entire universe. We need to see, though, that it is not the thing itself, but the process of holding on to it that is the separation. A single thought, a single feeling, a single idea—if we attach to it—separates us from the myriad things. It doesn't mean not having thoughts, feelings, and ideas. It means not attaching to them, not recreating and sustaining them moment to moment after they pass. When we separate from the totality of being, we separate from ourselves, from our own buddha nature.

Every time a thought arises in working with Mu, there is you and there is Mu. Every time you move, you re-establish and reinforce the idea of a self. And when you do that, everything else is distinct and separate. When you've merged completely with Mu; when you are Mu with every thought, every breath, every action; when Mu sits and walks and chants and bows without reflection; then Mu fills the whole universe. But let one thought of "I see it!" settle in, and the intimacy is gone. The reality is no longer there. What remains are the words and ideas that describe it.

So, what happens when you abandon eye, ear, nose, tongue, body, and mind? What happens when you abandon "yes" and "no," body and mind, buddha nature? What's left? Everything.

The whole universe, but with no abode, no fixed place. That's the nature of life.

That's the nature of each one of us. But if you "chase the air pursuing fragrance," then all you are creating is noisy confusion, making excuses, explanations, and justifications.

In noisy confusion they make excuses and explanations. Making an even presentation, he throws the shop wide open. "He throws the shop wide open" refers to Chao-chou exposing everything. He is not being divisive with this. Don't blame him for not being careful in the beginning. This was not a rehearsed script. Chao-chou didn't figure this out. He didn't say, "Oh, they're going to pick two of my koans and put them in a collection, so let me show both sides." He was just responding to circumstances.

Chao-chou had somebody come up to him with great doubt, wanting to know if a dog had a buddha nature, and he said, "Yes, he does." "Then why is he in that smelly skin-bag?" "Because he dares to offend," Chao-chou answered. Another monastic filled with great doubt came and asked, "Does a dog have buddha nature or not?" and Chao-chou said, "No, he doesn't." "Everything has buddha nature. How come a dog doesn't?" "Because of his karmic consciousness." What was Chao-chou getting at? He wasn't searching for the right answer. He wasn't thinking, "I told the first monastic 'Yes,' I have to be consistent and tell this one 'Yes.'" He was teaching both of these monastics. He was treating poison with poison. He was curing sickness with sickness. He was building a cage because he saw a cage. What's the cage he saw? What's the cage he built?

Don't blame him for not being careful in the beginning. He didn't reflect on what he was going to say. He just said it. He responded to the situation. He wasn't responding in a Buddhist context. He wasn't quoting the sutras. He was responding to the needs of a human being, right at the very instant, in both instances. He gave answers which, placed side by side, seem to contradict each other. Yet both are absolutely, unequivocally true and consistent with the Buddhadharma.

The poem says, "Pointing out the flaw, he takes away the jewel." Both of these monastics came to Chao-chou with a little gem, a little jewel, and Chao-chou, being the expert thief that he was, said, "Look! This is not really a jewel. It's got a flaw in it." And he stole it. He didn't physically take it away, but he made it useless to them. It was no longer a jewel. They were walking around with this wonderful thing that they thought they had, reflecting, "Isn't this gem wonderful?" But when they took it to the jeweler, they suddenly found out it was fake. It was not a diamond. It was made out of glass.

And that ends that. Only someone with the gigantic heart of a bodhisattva can do something like this.

What are your bags of treasures? Whatever they are, you've got to unload the pack, put it down, take off the blinders, strip everything away, and get to what has always been there—the ground of being, beyond the conditioning, beyond words, beyond Buddhism and buddha nature. Where is that? What is that? See it, and then live it.

Unromancing No

Joan Sutherland

THE ROMANCE of realizing a first koan like Zhaozhou's No is a powerful and beautiful one. It offers us the possibility of experiencing what we know must be true: There is a vast and wondrous dimension to life, whose revelation will put doubts to rest and support a deep and abiding happiness for ourselves and others. And the stakes are so high.

Pablo Neruda (as translated by Stephen Mitchell) wrote:

> *If we were not so singleminded about keeping our lives moving,*
> *and for once could do nothing,*
> *Perhaps a huge silence might interrupt this sadness*
> *of never understanding ourselves*
> *and of threatening ourselves with death.*

In the face of this urgency, Zhaozhou's No can become a kind of prayer for salvation. The old Zen stories that end with the student suddenly experiencing enlightenment are like the fairytale "...and then they lived happily ever after." The promise in such stories attaches to a deep human longing: Enlightenment will reveal a timeless, unchanging state truer than our ordinary way of experiencing things. And we will be made timeless and unchanging ourselves—ever peaceful, ever free from suffering, ever wise. No will save us from having to be our unsatisfactory selves and live our messy lives.

As compelling as this romance is, it misses something actually richer, stranger, and ultimately more beautiful than the search for happily ever after. Far from saving us from our own lives, No leads us right into the heart of life. It invites us to see the world as it is and to love it, in all its tenderness and misery. It shows us how to loosen the compulsions of the self and let the space that's created be filled with care for others. It asks a lot of us, and it offers us a genuine life in return.

Here, then, are some notes toward unromancing No.

The first thing I want to do is set aside the word *enlightenment*, which is obscured behind a cloud of mythology and projection. Instead, I'll speak of awakening, which is a journey that unfolds over a lifetime, in the way particular to each person who makes it. Awakening is the process of opening the heart and clarifying the mind that is made real in a person's life. It isn't a destination; it's the path each of us is already walking, and it's unfolding in big and small ways all the time.

A breakthrough is what I'll call that sudden opening to the vastness sometimes referred to as "passing through" the gate of No. It's a transformation of consciousness that is a significant though small part of the larger process of awakening. What is revealed in a breakthrough isn't something truer than our usual experience: It is an *aspect* of reality, just as the way we ordinarily experience the world is also an aspect of reality. We know the limitations of our ordinary way of seeing things—it's often what provokes people to take up meditation in the first place—and opening to the vastness does make a difference. But thinking that the breakthrough view is more real misses what is actually so: The world is one whole thing, and it is only our human perspective that creates categories of vast and ordinary. Working with koans is a way to integrate these two views, to experience the one whole thing. Happily ever after? Sure. And also painfully ever after, and no before and no after, and no ever and no ending of ever. And all of it just fine.

While No has a venerable tradition as a first koan, there are others that work just as well, such as Hakuin's Sound of One Hand, the Original Face, or Who Hears? The truth is that any koan might light up for someone, and it's always thrilling when a person's eyes start shining about some koan I'd never thought of as a first. Everything I'll say about No also applies to these other koans when they're taken up in the same way.

To start, it's good to let go of your ideas about what awakening should be and notice what's actually happening. Mark Bittner, author of *The Wild Parrots of Telegraph Hill*, describes how he was holed up in a cottage near where the parrots live to write a book about them. After a few days they found him and came to squawk and peck at his windows. He'd be writing about how wonderful the birds were and how much he loved them, and then he'd get up to shoo them away. "Leave me alone, I'm writing an important book about parrots here!"

The parrots of awakening are always beating at the windows, but if you're caught up in the romance of No you might shoo them away, because you've got some important concentration on your koan to do. Maybe you're taking Neruda's huge silence literally, thinking it has something to do with quiet and calm. Concentration practice is incredibly important as long as you remember that it's a method, not a goal in itself. It has its virtues and its vices like all methods, and it might not be the answer to every question. There are times when it's just right to dive deep and stay there, going after *No* with a great ferocity. And there are other times when something else is in the Tao: Letting your meditation be dreamy, say, or meditating on the fly—three deep breaths at the stoplight—because of some urgent circumstance in your life.

One of the reasons we translate "Mu" to "No" is because Mu can reinforce the sense of a first koan as talisman, a special focus of concentration so unrelated to anything else that it pulls your attention away from the world around you. No, on the other hand, is vivid and even startling. Why No? No to what? What's it like to breathe No every time you have a reaction to something, or see the face of someone you love? It's powerful to question even the positive ways you're used to seeing people and things you care about. A woman went to pick up her dog after a retreat in which she'd had a glimpse through the gate of No. As the dog came bounding down the path toward her, the woman saw that all her habitual and mostly unconscious ways of experiencing this creature—she's my dog, I love her, she loves me—were just not there. Instead, here was this luminous and completely autonomous being appearing before her. When even the woman's positive filters were gone, the dog was never more beautiful to her, or more beloved.

From the moment you take up No, nothing you do is a detour. Everything that happens is the journey itself: You love the koan, you hate the koan, you're frustrated, you're blissful. Life goes well for you, life falls apart, nothing much happens at all. No doesn't mind. You can't bribe No with good meditation or good deeds. Working with No is something more challenging than a self-improvement project: It's a radical deconstruction of what you're sure of—your hard-won assumptions about life, habits of mind, and usual sense of yourself—so that the world as it actually is, rather than the stories you tell about the world, becomes increasingly visible. As the deconstruction begins, people sometimes wonder whether they really want to go through with it. It's becoming clear that this transformation thing is actually going to require some change, and that isn't always easy.

If nothing is a detour, you don't need to turn away from anything, including your own doubt about whether you ought to be doing this. Paradoxically, No is profoundly nondualistic: It contains a great *Yes*, a growing willingness to meet the world and your own inner states with warmth and curiosity. If you've been rejecting anything, refusing to feel some pain or anxiety, No will show you that, too, in the small moments and the large. The difficult relative, welcome. The blank computer screen of death, welcome. The war in Iraq, come on in. Sit down, war, we really need to talk.

The other side of that coin is noticing that your thoughts and feelings don't actually go away if you ignore or reject them. If you believe that they don't belong in your meditation, you risk creating a split between the "purity" of meditation and the complexities of your own inner life—in other words, with who you actually are. No works against this kind of split by breathing spaciousness into everything. Over time, you see that there's not much need to suppress thoughts and feelings, because they become just things rising in a very large field that is filled with many other things, too. And naturally, without having to engineer it, they become less compelling; your attention isn't captured so much by them, and they grow quieter on their own. Thoughts and feelings are welcome, but now they're like travelers to whom you offer hospitality but not permission to build a fire on the living room rug. You no longer take these visitors at face value; you question and wonder. *I'm so tired and frustrated—and the problem is...?* People find that they get two or three sentences into one of the old scripts—*She always* and *I never*—and they just can't go on; it becomes almost comical. This No inquiry is a more genuine relationship with your thoughts and feelings than either suppressing them or giving them the run of the place, neither of which, when you think about it, is really much of a relationship at all.

No also works on any residual split between meditation and "the rest of your life." It's constantly mixing things up: Where's the moment when you've stopped meditating and gone on to something else? Is that such a bright line anymore? What's it like to greet the rise and fall of thoughts and feelings with the same warmth and curiosity you're bringing to your family or your work? How are your sleep and your dreams? One of the lovely things about koan practice is how completely portable it is, requiring no special apparatus or elaborate preparation. It can be practiced in the space of a few breaths, anytime and anywhere. As someone takes up a first koan like No, I also give her "Koans to Carry in Your Pocket," a collection of short phrases from the koans that can be pulled out and used at any time, koans such as: "There is nothing I dislike." "Luckily no one is looking." "What is most intimate?"

This last question points to perhaps the most painful split that No can address: the one that causes us to feel separated from the rest of life, bounded by our skull and skin in a kind of perpetual exile. At the same time that No is creating more space inside us, it is also making us more permeable to the world around us. Like those wild parrots, life is always coming to fetch us, and taking up No helps make us fetchable. The koan tradition is full of such moments: Seven hundred years ago, someone has been meditating in the garden deep into the night. He gets up and reaches for the wall to steady himself, but the wall isn't there, and when he falls there is only falling going on, and he drops all the way into eternity. In our own time, a woman is looking at her computer at work. She stumbles across a description of a breakthrough she had a few years ago and suddenly she's there again, completely, and the world is full of light. A breakthrough often begins with surprise, when there's a moment of freefall before the world snaps back into focus in the usual way. If we don't struggle to stop the falling, when the world does reconstitute itself it will seem different, more like home in the deepest sense. The Chan teacher Dongshan wrote of an old woman who awakens at dawn and looks into the ancient mirror, only to see a face entirely her own.

At any time, No or a Pocket Koan might invite us into an instant of falling freely. When you can't keep going with one of your tried-and-true stories but dissolve in laughter instead, that's the everyday version of what happens in a breakthrough. Instead of asking No to do the work for you, to provide you with a thunderclap of happily ever after, your awakening is becoming a collaboration with No and the world. You're changing, the world around you seems to be changing a little, too—even No changes as you go on. Difficult things keep happening, but you feel as though you have more resources for meeting them.

The presence of the vastness becomes palpable in the everyday world. More and more, you experience the dreamlike quality of things, the provisional nature of consensus reality. No can reveal the language of the trees, the bright, grainy texture of the air, the way everything blinks in and out of existence too rapidly to see with your usual eyes. This is another aspect of the one whole thing, and it is both wonderful and profoundly subversive of our usual habits of mind.

Keeping company with koans like this is a complete and satisfying way to live. It's also possible that you'll have, once or many times, a breakthrough experience. No two breakthroughs begin or unfold in exactly the same way, even for the same person. Sometimes it's not so much a vivid flash as a slow-rising dawn, gradually lightening the sky, and it's only by looking back that the change becomes clear. Sometimes a breakthrough comes when it seems most unlikely, when you're full of illness or pain or doubt.

In the same way that Zhaozhou said "No!" the Chan teacher Yunmen used to shout "Barrier!" referring to a massive, locked gate at the frontier. There are times in working with No that you face such a barrier, blocking you in on all sides, making it impossible to move. There's nowhere to go, and yet if you stay where you are you feel as though you'll die. This is the full-on, unrelenting, charged-with-energy No: *No to everything you know, No to everything you're good at, No to plans and prayers and negotiations.* When there's no way out and you can't keep doing what you've been doing, what do you do?

In one of the old koan collections, Yunmen's "Barrier!" is followed by someone asking Zhaozhou, "Who *are* you?" Zhaozhou replies, "East gate, west gate, north gate, south gate." I've always been a little queasy about the thought that everything is a Dharma gate; it so easily lends itself to the idea that the value of others is in their usefulness to us, and that we somehow step *through* them into something more important. For Zhaozhou the barriers are inside *us,* and No helps us pick the locks.

Look, he says, when the barriers are gone you are a city with open gates, where all are welcome and there's not a gatekeeper in sight.

The city of open gates is a joyful place to spend a while. And then, over time, the intensity of a breakthrough begins to recede, and the concerns of daily life roll back in on the tide. This isn't a failure or a loss; it's exactly what's supposed to happen, because the next stage of awakening is to embody this experience in your life. Realization means understanding something, and it also means making it real—tangible, having an effect in the world. We tend to think of our awakening as something deeply personal, but it also belongs to the world in some way; the world, after all, has come to fetch us, to welcome us home, to invite us to turn our awakening into matter.

Often people describe a kind of game they play while a breakthrough is still vivid, holding things up to their experience and checking: Is it this? Is it washing the dishes at the end of an exhausting day? Is it a harsh word from a friend, a bounced check, a troublesome vote in the Senate? At some point, weeks or months after a breakthrough, the stakes get raised, and many people experience a kind of crash back into life. It can be physical, like an illness or accident; psychological, usually in the form of depression or fear; or spiritual, a crisis of doubt. Often it's a chaotic and destabilizing time, when the whole meaning of awakening can be called into question. It's as though the world is playing its own version of our game: "That's all very well, your experience of the shining whole, but what about *this*? Is this it, too?"

If hope remains anywhere inside you that awakening will save you from having to live your life, that illusion will now be well and truly shattered. Here is your life, demanding to be lived. Here is the next gift of the koans, provoking you to discover whether you really can integrate what you've come to know of the vastness with what you've come to see more clearly about the everyday. This can be a difficult time, but if you hold through, something genuinely transforming happens: You find that you are content to be living this human life, and you no longer need things to be different in order to be happy. This sounds rather unromantic and small, but to genuinely feel like this is to be free.

Hand in hand with this is the deep desire for things to get better so that others can find their own way to happiness. In the world view of the koans, it somehow makes perfect sense to be committed to changing things for the benefit of others without needing to change them for yourself. The level at which you might do this isn't grand: nothing about trying to convert people or invading to bring them democracy. What seems self-evidently desirable are the fundamental things that make it possible for others to get free: clean water, no bombs or landmines, intervening in global warming before people's homes start disappearing under the waves.

Once Zhaozhou asked another teacher, Touzi, how he'd describe coming back to life after a profound breakthrough, which is sometimes called a great death. Touzi replied that you can't do it by walking about in the night, by which he meant by clinging to your breakthrough; you come back by giving yourself to the daylight. To fully realize No, you have to give yourself to the sunlit, everyday world. You have to care, to make art and babies and run for town council. You crash back into life because life, with all its complications and disappointments and heartbreak, is the ground of our awakening.

As you step back into the everyday you're not abandoned to fate and blind chance, because there are all the other koans. If you keep company with them, they'll show you how to deepen and widen the opening that started with No. At first they show you where the light shines brightly for you and where it's obscured, and they help the light spread to the shaded places. Then they ask you to articulate your experience as you go, which refines your understanding. And all along they're pushing you to integrate the big view with your everyday life. Koans make sure that once you've been transformed you stay transformed.

I can't say I completely understand how koans like No work. I can't say that they cause awakening in any sense that we usually mean "cause." Perhaps they just keep us open, or off-balance, so that other things can act upon us, so that we're fetchable. This week I think that their importance as a spiritual technology lies in their ability to reliably show us three aspects of awakening: the shining, eternal face whose revelation is one of the deepest graces we humans can experience; the shape-shifting face that invites us, along with everything else, to dream the world into existence; and the complicated earthly face, in whose presence we have to care about the world and exert ourselves on its behalf.

And the koans encourage our doubt, and ask us to trust our own experience, and don't give an inch on the important things. And I do notice that if people are willing to take up a koan like No with their whole selves, they tend to get kinder and wiser and more courageous.

I don't know about happily ever after, but that sure seems like happily right here and now to me.

Practicing Mu, Arriving Home

Ruben L.F. Habito

1. Zazen Is Not a Means to Enlightenment

LET US BE CLEAR from the outset that zazen is not a "means" that we undertake to obtain a desired goal called "enlightenment." Zen Master Dogen has emphasized this point, affirming in his "Discourse on Discerning the Way (*Bendowa*)," that "practice and realization are one." In other words, zazen is not a "technique" or "method" we employ so that we may obtain enlightenment as an outcome or result of our efforts. Rather, the practice of zazen, most notably in its purest form that we refer to as "just sitting" (*shikantaza*), is in itself the very embodiment of the enlightenment that is our true and original nature. Underlying this statement is the affirmation that all sentient beings, yes, you and I included, are enlightened right from the start.

But then you ask: "If this is so, how come I don't realize it as such?" "If I'm supposed to be already enlightened, how come I don't know it?" Or, some may ask the question the other way around. "If we're already enlightened, what's the point of getting into this back-breaking rigmarole of folding our legs and sitting up straight and quieting our mind?" This is in fact the very question that Dogen himself struggled with early in his life of practice, which led him to seek guidance from renowned masters in China. Fast-forwarding to how this turned out in his case, he himself proclaims that he came back to Japan "empty-handed."

What does this mean? Coming back home "empty-handed"? This is a very important message Dogen is conveying to us here. We are invited to open our spiritual ears, and listen with our whole being, to let this message ring through.

2. Why Zazen?

People get started into this practice of zazen motivated by different kinds of factors. It may be out of curiosity, perhaps to check out what is behind all these ideas one gets in books somehow linking Zen to such things as the art of motorcycle maintenance, or golf, or vegetarian cuisine. Curiosity may then just wear out, and one either stops it altogether, or it may turn to something deeper in a way that can sustain the practice.

One may turn to this practice out of the need for healing of some physical condition, such as cancer, or a psychological condition, or a situation of chronic stress that affects one's general health. And in engaging in this practice out of such an initial motivation, one may find that it not only enhances one's physical well-being, but also enriches one's life in different ways, and is thus spurred to go on.

One may get into this practice led on by genuinely spiritual motivations, such as a nagging sense of dissatisfaction with the way one lives life on the surface level of consciousness, usually coupled with a felt need for deepening one's outlook in life. Such a sense can come home to us especially as we face the fact of our own mortality, or experience what can be called an "interrupt" in our usual way of going about things, such as the loss of a loved one, or failure in an enterprise that we thought meant our whole life to us. Or it may come as a flash out of the blue right in the midst of a hectic pace of daily existence, with a question that is thrust like a dagger at the very heart of our being: "What am I doing all this for?" Or, it may come in the form of the question Peggy Lee asked on behalf of all of us, in her song, "Is that all there is?" Egged on by this question, we begin to seek "something more," in a spiritual practice that we may have read or heard about, and are thus led to a Zen center nearby—and here we all are.

There are those of us with a philosophical bent, or with a temperament naturally inclined to the kinds of questions raised by existentialist philosophers we may have read in a sophomore college course, or as early as our adolescent years. Or such questions may come to us later on in our life journey, having tasted some of the usual run of human life, going through school, finding and holding on to a job, getting married, raising children, and so on, not necessarily in that order. In any case, at some point in our journey through life, these questions get the better of us, and we find that we cannot go on and be at peace with ourselves without doing justice to them and actively seeking answers to them. Such questions may be couched in different ways, such as, "Who am I?" "Why am I here?" "What is the ultimate purpose of my life?" "How may I live true to myself and to the entire universe of beings?" Or, "knowing that I will someday die, is there such a thing as infinite life?"

Those of us raised in a monotheistic religious tradition, whether Jewish, Christian, or Muslim, may tend to ask questions in the context of our religious upbringing or cultural background. "Does God really exist?" Or, opening our eyes to the overwhelming amount of suffering in this world of ours, we may ask, "If there is a God, does God care *at all*?" Such are questions that come from a state of mind characterized in the master Wumen as "having one's hair on fire."

Each individual who comes to the practice of zazen does so led by a particular set of motivational factors coming from each one's unique background. The Zen teacher listens in the one-on-one encounter, and offers very concrete recommendations for each given individual as to the most suitable form of practice in the context of zazen for that person.

Those seeking to deepen their spiritual outlook are offered practical guidelines in practice that eventually lead to the form known as "just sitting," or *shikantaza* in Japanese. I will not dwell further on details involved in this very powerful mode of practice here, and simply recommend another book in Wisdom's Essential Writings on Zen series, entitled *The Art of Just Sitting*, a collection of pieces from Zen masters of China and Japan, as well as from contemporary masters still active and teaching in the Western hemisphere.

For those who come with the burning questions that cause the feeling of having one's hair set aflame, a koan can be offered that may enable one to get to the heart of the matter. A koan is like a "working tool" or "device" offered to a Zen practitioner in a suitable state of mind, which cuts right through one's discursive mind, and confronts an individual with *the naked fact* that cannot be reduced to a concept.

Among the so-called "entry level" koans in this regard, *The Sound of One Hand*, and *Who hears?* (in Japanese, *kikunushi*, literally, "one who hears") may be offered. The first invites the practitioner, as one sits with a conducive posture, breathing attentively, and silencing the mind, to listen with one's whole being, to the Sound of One Hand. The second invites the practitioner also to just sit in silence in a similar way, and penetrate through the phrase "Who hears?" in a way that breaks through the duality of the "hearer" and the "sound" that is heard.

Or, one may be given the Mu koan, which goes like this:

> *A monk asked Joshu (Chao-chou) in all earnestness,*
> *"Does a dog have buddha nature?"*
> *Joshu answered, "Mu."*

We will unpack this further, after taking a cursory look at the things that can happen in the life of one who engages in the practice of zazen.

3. THREE FRUITS OF ZEN PRACTICE

A person who, for any one or more of the various motivations that can lead people to the practice of silent meditation we know as zazen, takes up this practice and continues it on a regular basis in one's daily life, may experience the ripening of what we can call "three fruits" of Zen practice. This is so whether one takes up forms of practice that help attuning the mind in stillness, like counting one's breath, following one's breath, just sitting, or practice with a particular koan given by a Zen teacher.

The first of these fruits can be described as a deepening of one's con-centration (and I'll say more about that unusual hyphen in a moment). The word in Sanskrit is *samadhi,* which means a "one-pointed awareness." The Japanese term is a compound made of two characters, *jo,* meaning "abiding," and *riki,* meaning "power." To render this first fruit of Zen in English, I use "con-centration," with a hyphen between "con-" and "centration." This is to emphasize that our use of the word in Zen is not the same as what we understand by the term in ordinary English usage. The widely known and often replicated sculptural piece by Rodin entitled "The Thinker" is cited as a model of "concentration," but this is not what we mean in the Zen context. Rodin's Thinker, with his hunched back and elbow propped against his knee, evidently in the midst of "thinking" about "something," appears to be caught in a dualistic kind of consciousness. This is a state of mind characterized by an inescapable opposition between the "thinking subject" on the one hand, and the "object of thought" on the other, the I "in here," and the world "out there."

In contrast, in the context of Zen practice, a person who arrives at a point of "con-centration" is one who is able to be present in the here and now of each moment. Zazen is a most conducive setting for this, as one comes to a point of stillness in one's seated posture, attentive to one's breathing, with one's mind fully at rest in the here and now. As a person deepens in this experience of one-pointed awareness in zazen, fully present in the here and now, its effects manifest an outflow into one's daily life, transforming one's mode of awareness in the day-to-day business of living. The disparate elements of one's life are gradually brought together, and come to a point of focus in a dynamic "center," ever moving, ever fluid, yet accessible in the here and now of each moment.

As one continues living one's daily life in a way that keeps "coming home" to the here and now of the present moment, sustained by the regular practice of zazen, an event may occur that could transform one's entire way of seeing things, one's understanding of oneself and of the world. This is an event that may come in an unexpected moment, wherein one is thrown off one's guard, and in a flash, see everything in an entirely new light. It may be an explosive event accompanied by laughter, by tears, sometimes convulsions, welling up from a profound sense of inner peace and joy and gratitude. Or it may be a quiet, unobtrusive, externally unnoticeable, emotionally unremarkable event that nonetheless makes a definitive dent in one's inner being, ushering in a deep sense of peace. This is an event whereby one "sees" through the nature of things, "just as they are." This is called "seeing one's true nature" (*kensho* in Japanese, from *ken*, "to see," and *sho*, which can be variously translated as "nature," or "essence," or "ultimate reality"), which is an event of coming to a point of awakening. "Awakening" is what we refer to by the phrase "becoming a buddha." This is the second fruit of Zen practice. We will come back to this later as we unpack what is involved in the practice of Mu.

This second fruit, the experience of awakening, or of "seeing into one's true nature," is to be sharply distinguished from those things that happen on the level of "insight" or "conceptual realization." One may indeed derive important and valid insights from reading, from reflection, or from discursive thinking about the nature of reality. Further, insights and concepts derived in this way may indeed be transformative of a person's outlook and behavior. Yet insights and conceptual pictures are not on the same category as the experience of awakening we are talking about. In the latter, there occurs a shift in the fulcrum of one's being that is bound to make its effect felt in the way one lives one's life, the way one sees and relates to the world.

In the Rinzai (Linji) lineage, formal criteria have been developed and handed down through the centuries for distinguishing genuine awakening experiences from those that are not. Harada Daiun Roshi (1870–1961) was a Soto Zen priest in Japan who also trained under and received formal Dharma transmission from Rinzai masters, and he adapted the Rinzai koan curriculum to form the basis of what we now have as a training program in our Sanbo Kyodan lineage. He passed this on to Yasutani Haku'un Roshi (1885–1973), who in turn transmitted it to my teacher Yamada Koun Roshi (1907–1989). We thus have a set of "checking points" in our Zen toolbox, developed and honed by Zen masters through the centuries, which are put into play when an individual reports an event or experience in the course of one's practice that appears to be significant. When an individual is so confirmed as having had a genuine awakening experience, he or she is now launched into a new direction in practice, which enhances the unfolding of the third fruit of Zen.

Whereas the second fruit may take only a moment to be realized, the third fruit takes an entire lifetime to mature. This third fruit is called the embodiment of the awakening experience in one's daily life. It is also called "the bodily realization of the peerless Way" (*mujodo no taigen*). This involves the cultivation of a way of life that is but an outflow of that infinite realm one has glimpsed in that moment of awakening to one's true nature. This is a way of life grounded in peace, sustained by an inner joy, and marked by a sense of wonder and gratitude at every turn. From an external standpoint, there may be nothing spectacular about this way of life, as it is lived in sheer ordinariness of every day, like everyone else, eating when hungry, drinking when thirsty, resting when tired, and so on. "Ordinary mind is the Way," as a well-cited Zen expression affirms.

But notably, in its ordinariness, it also is a way of life that flows out in com-passion toward all sentient beings, in different levels and degrees of manifestation and expression. For what one "sees" in that glimpse of one's true nature is no other than the "emptiness" of one's self-nature. At the same time, one experientially grasps the corollary of this "empty" self-nature, that is, the truth of one's interconnectedness with all beings in an infinite circle of compassion. This realization of one's interconnectedness with all beings is what breaks down the barrier that separates the "I" from the "Other," enabling one to experience another's pains and joys as one's very own. This realization is also what brings forth the power of com-passion and sustains its activity in a person's life.

With this overview of the three fruits of Zen practice in the background, let us now consider a form of practice that provides the ground for and nurtures these three fruits of Zen in a distinctive kind of way.

4. Practicing Mu in Earnestness

A monk asks Joshu in all earnestness...

This attitude of earnestness underlies all genuine Zen practice as such. It is the earnestness of one who is faced with a matter of great importance, a matter of life and death.

If you come to this practice in a willy-nilly kind of way, just to "check it out," or to attain some kind of benefit, whether physical or psychological or spiritual, that is fine. But hopefully, as you go on in this practice, and begin to taste the fruit of "con-centration" described above, experiencing your life with a greater sense of cohesion and inner tranquility that is part of the first fruit of Zen, you may be led to ask questions about your life, about the world, in a new kind of way, and thereby drawn to something deeper in and through this practice.

Momentary glimpses, or tastes, of an inner world of stillness, marked by an indescribable sense of peace and acceptance and quiet joy, may be opened to one who has embarked on this practice of zazen, even one who has started out in a willy-nilly kind of way. These tastes given to one along the way may then bolster in oneself a deeper level of earnestness in this practice, realizing that it is not just another kind of useful pastime or beneficial activity in the same way as jogging or working out at the gym or spiritual reading may be.

This is not to demean these beneficial or in many cases necessary kinds of activity we take on to maintain our physical or psychological or spiritual well-being. However, this practice of sitting in attentive silence may bring about a different level of appreciation of the ordinary events and encounters that happen in one's daily life, in a way that ushers in an earnestness in the practice. This practice then is no longer something I take up "in order to" attain some kind of benefit for myself, or even for others, but comes to be something I take up in and of itself, as an end in itself. In short, we are now a bit more disposed to understand this statement that we may have found puzzling as we began the practice "seeking some benefit" in our life: zazen is its own reward. "Just sitting" is its own reward. And so with just standing, just walking, just eating, just laughing, just crying, just washing dishes, and so on. We can begin to taste each and every event and every act in our life in and of itself as its own reward.

This does not mean to say, for example, that in walking, we do not actually get from place A to place B, which is undeniably a result or outcome of the action of walking, or that in eating, our body does not get any less benefit in the nutritional value of what is eaten. It does not deny the fact that in laughing, our nervous system is thereby favorably affected in a way that benefits our health, or that in crying, we are able to express certain emotions that bring about a cathartic and generally wholesome effect. Nor does it deny what the action of washing dishes generally results in, namely, that the dishes actually do get clean, or at least, clean*er*. These "rewards" also come in as part of the entire process.

To say that to do something is to do it as its own reward is simply to affirm that we are now able to appreciate our life, in every particular movement or act or sensation that we experience, for what it is, just as it is, and not as a means toward something else. It means that we are no longer attached to the outcome or results of our actions, and are simply able to experience them for what they are. In experiencing the daily events of our life in this way, we find ourselves no longer bound or enslaved by the idea of linear time, whereby we are doing things now with a reference to an idea of what might happen in the future. Rather, we are able to live in the Now of each moment, and therein glimpse a realm beyond time, a realm that is Infinite, opening out in each here and now.

This is the kind of earnestness I refer to as an underlying dimension in authentic Zen practice. But we need to clarify this. We are here describing a state of mind that some or many of us may not have begun with as we entered this practice. Many of us may have been drawn to our Zen practice with some idea of getting some benefit out of it. All of us with common sense will admit that we begin to do something, anything, with the expectation that we will get something as a benefit. Given this then, the "earnestness" we are talking about may not have been there when we started the practice, but it is a way of being that we gradually arrive at and continue to cultivate as we deepen in this practice.

This is the earnestness that Joshu, with his sharp eye and exquisite skill in offering exactly the turning word needed to open the eyes of those who asked for his guidance in the path, was immediately able to discern in the monk who asked him the question.

Does a dog have buddha nature?

Faster than the snap of a finger, Joshu answered, "Mu!"

If the monk were asking a question on the doctrinal level, out of curiosity, or even out of a sincere desire to understand Buddhist teaching, it would have been dealt with in a different way. A doctrinal question calls for a doctrinal answer. Does a dog have buddha nature? Well, for one, the Mahaparinirvana Sutra says that "all sentient beings are endowed with buddha nature." It is also generally accepted in the Mahayana tradition, the larger stream out of which Zen flows, that indeed, this is so. All sentient beings are endowed with buddha nature. And of course a dog belongs under the class that we call "sentient beings." Therefore: "Elementary, my dear Watson! Indeed, we can concur, a dog has buddha nature. Q.E.D."

But look again. This is a monk asking not a doctrinal question, but *in all earnestness*, as a matter of life and death. The response he gets from the Zen master is likewise a response that cuts right through this matter of life and death: *MU!*

Now what on earth is this?

Let us take a step back and look at the question posed by the monk again. *Does a dog have buddha nature?*

The term *buddha nature* is used in Mahayana Buddhism to refer to nothing other than what you and I and the dog, and for that matter, mountains, rivers, the earth, the entire universe, are all about. We will not go into a historical analysis of how this notion of buddha nature developed from the early Buddhist teaching on the Selfless (*anatman* in Sanskrit, also translated as "no-self," or "non-self") or the Mahayana teaching of Emptiness (*shunyata* in Sanskrit, which, incidentally, is also said to derive from a mathematical notion of "zero," or *shunya*, as a matrix of all integers. Let us only note that this term points us to a realm that is most intimate to us, wherein we may uncover who we truly are, at the same time as it points us to a realm that is infinitely beyond what our puny minds can grasp.

We have already made the disclaimer that we are not dealing with a doctrinal matter here. Therefore we do not need to dilly-dally with contexts, translations, linguistic, syntactic, or semantic nuances, and so on. We will not tarry with the comment that in Chinese, the answer Joshu gave could actually be construed as "No." Nor will we need to recall that on another occasion, asked by another monk, Joshu gave the exact opposite response, that is, "Yes."

We are here concerned with a matter of life and death, a matter that cuts right through our entire being, each and every one of us. So how do we deal with this Mu? The practitioner offered this koan is told: "Your mission, should you decide to accept it, involves taking this work of Joshu to heart, receiving it and plunging your entire being into it."

Joshu answered, "Mu!"

So what is Mu? The only way to go about this is to plunge right into it, to sit in *zazen* with it, and with every outbreath, slowly, silently utter *MUUUUU*, emptying out one's thoughts and concepts and emotions and simply let them be totally absorbed, or better, dissolved, into Mu. Just that. Let everything dissolve into Mu.

With the same earnestness that enables one to taste every act and event as an end in itself, standing, sitting, walking, running, and thus taste the realm of the Timeless in every Now, just let everything be simply what it is in itself, dissolving it all into Mu. In *zazen* in particular, just *Mu, Mu, Mu,* emptying out everything into Mu with every outbreath.

As you meet your Zen teacher in dokusan, you will be asked, time and again, "What is Mu?"

It is important to realize that what we are after here in this process of practicing Mu is not a definition that goes, "Mu is…(whatever it is that may come up in our head, or in our heart, or in words from our mouth)." Any such answers will just be met with a nod, and the bell will ring, indicating "Dokusan over." So don't bother about thinking beforehand what you are to present when you are asked the question. Just go to dokusan, in the same way as Dogen returned from China back to Japan, *empty-handed.*

Here is a hint. To practice Mu is to be totally enveloped in Mu, in fact, to be dissolved into Mu, to *be* nothing other than Mu.

To practice Mu is not just limited to the time of zazen. One who has taken up this practice with one's heart and mind and entire being is invited to practice Mu not just with each outbreath in zazen, but in each and every waking moment, as one gets out of bed, washes one's face, takes breakfast, drives to work, meets friends, goes back home, takes a walk, looks at the sky, feels the breeze, and so on with everything that happens in one's day-to-day life.

But there is an important clarification to be made here. This does not mean that one is meant to keep the *idea* of Mu in one's mind while engaging in the different things of everyday life. No, that would totally drive one crazy. To take it in this way would be missing the point of Mu practice entirely. It would be like doing two different things at the same time, like stroking one's head with a circular motion of the left hand, and patting one's belly gently with an up and down motion of the right hand, and then trying it the other way around. One is bound to get confused if this is the way one goes about it, and sooner or later will be tempted to give up the practice altogether as doing it this way would lead to a more confused, even more frustrated, state of mind. Or taking it in this dualistic way would be like walking while riding a water buffalo. No, it is not a matter of doing each or all of these things, all the while *thinking* Mu or *muttering* Mu as a *separate act* from these things one is already doing.

The crucial word here is "separate act." Doing so would just add another extra layer and aggravate the kind of dualistic state of being that already plagues us in our ordinary consciousness.

Rather, to practice Mu in one's day-to-day life is simply to go about each and everything as each and everything needs to be gone into, but yet with a total outpouring of one's being in whatever it is that is before us. In zazen we are enjoined to pour out everything into Mu with each outbreath, thereby letting everything be nothing other than Mu, and Mu nothing other, nothing less than everything. In the same way, we are enjoined to pour out everything we see, hear, taste, touch, feel, think, do, into Mu, such that everything dissolves into Mu, and Mu into every-thing. And this in a way that is *not separate* from whatever it is we are seeing or hearing or tasting or feeling or thinking or doing. Just Mu. And that's all there is to it. Just that.

5. Arriving Home

So far I have been talking of Mu from the *perspective of practice*, inclu-sive of zazen as well as everything else that we do in our everyday life. Now let us turn this around, and talk of *zazen* and everything that we do and everything that happens in our everyday life, from the *perspective of Mu*. Rather than "practicing Mu," let us "let Mu practice."

By this I mean letting the pure light of Mu shine on each and every-thing we see, hear, smell, touch, taste, feel, think, and do in our daily life. The "pure light of Mu" here is like the pure light of the sun, in itself invisible, unfathomable, immeasurable, beyond all our sense perception, but yet, is what enables everything to become visible and perceptible, as it branches out into the colors of the spectrum, enabling each and everything to manifest itself in its own brilliance and lumi-nosity and transparency.

The particular colors of the spectrum, for example, green, or red, are not at all different from the pure light of the sun. They are only the par-ticular manifestations of it. The pure light of the sun is not different from the individual colors, green, red, violet, and so on, as these are no other than the same pure light but manifested in this or that particu-lar hue. Thus, all the myriad things of this universe, be it mountains, rivers, the moon, stars, lions and tigers, worms and dragonflies, you and I, are not different from Mu. They are only particular manifestations of it. Likewise, Mu is not different from the particular phenomena of the universe—mountains, rivers, you and I are simply the particular manifestations of Mu.

Perhaps this is already saying too much, and giving you some "ideas" about Mu that may serve only as obstacles to your experiencing Mu itself. Offering such a description of Mu is like giving you a postcard with a picture of your own home. You may send the postcard to a friend to impress them and give them an idea of what your home looks like, or you may even send it to yourself, and go on admiring the picture. But it will remain only a nice postcard that you might be able to gaze at. The postcard itself cannot shelter you from the storm, it cannot protect you from the elements, it cannot keep you warm in winter. You need to put the postcard aside, and recognize and claim your own home where it actually is, and settle down and relax inside.

Once you have recognized and claimed your home, and have begun to "find yourself at home" in it, then you are able to open the doors generously to the entire universe, welcoming everyone in with warmth and hospitality, sharing the abundant treasures therein with all beings who come your way.

If you have come this far, or better, "this near," that is, if you have arrived home, then there is a whole new world still waiting for you to discover. There are many interior alleys and corridors and rooms and nooks and crannies still to be explored within. Our Zen toolbox has a whole variety of devices, pointers, drivers, keys, to help explore those manifold dimensions of this infinitely vast, and yet uncannily familiar place called home, that you have now realized is indeed your very own.

So don't just tarry and stop there after you enter the front gate, though that point of entry can indeed be dazzling and surprising, and our tendency is just to linger on and stay there and marvel at what we have begun to see at that point. Go further in, and open your eyes and ears and explore. As your eyes get used to the dazzle, you will recognize all the ancestors, beginning with Shakyamuni Buddha and his aunt, Mahaprajapati, all the Indian and Chinese and the Korean and Japanese masters, down through Dogen and Hakuin and all the others, smiling at you and welcoming you. Together with your Zen teacher, they will be leading you by the hand through the contours of this exhilarating path, deeper into the recesses of your own home.

Even a Dog...?

Mitra Bishop

A monk, in all earnestness, asked Joshu, "Does a dog have buddha nature?" Joshu answered, "Mu!"

This is perhaps the most famous of what are known as "breakthrough" koans—one of the small selection of koans given to students as a first koan. In the Rinzai, Sanbo Kyodan, and Kapleau lineages, the student chews on this koan for years, even decades, until a "breakthrough," or first *kensho*—a "seeing into" the True nature of reality, occurs. Although this is usually a relatively small awakening experience, it is nonetheless significant. But one must not stop there!

In ancient days—and in some Japanese monasteries still—a person works on that koan his or her entire life, probing it more and more deeply, ever more clearly comprehending the ultimate truth of all existence. We are not speaking of an intellectual understanding here, but a right-into-our-very-bones understanding. Only that kind of understanding brings true freedom.

"Mu," as this koan is known, makes no sense at all, and this is the core of its power; it serves to confound the thinking mind, bringing it to a dead end and to relinquishment—at least temporarily—of its overwhelming hold over us. As it does, we come to recognize that seeming reality of our thoughts is far from the True Reality of life, death, relationships, trees, plants, rivers, mountains—of existence itself. It is only when this thinking mind is dropped, at least temporarily, that we can break free of our conditioning, our misperceptions, greed, anger, and delusion. It is only when we have seen to a certain degree into how this "thoughting," as Kapleau Roshi used to call it, creates a story all its own, independent of the real truth of the moment, that we can experience the clarity, the joy, the compassion and Wisdom that arises as we free ourselves even briefly from these deeply ingrained habit patterns.

Mu means "no" or "negative" in Japanese; the identical written character 無, pronounced "wu," has the same meaning in Chinese. When Joshu answers "Mu" to the monk's question, he is directly contradicting the Buddha himself, who in essence said that all beings have the buddha nature. Yet Joshu was a renowned, deeply enlightened Zen master. How could he be wrong?

Both of them are correct. A dog has buddha nature; at the same time, a dog doesn't have buddha nature. How can that possibly make sense?

This is the core of it. A dog has...a dog has not...

When we further examine this koan, entering into the culture of the great Tang Era in China, we see that the monk who asked the question was further perplexed. He must have heard Joshu say at some point that all living things have buddha nature and he wanted to really be sure he'd heard right, so he asked specifically about dogs. In that era, and even now—not only in China but elsewhere in Asia—a dog is considered a dirty, lowly creature.

Many years ago we were living in the country the British had called Burma. (It is now called Myanmar, which is its Burmese name.) My husband at the time was assigned to head the American consulate in Mandalay. Among our duties was getting to know local Burmese, and commonly this was done through entertaining. So we organized a Fourth of July party and invited four hundred local guests. Being young and poor (Foreign Service officers' salaries begin below the poverty level and this was only our second post) we lacked enough party trays to serve such a large number of guests, and because there were none available locally we bought winnowing baskets in the local market.

These handsome baskets were flat and beautifully woven, and seemed a creative solution for serving finger foods and red-white-and-blue-iced cakes to our guests. Luckily we had the foresight to put a clean napkin on each of the trays before placing the food on top, for the morning following the party we found ourselves the subject of an editorial in the local English-language newspaper. It seems that when someone in a Burmese town or village is sick, food is offered to the malevolent spirits that caused the illness and set out on the outskirts of the village, where wild dogs (the

Burmese did not keep dogs as pets) would scavenge off these trays. The conclusion drawn by the writer of the editorial was something akin to our offering food to our guests from the buckets used to bail out the toilets in Japanese monasteries: We had presented food to our guests on trays used to feed dogs. The Burmese were dismayed. (So were we.) It would have been very easy for a Southeast Asian in the 1960s to be as perplexed as that monk in Joshu's temple: How could a *dog* have the pristine, perfect, buddha nature?

In our culture, questioning, "How could Hitler have buddha nature?!" Or, "How could Osama bin Laden have buddha nature?!" might approximate the monk's bewilderment more than "Does even a dog have buddha nature?"

It is this perplexity that is the core of the koan. The koan cannot be answered through thought. Our intellect, upon which most Westerners have learned to depend completely, is of no use. How on earth can we solve this puzzle then?

Quite simply, it is through activating our bafflement again and again that the answer suddenly comes forth.

The practice of *sussok'kan*—of evenly extending the out-breath naturally, without "controlling" it—is a masterful tool in this endeavor. Coupled with a wordless probing from deep in our *hara*, or belly, if we use it with full commitment, concentration, and awareness, we cannot fail to eventually comprehend the answer to this koan and to experience the joy and freedom that comes of that comprehension. Gently drawing the out-breath further and further out—and with practice this can be quite far—requires attention, a relaxed body, and a focus that is at the same time an expanded awareness. Allowing ourselves to be aware of the physical experience of that extension of the out-breath—and not shutting out the sound of the cars going by, the airplane overhead, someone coughing—the relinquishing of attention to thought naturally occurs. This is a vital aspect of this practice. Quite simply, practicing sussok'kan will significantly speed up the process of finding the "answer" to that koan—or any koan. But that will happen only if we maintain our focus on that experience of the out-breath, and on the sense—beneath or beyond thought, necessarily!—of puzzlement and mystery engendered by the knowledge that this koan does have the power to lead us to a transcendent truth, if only we can reach far enough within to grasp it.

And it will. Countless human beings for more than two and a half thousand years have done so, and there is no reason why we cannot, if we deeply commit to that process, persist, and have faith that it can indeed bring us the freedom that we yearn for and that has been experienced by so many other people just like us.

Persistence is vital, for along the road, every place of greed, anger, or delusion within our own psyche will be revealed, and that is not something most people are comfortable with. In fact, when such insights even threaten to begin to surface, many people become so discouraged or so frightened that they quit practice. Or they decide that that particular practice or teacher isn't for them and they change practices and teachers, thus diluting the process. But those who do persist, seeing clearly where they are caught in conditioning, habit patterns, greed, misperception, anger, and ignorance of the True nature of Reality, will be honed and humbled, and will ultimately lay aside their investment in these deluded mind states. Little by little, like so many people before, they will become more clear, more free, more at ease, more joyful, more compassionate, and more wise. "Like a mute trying to tell a dream," this freedom and joy is beyond ordinary comprehension, beyond explanation, beyond anything words can describe.

The potential to experience it lies within each one of us.

Persist, and you will know it for yourself!

Always at Home

Jan Chozen Bays

ALTHOUGH WE TALK ABOUT "working on Mu," this is not what actually happens.

We work at "working on Mu" until we are able to let go and let Mu work on *us*.

This happens when Mu penetrates every breath, every footstep, every blink, every touch, every sound.

Raindrops falling—Mu, Mu, Mu.

Crows calling—Mu, Mu, Mu.

Hands pick up Mu and spoon Mu into Mu.

When our awareness is completely filled with Mu, when thoughts are replaced with Mu, then the habitual flow of energy reverses. Usually our energy is directed inward in the direction of self-protection, a form of fear. This fear is carried by anxious, obsessive thoughts and emotions, which reinforce the experience of the small self-as-core-of-being. In this habitual mode our life energy is only occasionally directed outward. It is usually in defense, in response to perceived threat.

When we give ourselves completely over to Mu, the awareness of a self-that-needs-protecting disappears, and the energy is able to reverse and flow in its natural direction, the direction of happiness, which is outward and generous.

Am I saying, "Don't work on Mu, just wait until it reveals itself to you"?

No. At first you *do* have to work. You have to work in a way you have never worked before, and harder than you have ever worked before. This unaccustomed work can be quite tiring. You have to work diligently and continuously to quiet the mind, but without any judgment of self or other.

This is accomplished in stages. You begin with a busy, complicated mind. You continually return to Mu, substituting Mu for each thought that arises, as soon as you catch it. At first you only catch thoughts when they have been going on for some time, and have branched many times. Later you are able to catch a thought as it is arising, before it takes shape in inner words.

After many days of meditation you may have periods of pure awareness, when no thoughts even make the effort to arise. Ultimately these periods of pure awareness expand, until awareness of *being* aware disappears. When the witness vanishes, time also vanishes. This is the realm in which cause and effect are one and everything is present, from all places and times. This is the realm of Mu.

Thus the mind goes from complicated mind, to simplified mind, to unified mind, to pure awareness, to no mind. This is the mind we call Mind. Although it is eternal, that does not means that our awareness of it is eternal. It cannot be, because of the truth of constant change. All states of mind change.

You hear people talk about "beating down the walls of Mu."

Mu is not some thing outside us that we must beat upon and finally get inside of.

We can't get inside it because *it has forever been us.*

It is closer than our tongue, breath, or beating heart.

It moves in and out freely, regardless of our awareness or our ignorance of it.

Mu is not a destination because it permeates everyplace.

In fact, there is no way to get away from it, even when you die.

Isn't that comforting? It is never anywhere else than here.

And yet it eludes us. Isn't that frustrating?

We begin practice because we heed the call of Mu.

Mu is calling to us, all the time, asking to be brought into the light of our awareness.

It is utmost health, making its way out through all the layers of thought and emotion.

Often students are inspired by reading old instructions such as "beat yourself against the iron wall of Mu" or "Mu is like a red-hot iron ball that you have swallowed and can't spit out or swallow down."

I find that for most students these descriptions are dualistic and mischief-making.

They arouse an effort in the mind that involves willpower and conquering, judging, and comparing. These all add layers of thinking, emoting, and reacting to the utter simplicity and accessibility of Mu.

The way to work on Mu is this:

Sit down and keep the body still.

Only when the body is still can the mind begin to become still.

"Still" means don't scratch itches, don't blow a running nose, and don't brush away insects.

Resolve to sit completely still for as long as you can—I usually sit at least thirty-five minutes.

Keep the eyes still.

The eyes are an organ of meditation.

When the eyes wander the mind also wanders.

Become uninterested in your thoughts.

This is not easy.

It may take days of sitting, or special practices.

A simple practice is to imagine that the mind is a radio that is able to turn itself on.

If the mind is agitated, Mu remains hidden.

When the mind settles, Mu is revealed.

A very good way to become open to Mu is through complete, deep, and undivided attention on one thing.

It doesn't matter what it is, it could be the word Mu, it could be a flower, or the sky, or a broken bit of concrete.

Attention to breath or to sound work particularly well.

They are at once inside and outside, they bridge conscious and unconscious awareness, they are always in the present moment, and they are always available.

Working on this elusive Mu is like working on making the shy forest animals come to you.

You must sit as still as a rock, forgetting that you have a human body.

You must withdraw your human personality, become an intention so pure that you drop all wanting, for if the wild and original ones detect its pushing, they will not advance forward.

Your body must become an unmoving rock or an upright tree, your breath a breeze, your mind without a single human thought, only wide open in pure awareness.

Then something emerges—utterly simple and fantastically complex, very familiar, known to you from ancient times and yet always hidden.

When it emerges, you realize that it has always been there.

On our side the door seems to be closed and then, occasionally and miraculously, to open.

On the other side there is no door, and no sides at all.

Everything is completely open and revealed. Yet we have to work to experience this for ourselves. If we do not, we will always be restless and ill at ease. If we do, no matter what our life brings us, we will be able to rest content, always at home.

At Home in the World

Rachel Mansfield-Howlett

FOR ME THE KOAN No is a good, big initiation koan that transforms your idea of who you are and your relationship to everything around you.

Some other famous koans like Yunmen's "Everyday is a good day" or Linji's "There is nothing I dislike" might seem more approachable because they have a surface level of meaning. If you ignore the question about the dog, or take it as standing for any question you might have, then No doesn't have much of a handle. There's no clear image, question, interchange, or other graspable feature, so it's a difficult koan both to enter and to navigate through. That of course is its strength, that it is not amenable to our usual artifices and strategies. No involves a process of working with your mind, without a map telling you how to go about doing that.

I came to the practice out of a desire to find the intimacy within life, to hear the call and response of this moment, to feel the connection between myself and the world, to find my place in the great way of things. I wished to bridge an essential estrangement I'd felt with my own life. I was drawn to the koan way because I thought it operated outside the known ways of doing things. It seemed to be connected with a knowledge contained inside the immediacy of life. I found the koan path also touched an area of my life I had a hard time reaching into by intention—the place of intuition and creativity. The laughter coming out of the teacher's interview room also told me that this path included a deep sense of play and an interchange that encouraged a view I subscribed to—and that was echoed in the wonderful stories of the old Zen teachers' antics I grew up on—that life was better described in the ridiculous than the tragic.

I was also compelled toward the koan No because it had a reputation of being a koan that would defeat you. I got hooked on the challenge. And

I was lucky too in having a teacher that I trusted who would stay the course with me.

There is a koan toward the end of the curriculum that says:

> At midnight before the moon rises
> don't be surprised if, without recognizing it,
> you meet a face familiar from the past

It's a passage that offers us an intriguing sense of a remembrance of awakening while still being submerged in delusion. We meet something true and can't quite recognize it. That's how I felt at the beginning of my koan work. I experienced this remembering and it seemed I could touch it if only I could discover how. I hooked my wagon to the koan way in hopes of finding out.

Undertaking the koan in earnest I read the commentary on No and the injunction to sit "as if your hair were on fire!" This was dramatic, and somewhat entertaining, but I didn't understand how I could go about meditating like this and so I set that approach aside. Perhaps my teacher understood and trusted the innate quality of buddha nature; in any event, he offered me a different kind of encouragement, to follow my nose. I had no inkling of what this would entail, but I later found it to be powerful advice I am still grateful for. It also mirrored my own understanding of what might be possible if I approached the practice in the skin I was in rather trying to adopt someone else's method or practice. And, it also called up that aspect of remembering the way, that intriguing sense that it was something I had known for a long time, a promise that was barely on the edge of my consciousness.

When I began to teach koans recently one of the most interesting and beautiful things that was immediately obvious was that each person's path looks different and holds its own wisdom. An artist's mind is different from an engineer's and the discovery of wisdom through those eyes is quite different, surprising, and appropriate to its own way.

Here are some of the ways I have spent time with No.

Field Effects

At first I worked with No in a wide field, allowing the koan to enter in whatever way it would, not holding too tightly to anything. I basically just threw myself at the koan and little phrases or bit of songs would come to me. I took these things as being part of the field of the koan and I remember meditating with these fragments as they arose and trying to not know or explain too much about anything: "neither lost nor saved," "not this or that," "nothing lost or gained." In my life, a sense of not over-rating my condition and opinions started to show its influence.

Cutting Through

The slash and burn technique has its adherents and although it's hard to get all the way using this technique, I have to admit that it had its value in the early days of working with No. I held a lot of opinions and judgments about the way things were supposed to be and the weed-whacking approach was helpful in cutting through some of them. The way it works is this: whatever isn't the koan is out, off the table, not wor-thy of any consideration whatsoever, gone. It's just No on every station, all night, all day, 24/7, no variation. If another thought, feeling, or sen-sation enters, you just put it aside and come back to No. It's an intense concentration practice; it revealed a kind of bright certainty and devel-oped my ability to sit through and not be too distracted by things. In my life I noticed I felt released from the social pressure of having to respond in certain situations in the ways I always had.

Sitting Through

Where's your koan when you're tired and sleepy in the afternoon? It's just tired sleepy No. I found if I continued to sit through, my tiredness would actually show me the way through and the koan would be gently waiting for me on the other side. This allowed me to see the ephemeral nature of conditioned states. I got unhooked from my condition; what was happening in my mind was just something happening in my mind. I realized I often refrained from life if it contained uncomfortable or unpleasant states, and I saw that I didn't have to hold back any more. It's cool not to hold your life hostage to your comfort and to be willing to meet whatever comes. The idea of what a bad state was began to blur and I was more willing to live in the middle of life rather than just in the margins, in the areas I used to call good.

Show Me

During the private interview with the teacher, two words sometimes strike fear into a student's heart. That's when the teacher says, "Show me." This is an invitation to present the koan without words or explanation. During one encounter with the teacher I made an attempt to explain my understanding of No instead of just presenting the koan and was told, "Don't try and make the room safe for your presentation." This helped me to be more willing to take risks, to act directly without thought and to allow something unstructured to occur.

The presentation can also be understood as asking where in the body the wisdom of the koan resides. Folks sometimes balk at this phase of koan work and see it as a kind of pantomiming of the koan. That's not it for me. There is a possibility of awakening in the moment of presentation if we really give ourselves over to it. There's a koan that is traditionally presented as just falling down. Between the time you are standing and the moment when you hit the ground, there's an opportunity for the wisdom of the koan to make itself known. It's a response that can come through us when we're able to get out of the way. Time inside the interview room is like no other: the teacher holds open the possibility that awakening can happen in any moment including this one.

Including Everything That Happens

After the period of clearing away I wasn't as plagued by the imposition of my thoughts onto the meditation and I became more interested in including what was happening into the meditation. Whatever arises that's it, that's No too, that's an expression of the koan. I became a fan of this technique; it's rich, and it especially encourages the integration process, moving the practice on the cushion into our lives. I experienced the light going both ways—the wisdom of the koan shining into my life and my life informing the koan.

I also worked with this as an image of a giant bowl in which all of my experiences could reside, whatever happened was included in the No bowl. It became a container in which many things were allowed without my needing to form an opinion or judgment about them. What arises from this kind of practice is not merely an accumulation of experiences but a generous openness about where the gate is. It's always right here right now, with this thought, with this feeling, with this person in front of me, with this event in my life, with this age, with this pain or hurt or joy or sorrow, with this condition of the world. There is an openhandedness that allows and includes all of life, all of ourselves, not only those aspects that we feel are worthy of being placed on the altar. The clarity comes from seeing the moment of awakening embodied in different circumstances, from hearing it in different voices, it's not so insistent on the path looking a particular way. Because the field of practice is always just this life, there isn't a distinction between what is practice and what is not.

LEAVING THE REALM OF THE KNOWN

This is the land where mountains aren't mountains and rivers aren't rivers and things get strange, but it's ok. I was so far into the process at this point that I didn't mind if things were beginning to lose their usual associations. There was a truth to this experience and that was all that mattered. I could see that moving toward authenticity held its own freedom and I was game for whatever was in store. An old koan speaks to this place:

> *Blossoms on a withered tree,*
> *a spring beyond the ages,*
> *Riding backward on a jade elephant,*
> *chasing the dragon deer.*

As a young woman I worked at a beautiful landmark nursery in Sonoma, California, for many years and developed a great love of big trees. We used the trees that grew there as directional devices for how to get around through the nursery. There was a weeping willow in the center of the nursery; we dubbed an avenue of Japanese maples and ginkgos "Shady Lane"; the "South End" held a tall row of gorgeous yellow poplars; and there were many trees throughout that had grown through their pots to become full size trees yet still held the square of roots where their pots had once been. This became one of the significant places in my dream life and showed the role trees play in my life.

I had a dream during this time with No where all of the trees in the nursery had been cut down. Where my beloved trees once stood, there was a vast hillside of stumps. Yet just over the rise of the hill I could see a magnificent long vista that I had never known was there because the trees had obscured my view. I was awed by what I saw; the sky was vivid with brilliant streaks of orange, yellow, and pink. Through my tears, I saw something that I had never imagined before. I understood this dream as leaving the familiar place beside the hearth to encounter something new.

Periods of Drought

There are times when the practice suddenly feels dry, the meditation is uninspired, our knees hurt, we've run out of ways to entertain ourselves, there's a fly droning somewhere, and it isn't funny anymore. I learned to walk through these desert places, and even to welcome them. I realized that dry places are way stations where we have exhausted the known and are waiting for the new. There is a patience and kindness with ourselves that develops when we're willing to wait through like this. We can't know what timeframe is appropriate, and it doesn't matter anyhow, our life is always happening right here while we're hoping for something else to happen. If I just sat not wanting very much to happen, little things would open up, and I found that just being given this task of sitting can itself be a form of grace.

Giving Up or Giving In

At the end of a year's intensive work with No, I remember finishing winter sesshin and standing in the dining hall looking out onto the redwoods steeped in mist on the last morning of retreat. I felt I had given it my all and that this wasn't enough, my responses to the koan hadn't been accepted. I was at an utter loss. I remember vividly the feeling of having spent every ounce I had. It seemed that there was nothing for it but to give up the possibility of getting through this koan and to continue the practice without hope. I don't know whether this is an essential step but it seemed to be for me. I gave up thoughts of achieving, acquiring, or wishing for something different than what I had, and this turned out to be the key for the next phase of practice.

AT HOME IN THE WORLD

After I had given up I just kept going and started having small but real experiences in which the separation between me and the things around me lessened. At other times, I would become whatever I was looking at, a rock, a shirt, a face. Everything seemed to happen without me needing to do anything about it. The walls met each other perfectly. There were many experiences like that.

Then at a retreat I was following along in the walking meditation line outside the main meditation hall in the parking area. The person in front of me was wearing a black silk shirt and I became interested in the finish of the cloth. The thought crossed my mind, "This is a regal procession." And that was it. The redwood branches parted in front of my eyes to reveal a whitish, granular, particulate quality to the light that seemed to be everywhere, like seeing between the atoms. There was no past, present, future; no me, no nothing. I don't know how long it lasted but before I returned all together I requested a phrase. I received two words: "No other." That was all. The experience seemed to come about as an accident and I'm not sure that the details of the experience are the point. I think the more interesting thing is what an opening allows for. I thought of some of the things other people had said, like, "From now on I won't doubt the words of a famous old teacher" or "After all there's not much to the Dharma." And for me "No other" was the only expression. I experienced this as a deep familiarity and kinship with life. It was impossible to feel alone or apart, and the questions I had about what use this life was, and what my place in it was, seemed to fall away. *Why* it all is became less important than the marvel of that it is. Then the blue of the sky seemed to come to my aid, my stubbed toe was helpful, the yellow of the hills.

After that, I could answer the teacher's questions, and the teacher finally passed me on No.

Turn the Light

Roko Sherry Chayat

THE MONK WHO ASKED JOSHU, "Does a dog have buddha nature or not?" was steeped in the Buddhist teaching that all sentient beings have buddha nature. It was as much a given in his cultural sphere as owning a car or a refrigerator is in ours. Why did he ask the question? Perhaps he couldn't fully comprehend this; perhaps he had not experienced this for himself.

Even a dog? Just picture it: a slobbering, bedraggled mongrel stinking from the sludge and carrion he's just rolled in. How is this possible, that Buddha can be found in such a beast? What, or who, is this dog?

Bringing it all back home, the question really becomes, do I have buddha nature? How could it be? I am so weighed down by my greed, my anger, my delusions, that monk—and we too—might feel. Perhaps we are filled with chagrin, thinking about how we lashed out in irritation at a family member, remembering that greasy doughnut we ate this morning, the bills we've been ignoring, the sick friend we haven't called. Recognizing our lack of virtue, we can't imagine how we can really have the capacity to be Buddha. We want some reassurance, just as did that monk.

And so we may go to our teacher and ask, "Do I have buddha nature?" and—this is an important "and"—we expect that the teacher will smile benevolently and say, "Yes, of course you do; practice more intensively and you will wake up to this, I guarantee it." But even if we get that reassurance, we don't feel at peace with it. Why? Because we haven't experienced it for ourselves. "U" or "Mu," yes or no, either one is "the answer" when we have insight. And indeed, in another koan, to the same question, Joshu answers "U!"

Joshu, in this koan, defies the monk's expectations. He gives him—he gives us—an abrupt wake-up call, as all teachers and indeed all our life circumstances do. The usual response to such calls is to turn off the alarm, or re-set the clock to "doze." And we go on dozing right into death, right into the next samsaric round. Mu! Wake up! Joshu said Mu, giving future generations of Zen students throughout space and time the sublime irritant, the red-hot iron ball that can't be spat up, can't be swallowed down.

Mu is sometimes thought of as a kind mystical symbol, a Japanese term that can't be understood but can only be used as a focusing device for meditation, since after all, as we are often reminded, Mu is beyond yes and no. However, it is essential to know that Mu is definitely No! How can we penetrate into Mu unless we understand the no-ness of it, the radical no-ness of it? To be permeated through and through with the experience of this beyond yes and no, we have to plunge into No. This No is not that of "No, thank you, I don't want any eggplant," but the No! that my mother screamed when the police officer came to inform us that my twenty-year-old brother had been killed while riding his bicycle, hit by a car. It is the No that rips through the fibers of normalcy—the No that tears apart the polite acquiescence based on temerity, the fear of others' opinions. Mu practice is to look deeply into our own yes's and no's and discern what is true, what is self-deception. Mu must be understood as that No in which simultaneously everything is swallowed up and everything is present. That Mu comes from the gut. It's not just a meditative device based on a sound. It's our life force itself, manifesting from emptiness, vibrantly present, yet without a trace.

Thus the phenomenal power of this koan. Generations of practitioners have struggled with it; just as did that monk, who must have thought, "Wait a minute! What's going on here? I have been told that all beings, without exception, have buddha nature. Then wouldn't a dog have it too? I don't understand! Joshu said no...Mu. Am I not a buddha? Mu. Buddha? I don't feel it. Mu!" The desperately logical mind gets trapped by this one syllable.

This short koan is the first in the *Gateless Barrier* collection put together by Mumon Ekai, who was born in 1183 and died in 1260. He was given the koan by his teacher, Gatsurin Shikan, and worked at Mu for six years. What is Mu? Why is Mu? How is Mu? For six years he was frustrated, for six years he couldn't get it, couldn't penetrate it. Finally he decided he wouldn't sleep until he got it. How many of us can make such a vow? Well, of course he got sleepy. He was doing *yaza*, late-night zazen, out in the corridor of the monastery. Fortunately right near him there was a post, so whenever he felt overcome by sleepiness, he just bashed his head against the post and woke up, but still he didn't wake up! Still, he felt, I can't understand, what's wrong with me?

Then one day, while he was sitting in the zendo, the noon drum sounded, signaling lunch: *Badum dum dum dum, Badum dum dum dum, Bambadum bambadum bambadum dum dum!* The same signal he had heard every day for years—but that day, he truly heard it, and suddenly, he woke up! Just as did Buddha Shakyamuni: sitting, sitting, day after day, and then, on the eighth morning, there was the morning star! It was the same star that had been in the sky every morning, but suddenly, suddenly! What does this mean, "suddenly"? For six years, Mu, Mu, Mu. Suddenly, six years were nothing but one moment, one everlasting moment. This is another way for us to look at practice. We may be grumbling along in our internal monologue: good lord, shouldn't this sitting have ended long ago? Will I ever be able to do Mu for more than three breaths? I'm such a terrible student—maybe I should just give up and try something else. Maybe my teacher doesn't really understand me, and it's a mistake for me to work with Mu.

There is a saying "Practice must be true practice." What is true practice? What is your motivation? Although no one is recommending that you bash your head against a post, to have sincere determination is crucial. Indeed, we cannot do Zen practice without this kind of death-defying dedication. The famous exhortation "Die on the cushion!" is not a literary statement; it is an essential fact. When we hear this, we tend to view it in a safely conceptual way—OK, all my self-centered, self-absorbed, self-defending concerns and anxieties will finally die, and then I'll feel better? Oh, good, then I'll die on the cushion, when do I go?—and of course all the while, in some tucked-away place, we're clinging to all those egocentric obsessions. What is necessary is the radical death that is Mu, to *diiiiieeeee!*—to have such a strong vow of practice that absolutely nothing is held back. When nothing is held back, there is also nothing that is projected, no prospective outcome. We cannot "get" Mu if we think it is something to get.

In another famous koan, Baso Doitsu (Ch.: Mazu Daoyi) was sitting alone day after day deeply immersed in zazen. His teacher, Nangaku Ejo (Ch.: Nanyue Huairang), asked him, "Why do you sit?" Baso replied, "So that I can become a buddha."

Nangaku picked up a tile and began polishing it with a stone.

"Why are you doing that?" Baso asked.

"I'm polishing it, so it will become a mirror."

"How can polishing a tile make it become a mirror?" Baso asked.

"How can sitting in zazen make you become a buddha?" was Nangaku's delusion-blasting response.

So what is zazen all about? Are we sitting in order to become something that we are not? Are we polishing, polishing, and regretfully seeing that it's still a tile? It's a really shiny tile, and maybe we can see our reflection in it, but it's still a tile! But what about just polishing, just polishing, without any idea of making it into anything else? From the beginning, tile-buddha. This is a buddha called a tile, this is a buddha called a stone, this is a buddha rubbing the stone against the tile. This is practice. We are not practicing in order to become a buddha; we are practicing buddha. Buddha practicing buddha.

My teacher has said that there are three essentials of Zen practice: cleaning, chanting, and zazen. Just as the story about polishing the tile points out, most of the time we clean with the idea of getting something. We clean so that we can get through with the job and go on to do something more enjoyable, like taking a walk, or something more important, like sitting down for the next period of zazen or chanting sutras. And then, of course, we find out that the presumed satisfaction in that projected next thing is lacking; that our absent-minded preoccupied cleaning has carried over to the way we take that walk, the way we sit: lackluster.

When we clean with buddha-cleaning-buddha mind, something very different takes place. With this mind, anything—the sound of the drum at lunchtime, a pebble hitting a bamboo stalk in the story about Kyogen raking at the National Teacher's gravesite, the sudden glimmer of a rainbow in a puddle at our feet—anything can be the trigger that brings us to the sudden recognition of wordless truth. It's never elsewhere. Then we might rephrase the koan: Does a buddha have buddha nature or not? Buddha-cleaning-buddha is Mu, nothing more, nothing less.

Everything in the zendo is arranged to create an atmosphere of clarity. The setting up of an altar is not haphazard. The traditions we uphold are not based on caprice. The conduct of a life is not haphazard, either. There is nothing casual about this practice, nothing whatsoever. So to clean with buddha-cleaning-buddha mind is to give full attention and full reverence to every detail—not only to a speck of dust, but to the position of each object, honoring the creation of an atmosphere in which every single form is cared for, including each one of us. Thus we embody Buddha; thus we understand the Heart Sutra's teaching that form is shunyata; shunyata, emptiness, is form.

The way we clean, the way we chant has a direct impact upon our zazen and, of course, upon our lives. If we just follow along, chanting by rote, we might as well be snoring on the cushion. That would at least be honest. To throw ourselves vigorously into the chanting, to throw ourselves away and allow Kanzeon (Avalokiteshvara) to manifest right through the pores of our skin, wow! This is chanting. And when we feel tired, or overwhelmed with physical or emotional pain, there is nothing better to revive our buddha-chanting-buddha mind than just throwing ourselves right into each syllable, with not a single drop of our energy held back. When we hold something in reserve, either out of self-consciousness or fear, all we get is that self-consciousness and fear. Our lives become nothing but self-consciousness and fear. To plunge into what we are doing and reserve absolutely nothing—not a trace—this is dying on the cushion, wherever we are. This is Mu. Then, Avalokiteshvara is nowhere but right here, right now. In our morning service, after chanting Kanzeon with all our might— forgetting self, forgetting everything—then we shout Mu! This is nothing but our own original buddha nature. Then: zazen. With newfound energy!

Daie Soko (Ch.: Dahui Zonggao) said, "If you truly wish to practice, just let go of everything. Know nothing, understand nothing, like one who has died the Great Death. Proceeding straight ahead in this not-knowing and not-understanding, grasp this single thought-instant. Then even Buddha can do nothing to you."

Let go of everything, as it arises: Mu to all of it! Does a dog have buddha nature? No! Joshu said no. This single word, no, is a weapon to destroy all our heaped-up facts and figures, all our opinions and preferences. Beyond yes and no, existence and nonexistence, just proceed straight ahead with Mu, time and time again, twenty-four hours a day, whether walking, standing, sitting, or lying down, whether driving to work or washing the dishes, Mu!

In his commentary, Mumon tells us exactly what to do; it's a step-by-step instruction manual: "To master Zen, you must pass through the barrier set up by the ancestral teachers." Just penetrate into Mu. "To enter into incomparable enlightenment, you must cast away the discriminating mind."

Cast away, cast away. This is a very active image. Dogen woke up when he heard his teacher say, "Drop off body and mind." Cast away body and mind. Cast away, drop off, discriminating mind. But for most of us, the fruit is not quite ripe; we hear this, or read this, and immediately, discriminating mind rears up. We demand an instruction manual that's written in a language we can comprehend, right? In the language of discriminating mind! Give me a plan—that's discriminating mind. Am I doing this right?—discriminating mind. Was it happening just then?—discriminating mind. Will it ever come again?—discriminating mind. I like it, I don't like it, I want more, I don't want that, I don't like the draft, I wish there were a breeze, I don't like the food, I want more food. There are so many ways we can reinforce our discriminating minds, even in the pared-down world of sesshin. It's amazing. We drop our daily lives and daily concerns so that we can be free of discriminating mind, but we are so good at it; we've come to depend upon nothing but! After all, this discriminating mind is based upon defending the central fiction of our lives: the fiction of an ego-entity, a self-identity, a separate selfhood. So of course it's difficult, and fearsome, to let go.

St. John of the Cross said, "To reach satisfaction in all, desire to possess it in nothing. To come to the knowledge of all, desire the knowledge of nothing. To come to possess all, desire the possession of nothing. To arrive at being all, desire to be nothing."

The *Tao Te Ching* tells us: "If you want to be given everything, give everything up." This is it! If we just remember this, we don't have to remember another thing. Give up everything, everything. This is Mu. Something arises, let it go let it go let it go. Right now, what's arising? Pain? Whose pain? Immediately we think, mine! And this is what we must give up! This is where it begins, *MINE*! The converse of "If you want to be given everything, give everything up" is: receive all beings' pain, and you will lose yours.

We may think we are practicing Mu, but indeed much of the time that little syllable being repeated is not Mu but *Me*—the universal mantra of me, myself, and mine. The efficacy of long periods of sitting is that we get pushed into a corner. There's nowhere else to go. The self-absorbed wanderer—depicted by Mumon in his commentary as "a ghost clinging to grasses and trees"—hits the wall, hits the barrier. Sitting after sitting, me, myself, and mine become very old, very boring; and there's nowhere to go but Mu. Something begins to change. Mu starts mu-ing. It's so simple, and so powerful, when we allow this to happen, just allow this without interrupting it to evaluate it. Then, the barrier dissolves; is seen as insubstantial, as insubstantial as that tyrannical dictator identified as the self.

Mumon says, "When you pass through this barrier you will not only see Joshu face-to-face, but you will walk hand-in-hand with all the ancestral teachers. Your eyebrows will be entangled with theirs. You will see with the same eyes, hear with the same ears." Intimate, intimate, to see with the same eyes, to hear with the same ears—to see and to hear with our own true sight and hearing. In a word, insight. "Don't you want to pass through this barrier?" he asks us. "Then throw your entire being into this Mu." Into everything that arises from discriminating mind, drive the piercing questioning, the pneumatic drill of Mu. "Make your whole body a mass of doubt. Day and night, keep digging into it, ceaselessly. Don't think of it as 'nothingness' or as 'has' or 'has not.'"

The well-known trinity of Zen is great doubt, great faith, and great determination. What is meant by great doubt? The discriminating mind thinks it knows everything. It identifies everything—cup, clock, time, floor, self, other—and assumes the reality of all of these seemingly separate forms. But we are called upon to doubt it all. Are you sitting on the ground? Oh, really? Where does the temporary arrangement of cells called "you" end and where does the arrangement of cells called "the ground" begin? What is the universe? What is this? What is today? All of these essential questions come down to one: What is Mu? This is great doubt. "Keep digging into it ceaselessly," Mumon says. Don't get trapped by form, don't get stuck in emptiness. Don't get caught in dualities, in positivism or nihilism or any concepts. What is Mu? You can't say the word Mu means nothing, means no, means not. Mu doesn't mean!

Then what? Then it's "like a red-hot iron ball that you have swallowed; you try to vomit it up, but cannot." Most people come to Zen practice looking for serenity and perhaps some clarity about the difficulties in their lives. It's shocking when someone says, "Oh you want to be at peace? You want to be enlightened? Throw your entire being into this Mu; it must be like a red-hot iron ball that you can't swallow and can't vomit up." This point is really the crux of working with Mu. As we sit, we begin to see things about our lives, about ourselves, about our M.O.— our method of operation. It's unavoidable. And when we get to that uncomfortable place, the tendency is to find any way, any way at all, to get away from it. The title of a wonderful book, later made into a film, was *Anywhere but Here*. We'll go anywhere but here in our practice, anywhere but this place of raw discomfort. But we must be here, naked, exposed.

This is why mistakes are so helpful, especially when we make them while holding some public position, like being an officer at sesshin. When we find ourselves face-down in the mud, when we can no longer keep up the farce of knowing what we're doing, then we are in Mu-*shin*, Mu-mind. It's no longer possible to shore up the defense mechanisms of a separated individuality, an ego-entity. We may feel horrible— humiliated—yet what a relief! In truth, we can only be free of our carefully manufactured identities when we're willing to stop defending ourselves; when we drop the expenditure of energy that it takes to keep that ruse going. When we drop it—usually unintentionally—there is a feeling of profound release. All the energy that we've used in protecting the illusion of self has been liberated! Then "anywhere but here" changes to "nowhere but here." We can enter into what causes us the most disease to be healed from disease. When you have great pain, whether emotional or physical or both, think of this: your body is giving you a great gift. It's reminding you that you have separated from this "here"; from Mu. Just come back. Just soften into it, right here, whatever it is. What else can you do? If you bolt—if you run anywhere but here—you just have to do it all over again, if not in this life, then in the next. The seeds are already planted! You're committed, like it or not, so you may as well commit yourself to this wonderful practice.

Mumon then tells us, "After a while, Mu will ripen; inside and outside will be understood as One." This is the quintessence of Zen, to experience for ourselves that inside equals outside, that the vast space inside equals the vast space outside. "You will be like a dumb person with a dream," he says. Indeed, when this happens, we truly can't speak about it; we can't say a word. No word can describe it; all words just add concepts to it. "You will know yourself and for yourself alone," he continues. There is another saying that reflects this: To drink water and know for yourself if it is cool or warm. Perhaps this doesn't sound like the bodhisattva way? But when you know yourself and for yourself alone, at one and the same time, you are a being of light for all other beings. Shakyamuni Buddha, upon awakening, said, "I and all beings *together* have awakened." Inside and outside, self and other, have never been apart.

At such a time, "If you meet a buddha you kill him, if you meet ancient masters, you kill them." What does this mean? Again, it is easily misunderstood. Of course Mumon is not advocating murder! What we must kill are any ideas about what is pure, what is not; what is worthy of reverence, what is not; all such notions in the mind. There is nothing to view as holy, since that implies its opposite. As Bodhidharma said to the Emperor Wu, the holy principle of Buddhism is vast emptiness, nothing holy therein: what is holy is no holiness, just Mu. There is no buddha, there are no ancient masters. It's right here, not something out there to be striven for or attained. This is great faith. It wells up from within. It's not about believing in something or someone; it's knowing for ourselves, and anything we can say about it is superfluous. This Dharma is like a raft, the Diamond Sutra reminds us; it must be relinquished. How much more so misteaching! Drop it. Cast it away. Let it go, let it go. Then:

"Standing at the brink of life and death, you are completely free." Here we stand at the brink, each one of us. There is no escape from life and death; when we understand this, when we are completely life-and-death itself, as it is, then we are no longer bound, and there is nothing to escape. In the midst of samsara, in the midst of the continual round of birth and death, we are completely free. It's difficult for us to just fling ourselves off the cliff in our practice, but this is what is required. And what we discover in this freefall is complete and utter peace. This is peace, not something we can bargain for or scheme to achieve.

"In the six realms and the four modes of birth"—wherever we have been, wherever we go, whether hell dwellers (and we've all been there, maybe as recently as last night!), hungry ghosts, beasts, fighting spirits, humans, gods, or devas—and whatever our modes of birth, described in the Diamond Sutra as "born from eggs, from wombs, from moisture, or by transformation"—"you live in playful samadhi." OK! Let's enjoy this, right here! My Dharma grandfather, Soen Nakagawa Roshi, loved wordplay. He used to say, "Nowhere, now here!"

Mumon concludes, "Now, how shall you work with Mu? Exhaust every drop of your energy in becoming Mu!" Simple enough. As we've heard—just hold nothing back. If we reserve a little bit of our energy, thinking, oh I'm going to need some energy for later, so I'd better not exhaust myself now, then there is no energy, either now or later! That attitude is what keeps us imprisoned. Exhaust every drop! Then he says, "If you do not falter, it's done!" Done! No faltering between should I or shouldn't I, now or later. Another way of putting it is, "A tenth of an inch's difference and heaven and earth are set apart." If you do not falter, there is no gap; you are *done*.

"When the Dharma candle is lit, all darkness is at once enlightened." When it is done, when the Dharma candle of our true nature is lit, this light illuminates the whole universe. This final line leads seamlessly to Mumon's verse:

> *Dog! buddha nature!*
> *The truth is fully manifested.*
> *A moment of has or has not*
> *and you've lost it.*

The truth is completely and perfectly revealed, now as dog, now as Buddha. The very question itself—has a dog buddha nature?—and the very answer itself—Mu!—are none other than the truth, fully manifested. Understanding this, faith is as natural as breathing. But beware! he reminds us. The moment the mind swerves toward discrimination—has or has not—and we're lost in the darkness of ignorance. Mu! Again,

Mu! Mu is not just a mechanism, a tool for us to achieve some new and better state. It's not something we do for a while until we get it; even though Joshu's Mu is Case One of the Gateless Barrier, it would be a mistake to think that Mu is something we pass in order to go on. To be done, as Mumon puts it, is to continue, ceaselessly. "However endless the Buddha's way is, I vow to follow it."

Soen Roshi used to say, "If you penetrate into Mu, I will write down all the answers to all 1,700 koans for you." If we truly understand this Mu, then indeed we will, as Mumon said in his verse to his Preface to the Gateless Barrier, walk freely through the universe! Walking freely, sitting freely together in silence, in deep and radiant silence, there is nothing that comes between what we call the self and endless dimension universal Self.

In January 1958, Soen Roshi wrote, "Human knowledge has come to the point where living beings can spin around outside the earth's orbit. If we do not turn the light toward true wisdom, we will go off the track and destroy ourselves. Does a dog have buddha nature or not? An ancient buddha said, 'Mu!' Investigating this Mu, we celebrate the New Year with a wish for humanity's inexhaustibility." And the haiku for that journal entry is:

> *Buddha Mu Mu Mu Mu*
> *Buddha Mu Mu Mu Mu Mu Mu*
> *Buddha Mu Mu Mu Mu.*

What will we bring to our community, our earth? What is our wish, our vow? What do we yearn for?

Beyond the seemingly real entanglements of our murky, self-absorbed, self-addicted bubble-being, what is here? Let us turn the light of our practice toward true wisdom; let us exhaust ourselves in this utter inexhaustibility. "If you do not falter, it's done!"

The Power of Possibility in the Unknown

Dae Gak

TRUSTING ONE'S INCOMPETENCE is the beginning of transformation.

Each of us has been trained to avoid appearing ignorant or needing to learn. We are trained early in life not to enter mystery and not knowing, but to pretend that we know, no matter what. Confronted with situations that reveal our basic ignorance, we are threatened and frightened. We engage in all kinds of distraction behaviors to avoid feeling that. We have learned to fear what we don't know. We have learned to believe that the status quo must be maintained. Yet it is our basic not-knowing that is the wellspring of all creative possibility. This is not the ignorance of mistaken beliefs or opinions, but true not-knowing, of having no idea at all, no opinion for or against. It is a mind free from right and wrong, picking and choosing.

In Zen training we often use koans as a dialogue point to expose this basic not-knowing. The first koan we, student and teacher, look into together is often JoJu's Mu.

A monk asked, "Does a dog have buddha nature?"

JoJu said "Mu."

For most of us, taking up the koan is terrifying and exposes our underlying fear of the unknown.

We start with what we know about Mu or what we can find out about it from others. "Translated, it means no or nothing." When this doesn't get us the approval we seek, we speculate from our theoretical libraries, "Mu means that...JoJu meant...JoJu was trying to get the student to..." and we continue with our speculations using our intellect. And yet the dialogue is lifeless. We don't need a teacher to reveal this. We feel it in our hearts, in our inner dialogue. This lifelessness and dissatisfaction was our entry point to spiritual searching in the first place. We know our betrayal and effort to "get by," without having to be told.

And yet we still enter the dialogue with our teacher nervous, and leave unsatisfied. We may be more interested in getting the teacher's approval than embracing our own Mu stuckness. Or we may want to find a conclusion, nail it down and put it in our pocket to use at will. This is our job as students. And if our teacher is particularly caring he will rebuff our attempts to manage this enigma. He will be unwilling for us to settle for less than the entirety of Mu, the living tissue of immediacy that is Mu, the vast not-knowing that is Mu.

Koan practice is not a device or method. It is our very life. This human life is koan. All we have is the rich fabric of this particular life we are living and we have no possible idea as to what it means or what it all adds up to. This is the essence and function of Mu.

When we evaluate this life, we stop living it as a vital koan and begin theorizing about it. Most of us live in fear and shame because of our past. We regret the things we have done and carry these regrets and shame into everything we do, or we regret what has happened to us and cannot live beyond our pasts. We have not learned to press the clear button on our computer, my teacher Zen master Seung Sahn used to say.

But our true life is immediate, without alternative. It requires no theoretical position nor does it require understanding based on our partial memories of the past. Memories and images rise, dwell, and fall away without fixing in time. The immediacy of our life is brilliant, outside of time and freshly alive. Dogen offers, "Tonight's moon is not last night's moon. Moon inherits moon." As humans we have the great gift of being able to follow the way of choiceless awareness. What Zen practice calls "suchness," "thusness," or "Tathagata."

The nature of all existence is change. This does not mean change into the familiar, but in spite of the familiar into the unknown. This is the heart essence of Mu practice. This is the bone of these Mu ashes left by JoJu for us to investigate, to manifest again and again, and make vibrant and brand new, alive.

Transformation is not from something into something else. It is a complete revolution, something brand new, without a referential past, not continuous. It is a leap beyond the past, the manageable, without reference to what was. Transformation is that "one more step at the top of the hundred-foot flag pole."

Our capacity for not knowing is boundless, so our capacity for possibility is also boundless.

When asked, "Does a dog have buddha nature," JoJu answered, "Mu." This Mu is the living embodiment of our practice. It is the roots and wings, the condition and function of possibility. But this Mu is also a disease. Like any strong medicine it can cure and it can kill. If one attaches to the medicine it will be worse than any disease it cures. When I first started to practice Zen I became very infatuated with Mu. I saw the solving of this koan as the route to my salvation. I searched and searched for a teacher to assign it to me with little luck. When I met my teacher Zen master Seung Sahn, he showed no interest at all in "assigning" me Mu. When I brought it up he would just say, "Put it all down; better than Mu."

One day my teacher and I were riding in the car. I was secretly practicing Mu silently as I drove. He slept in the passenger's seat next to me. Mu had become such a part of my inner voice, I had forgotten that I was turning it in my mind. My teacher woke suddenly and said, "Mu practice is wrong." He immediately went back to sleep. This startled me and penetrated my entire body. Great doubt appeared in my mind. "Why do some teachers revere Mu with such intensity and my teacher said it is wrong?" Later when I asked him about this he said casually, "Mu is not so interesting, find JoJu's mind just before he said Mu." I asked him how I could find this and he said, "Don't ask me, ask a tree."

I did ask a tree about Mu and JoJu's mind; in fact I have asked many trees and have taken up a devoted mentorship under the trees of the earth. A tree's answer is always resolutely sincere, penetrating, and never conclusive. So if you want to know the true meaning of JoJu's Mu, ask a tree, but be sure you listen with every pore of your skin and every organ of your body. It is a work of ten thousand lifetimes.

Our future is here and now. If we can learn to take care of this moment, the next moment will take care of itself. This is our correct function as human beings. How do we take care of this moment? How do we appreciate this very unfolding moment with great faith, great humility, and great compassion? This is the point of Mu practice. It is a gate from nowhere to nowhere. It is the gate to just now where you are sitting reading this. It is the first gate to being a true, compassionate human being.

As friends, finding this point is our gift to our beloved. As parents it is our legacy to our children. As students it is our responsibility to our teachers, and as humans it is our vow to all sentient beings.

It is my boundless hope that all beings will find their original Mu, and manifest this Mu point, without hesitation, as wisdom and compassion for others.

A THOUSAND MILES THE SAME MOOD

Susan Murphy

THE FIRST CASE of the Gateless Gate is "Zhaozhou's Mu (or Wu)," and the first case of the Blue Cliff Record is "Bodhidharma's Great Emptiness." It's as fine a way as any of approaching Mu. Every koan picks up the light of Mu, the first great gateless gate, which is your first encounter with the vast fact that there is no barrier, no impediment, that everything gives way.

The people we meet in the first case of the Blue Cliff Record are Bodhidharma and the Emperor Wu of Liang. Bodhidharma, ancestor in the Dharma of all Chan teachers, was newly arrived from India at this point. The encounter with Emperor Wu was perhaps his first formal engagement after his three-year journey from India into China. Fresh from India with a big bushy red beard, something that nobody else in China had, he was known as the red-bearded barbarian. Barbarian in more ways than one—it turns out he had no Chinese manners whatsoever. He was in fact the twenty-eighth teacher in the lineage from the Buddha and he's taken as the founding teacher of Chan, which became Zen, Buddhism.

This was happening about five hundred years after Buddhism had begun to percolate through, by way of trade and travel, from India into Chinese culture. But it is Bodhidharma who initiates in that tradition a profound insistence upon direct experience of great emptiness, which cuts away all other formalities and pretty much burns down the cornfield. That is Bodhidharma's Buddhist legacy to China, and to us. His encounter was with a most interesting emperor, Emperor Wu, who was popularly known as the Imperial Bodhisattva—I hear a slight contradiction in that title, don't you?—to mark the fact that he was a great benefactor of Buddhism. He was responsible for endowing hundreds of temples and monasteries and sometimes giving his own personal treasure to found a monastery. In other words, he might have thought he had acquired a certain amount of merit as one who was sincerely dedicated to opening the Way.

And indeed the encounter that we come across in Case One of the Blue Cliff Record actually begins with a direct question about merit from the Emperor, a question that is not included in the case. Emperor Wu said, "I have endowed hundreds of monasteries and temples and endorsed the ordination of thousands of monks and nuns. What is my merit?" Bodhidharma replied, "No merit, no merit at all." Now *dana* was extremely well established as the first and greatest of the paramitas, or perfections, the one from which all the others seem to flow. And that's what's behind the next question, which is the first question of the case. Let's read the case right through and then we'll come back to it bit by bit. "Mercifully," says Bodhidharma, "no-merit is abundant everywhere. Have you seen this yet, Emperor?" Obviously he had not, as we see from his next question, which initiates the case.

Emperor Wu of Lian asked Bodhidharma, "What is the first principle of the holy teaching?" In other words, he asks, "Then what *is* the first principle of the holy teaching, if it is not dana?" Bodhidharma said, "Vast emptiness, nothing holy." The Emperor said, "Who is this person confronting me?" Bodhidharma said, "I do not know." The Emperor could not reach an accord with this.

Bodhidharma then crossed the river and went on his way—that's the Yangtse River. According to legend he crossed that immense river on a single reed. And he went on to Wei, which is in Hunan province in Western China. In other words, the far side of the moon from Emperor Wu.

The Emperor later took up this matter with Master Zhigong, who was his spiritual adviser. Zhigong asked, "Does your majesty know that person yet?" The Emperor said, "I don't know him." Zhigong said, "That was the Bodhisattva Avalokiteshvara conveying the Mind Seal of the Buddha." The Emperor felt regretful and at once sought to have a messenger dispatched to urge him to return. Zhigong said, "There is no use in sending such a messenger. Even if everyone in China went after him, he would not return."

So the encounter recorded in this case begins with Bodhidharma's extraordinarily uncompromising reply to the question "What is the first principle of the holy teaching?" *Vast emptiness, nothing holy.* Hardly a cloud in the sky up there, and the wind's in the trees. Currawongs are celebrating the fact of being.

This uncompromising reply has echoed down through the entire tradition. Zhaozhou's uncompromising reply to a monk's implied question, "Does a monk have buddha nature?" resonates with Bodhidharma. He replied even more simply, "Mu"—"No." No having or not having, if you really dare to look. No monk or Zhaozhou. The great amplitude of this fact. What we are facing—at every moment of our lives, in fact, whatever we may think or dream up about it—is just this barrier of emptiness.

Wuzu, teacher of Yuanwu who compiled the Blue Cliff Record, said this about "Vast emptiness, nothing holy": "If you can just see into this vast emptiness, nothing holy, then you can return home and sit in peace." Return home. Sit in peace. It's vast like the night sky last night blazing with stars, blazing with ten billion bright particulars. And don't be misled by "nothing holy," don't fail to hear the fire running through it.

There is a fire that runs through all things and "nothing holy" is the road to seeing it. Curiously if nothing indeed *is* holy, then everything is endowed with completeness, sacredness; everything matters. There is nothing that is not sacred. All is blessed. Everything counts.

Can you feel how this is so? Where does it leave you in the actual living of your life? What does it mean when you are wrestling with a particularly dirty pot in the washing up? What about dealing with a work colleague? A difficult work colleague? How can this "nothing holy" be a blessing upon that interaction? If nothing is holy, then what is your freedom at such a moment? How are you unimpeded in the most essential way? And what, then, is right action? When dealing with that most difficult person in the world, your partner, how do you meet this "nothing holy"? How do you meet this quality of *It is Unknown. There is Unknownness, right here.*

This becomes more acute next moment when the Emperor says, "Who is this person confronting me?" This obdurate person, this unfettered human being? The Emperor Wu was not affronted, I sense, but deeply curious: "Then who *are* you?" What manner of being human do you present? And Bodhidharma replies, "I do not know." Like the note in the wind, in the breeze right here right now, you will be able to hear that this is again a great blessing. This enormously open position: *I do*

not know. In such a condition there is no merit. There is no first principle. There is no teaching, no emperor, no sage. There is nothing holy.
There is nothing at all. There is a sense of "I am unknown to my deepest
self," the "I" falls away as unknowable. And surely every one of you has
stumbled on that first inkling of the plain fact that you are unknown, that
you are unknowable, and that this is a vast dimension in you and every
detail of your life—everything holy has its lodging there and every joy
is connected to it. We are that *unknown*. It is our most intimate fact.

Robert Aitken turns Wuzu's words slightly, to comment, "Unless you
can acknowledge I don't know to the very bottom, you can never return
home and sit at ease in peace. Instead you will live your life to the very
end in meaningless yackety yackety yack."

Later on the Emperor is asked by Master Zhigong, "Do you know that
person yet?"—that one who flashed past you, so near and yet so far
away—and Wu said, "I don't know him." It's very important to feel the
difference between Bodhidharma's "I don't know" and Wu's "I don't
know." There is great honesty in Wu's "I don't know him," and there is
the beginning of intimacy in that honesty, a door opening. But one "I
don't know" has infinite provenance to be found within it, and the other
is not yet aware of its presence.

Later on, the Emperor Wu, hearing of Bodhidharma's death,
inscribed a monument with the words "Alas, I saw him without seeing
him. I met him without meeting him. I encountered him without
encountering him. Now as before I regret this deeply." Now as before I
recognize the true extent of yackety yackety yack in my life. The
moment he hears from Zhigong that this had been compassion itself
speaking directly to him, conveying the Mind Seal of the Buddha, he
immediately "felt regret"—a most delicate understatement. He immediately knew that he had missed it. It had rolled over and shown its belly
and he had not been looking. And he said, "Send them out, bring him
back!" As an Emperor, you can say things like that. But even an Emperor
could not make Bodhidharma come or go. Zhigong said, "No, even if all
the people in China went after him, there's no coming back." No coming or going, nothing holy, no one to be lost, no one to be found. So nothing to attach an order to at all, sadly. Nothing for a thousand miles but
tremendous freedom.

That freedom took the red-bearded barbarian to an old run-down ruin of a temple that wasn't actually fit for habitation, so he adopted it as his and took up residence in a cave behind the temple. And there he sat for nine years facing the cave wall in deep zazen. Eventually three or four disciples gathered around him. One was an unknown woman, another one of the unknown women, no name. A great name, that—"no name." At large in the unknown. And among them was Huike, who became the second ancestor, who gave rise to the third ancestor and the fourth and so on down through all the founding teachers, as they were called then. Some said Bodhidharma faced the wall because he didn't know any Chinese. But if you've sat for a little while you'll know he faced the wall because he was prepared to face himself. Unimpeded, unafraid. Clear right through, no front, no back. Yunmen in a very different moment some six hundred years later was asked by a monk, "What is the Tao?" That's a bit like saying "What is Buddha?" or "What is self-nature?" Which is to ask, "Who am I really?" Yunmen said, "To break through this word." The monk then said, "What is it like when one has broken through?" And Yunmen said, "A thousand miles the same mood."

Perhaps that's a clue to why there was no bringing Bodhidharma back. He traveled on for a thousand miles. "A thousand miles the same mood." What is that one great mood that you realize when you are not in your own way? There is another koan which says, "A thousand mountains are covered in snow. Why is one peak not white?" A thousand miles the same vast mood, and yet one Bodhidharma, so unrepeatable, red beard, barbarian, and all? Look at us. We're also unrepeatable. Never will be seen again. None of us. Nothing like us.

So you can see that in the company of Bodhidharma, we're very much in the territory of the koan that asks us simply to break through this one word "Mu," to admit ourselves fully and completely to Mu. So how do we do it? Every mindful breath is an approach to the gate of Mu. So breathe Mu, let it soften and take your thoughts away, just fast your mind on Mu, for it will provide all that you have ever needed. And fasten your heart on Mu.

There is a strange category of Celtic fairy story, repeated in many forms, in which a young girl takes shelter on a stormy night in a strange house, and the people there have a corpse laid out in the front room. It is the body of a man who has died, and the young girl is granted shelter on condition that she sits up and watches the body all night. She agrees that whatever happens, she will never take her eyes off the body. So when that man's body suddenly sits up, stares at her, and flies out of the window, she goes with him, clinging on for dear life. He plunges through seas, he thunders across moors, he dives into rivers, he flings himself over mountains, and she never lets go. She has fastened her heart on this unknown business. And at the end of this truly amazing night, they come back to where they began, and she finds that she has, by her absolute fidelity to the task, released him from a spell. He can show her his true face. You could also say she has released herself, when his true face becomes clear to her. It is the face of unconditioned love, and nothing is missing anywhere in the world.

So the business of Mu is the task of lovingly keeping watch over a difficult question, through all the long night and wild journey. It is the business of learning how to love a slippery, ungraspable question—a question exactly as slippery and ungraspable as you are. If you can learn how to love the inexplicable nature of this question Mu, you have reconciled with yourself. What is Mu? What is this strange untranslatable word? Why is it the way through? How? How? *Knock, knock*—come to the gate and knock. Let your heart knock. Let your heart fasten on. Great life may well be worth the price of admission, the one we usually call "suffering."

Rilke says in his *Letters to a Young Poet*: "This is in the end the only kind of courage that is required of us. The courage to face the strangest most unusual most inexplicable experiences that can meet us." And Mu is certainly of that category. Inexplicable, strange, unusual, and yet wholly familiar. Wholly familiar. Your family of origin, in fact.

Live Mu, live the question "What is Mu?" in any way that you can discover. And you will live your way all the way in. Every path to this gateless gate is different. There is not one that has ever repeated itself. You are the first theory of Mu in the universe. Your path to Mu is its own theory of Mu. Find your way. Break through this word. Live your way into the answer to the question, "What is Mu?" Trust that this question arises out of necessity. It's the necessity to go into your own nature as far as you can go, and to see how deep is the place from which you spring, from which your life flows, and how strange is the place from which your life flows. Great emptiness. Nothing holy. This trust, this courage depends on a certain kind of unquestioning fidelity, on a sense that there's something stored up in you as your forgotten legacy, your long-forgotten inheritance. It belongs to nobody but you. It's a blessing so large that you can travel as far as you wish without ever having to step out of it. A thousand miles the same Mu.

Trust the apparent difficulty of Mu. Trust it. That very difficulty is its own gold-clad guarantee. The general bent of human life—the general technological, itching, searching bent of it—seems mainly to be a hopeful search for the easy, the dream of finding the easiest side of the easy. But there's nobody on earth who doesn't secretly know that the greatest experiences of life blossom from the difficult, not the easy and the comfortable. We're all artists of ourselves, and we know it and artists know it—the difficult is where you go. That's where the juice is. Creativity begins in exactly the right impossibility.

Rilke says again, "It is clear we must trust what is difficult. Everything alive trusts in it. Everything in nature is spontaneously itself, tries to grow and be itself against all opposition." So human lives are only barely large enough for the reality of this one word Mu, when all the locks click open. My favorite Japanese filmmaker Yasuhiro Ozu has inscribed on his gravestone just that one word *Mu*, no other particulars at all, no dates, no name, just that one word. You could say that the dead have melted back into that one same mood a thousand miles. The unborn too are there in timeless accord. We come and go from it a thousand times a day, before we go back in, if we let practice grow us aware enough to know it.

In searching for Mu, look right where you are, obviously. Where else in the universe is there to be or to look? Look right where you are and maintain the bare and simple attention that sesshin provides for you. If you trust in the small things that are so easily overlooked they can suddenly become huge, immeasurable, clear, one great shout of your own self-nature. Serve the small things with confidence and let them confide in you. They can be so strange. It can be a key dropping onto the table. The bite of an apple. Watch out for the bite of an apple, it can be very painful. It can be a sneeze. It can be the music of pebbles as you walk, the sound of your own footsteps, the passage of a leaf from a tree. Just in one small face of it you can find Bodhidharma's "Vast emptiness, nothing holy." When you're not separate, the whole universe can wake up in just that articulation of what is.

So Mu is like placing a stone in your shoe. It goes with you everywhere. You never forget its presence. It irritates you badly at times. That's OK. Or perhaps it's like losing a filling in your tooth. Your tongue goes to it all the time and marvels at the crater it has just discovered. That's Mu. Mu is as close and intimate and vast as that.

You can't will yourself through this barrier. You can't cross the barrier at all, because it is no barrier at all, when you realize it. But suddenly it will be crossed. It will be crossed. It happens that way. If you approach the gate again and again with a simple sincerity, you will be flung through by some mistake, which is also called a miracle. Mu is not a metaphysics that you can read in books or that your mind can grapple. It is nowhere but in living beings and in the life of stones and trees and clouds. So please just keep coming up to the gate of the mystery. The gate of your life, of your next breath, this breath. To find vast emptiness, just embrace the small and the near. It's so simple that it presents an almost scandalous barrier to the kind of mind we've learned to build to house the ego.

I'll end with a little poem by Ryokan. Ryokan is that lovely playful monk whose life is simplicity itself. Ryokan said:

> *In all Ten Directions of the universe*
> *There is only one truth.*
> *When we see clearly*
> *the great teachings are the same.*
> *What could ever be lost?*
> *What could be attained?*
> *If we attain something*
> *it was there from the beginning of time.*
> *If we lost something*
> *it is hiding somewhere near us. Near.*
> *Look at this ball in my pocket*
> *Can you see how priceless it is?*

Ryokan was always playing with children. Hard to imagine him without a ball in his pocket. One time someone found him hiding behind a tree, long after dark, long after all the children had been called in from the game of hide and seek to their baths and their suppers. But Ryokan wasn't letting anybody down. The person came up to him and said, "Ryokan, what's going on?" Ryokan turned, and smiled, and put his finger to his lips, and said, "Shhhh." Always at play in the dark of Mu.

And Mu responds well to that spirit of play and laughter. Bodhidharma did not persist with the Emperor Wu. He left him to his path of devotion and study. He saw that he was not yet clear enough to catch the vast laughter. He smiled, and said, "Shhhh!" and vanished back into the dark.

Each moment, that's the gate. There's nothing lacking in the universe.

Mysterious and Subtle, Simple and Straightforward

Elihu Genmyo Smith

Zazen is Mu.

Even to say that is extra.

Nevertheless, we need to say more in order to see that it is extra.

In the exploration of Mu that follows, the guidance of my teachers, my own teaching, and my ongoing practice are intertwined. I will at times speak as a student, at times as a teacher, and always as an ongoing practitioner of Buddhadharma. I am grateful and fortunate to have practiced at various times with my teachers Soen Nakagawa, Eido Shimano, Taizan Maezumi, Bernie Glassman, and Joko Beck. Though working with a teacher is vital in Mu practice, Mu practice must be our own. Nevertheless, unless a teacher is consulted, it is easy to go astray or quit due to frustration. Even if we "accomplish something" in Mu practice, without guidance from a teacher it is possible to be satisfied with a little bit, with a shallow opening or understanding. The goal is not "passing" Mu because Mu is a lifetime practice, not a means to get somewhere or something. Over and over we clarify, realize, and actualize this life of Buddhadharma, this ongoing practice of everyday activity.

When I began Mu practice I was told, "Do Mu." After initial attempts and asking for more instruction, my teacher suggested that I look at the first case in the Gateless Gate, Joshu's Dog. Reading the case and commentary, I thought that I knew what to do. Teishos on Mu also seemed to point practice in certain directions. But very quickly, what I knew, my interpretations, seemed to be of little value. Presenting Mu to my teacher(s), little by little I was disabused of the various notions and strategies I had adopted in trying to do Mu.

Mu practice was a natural deepening of my practice and my desire to grasp the Buddha's teaching, to see and be this joyful life, to take care of my suffering. At the same time, in the back of my mind was a notion that this koan would get me somewhere, would allow me to enter a mysterious world that I thought was expressed in the various koans I heard and read about but could make little sense of.

Being told to "do Mu," I assumed that there was something to do. So I tried to figure out what to do. As my zazen initially had been breathing practice, breathing Mu seemed sensible. I combined Mu and breathing, so the out-breath was Mu, in-breath Mu. My teachers did not discourage Mu-ing breath. And in fact this is a good way to proceed, not just Mu breath but Mu whole-body breathing.

Doing and *being* seemed different to me, yet I was urged to do Mu and be Mu, told, "throw your self into Mu." At this point, practice was my self going forth and practicing Mu. I was doing Mu, and being urged to be Mu; this was especially frustrating when my "trying to get somewhere" seemed to not get anything except blows from my teacher. I assumed that blows from my teacher were a criticism, a negative evaluation of my presentation. What are blows? Are blows Mu? Blows are easy to misunderstand, especially if we are looking for Mu as "some*thing*." In trying to figure it out, I kept coming back to the question, was being different than doing? I had a sense of other practitioners forcefully Mu-ing, whether in the dokusan room or at other times. And in fact in teisho we often heard just that, "work on Mu in your lower abdomen," and "become Mu yourself from morning to night." And we were assured that in maintaining such a state we would become totally such a state. This effort and concentration seemed to be what was called for but seemed to get me "nowhere," at least nowhere that I thought I was supposed to get to. What is Mu? What is being Mu?

The commentary by Mumon states, "concentrate your whole self, with its 360 bones and joints and 84,000 pores, into Mu." Misunderstanding these and other "instructions" of Mu practice might lead one to think that a forced concentration effort is valuable. Unfortunately, practice that is primarily this concentration also may make for a sense of power and accomplishment while creating a tension and subtle self sense that actually perpetuates self-centeredness.

As Mu practice continues and various byways and deadends of the "effort to accomplish" are abandoned and fall away, body-mind is more and more Mu. Concentration can lead one to attempt to push everything else away in just holding on to Mu, just Mu-ing. While at times this may be necessary and useful, if pushing away is always the practice style then a dualism is perpetuated, a dualism of Mu and not Mu. More useful is opening Mu to include whatever physical and mental states arise. Everything is thrown into Mu, Mu swallows up our whole life, Mu lives our life. Therefore, Mu is being body-mind present to this moment as is, each moment as is. Not body versus mind, but this emotion-thought-body-state, being Mu. What is this?

What reactions, what emotional states, do we get caught up in? If there is gain, is gain experienced, is gain Mu?; if there is loss, is loss experienced, is loss Mu? Seeing what beliefs we hold to as true, as real, is seeing how we exclude Mu. Right here is the opportunity of bodily experiencing, of being Mu.

In deepening Mu practice, Mu pervades the whole of being; the whole of being is Mu. Zazen is Mu, daily activity is Mu, Mu washes up, Mu lies down. Mu breathes in, Mu breathes out. A state of clarity and presence may eventually develop. Yet this state is just that, a particular state. It may be important, an indicator of the quieting of body-mind, and yet it is but a way station of Mu. Though the state of body-mind is good, if we attach to it, think "I have to keep this" or "that will interfere with this state," we are blinded by delusion. There is still some hindrance. We may remain stuck in this clarity and stillness until our teacher and circumstances push us, expose this attachment.

Sometimes Mu practice includes a subtle or not-so-subtle hope, looking for an "experience" of a certain type. Hearing words like "opening," "enlightenment," "satori," or "kensho" (seeing into one's nature), it is easy to expect this to be some "experience" or state of being that will come when working on Mu, when accomplishing Mu. We might even turn having this experience into the aim of our Mu practice. Unfortunately, this desire and hope is another sidetrack that detours practice and may actually create attachment and delusion that further perpetuate self-centeredness.

Mu is not an experience but seeing. Seeing is not something created by us, by "my action." Though we may use the word insight, it is not conceptual or intellectual. And it is not insight as opposed to presence or awareness. It is experiential insight. Seeing is not something extra. Seeing is natural functioning of being, yet a natural functioning that may seem unusual and special because in so much of our life we are blinded by the lens of self-centeredness through which we see. Because our habitual seeing is through the lens of self-centeredness, Dogen Zenji in Genjokoan encourages us to forget the self; forgetting the self, we are awakened by the dharmas of life, to "see" and be our life functioning. Dropping away body-mind, Mu reveals our life, Mu is our life. This enlightening, seeing, is insight of the nature of our life, the life of the universe, which is not two. Again, seeing is certainly not some intellectual or conceptual matter, not some extra "thing." Being Mu, Mu is seen; the functioning of great joy is encountering our original face. We encounter our face from morning to night. To pass the barrier of no-barrier is to pass through the self-centered dream we maintain. Though Mumon says this barrier is set up by the Zen ancestors, there is no barrier except that we are unable to forget the self. We create the barrier. Because we create and maintain the barrier, we must pass this barrier of our ancestors. Only in forgetting the self, as Mumon says, "you will know it yourself and for yourself."

For the practice of Mu, explanations are of no use. Discussions of emptiness and Dharmakaya have no place in Mu. Explaining Mu is more than worthless. One might even believe the explanation to be some truth, further entangling life in the self-centered dream, even if it is a new "enlightened" dream.

Seeing is our life as is, seeing is being *thus*. Therefore, the practice of Mu, the seeing of Mu is whole body-mind, is dropped away body-mind. A teacher can detect when a practitioner has "seen" Mu by the way the practitioner is, the way he or she walks into the room, and so forth. Seeing naturally manifests being, not something extra.

Seeing Mu, being Mu, varies with person, with circumstance. It is so even if it is shallow, even if just for an instance. Depth and breadth vary. Yes, attachment and delusion, habit of body-mind, may arise. Many ancestors, after an initial or early opening, or even after later practice, went through periods where attachments and habits of body-mind arose.

Hakuin Zenji's Mu enlightenment led him to believe that "In the past two or three hundred years no one could have accomplished such a marvelous breakthrough as this." Nevertheless, by his own account, after this his pride and arrogance would earn him the pounding of his "delusions and fancies" by Master Shoju (Dokyo Etan). Even after resolving this matter further under Master Shoju, Hakuin was encouraged to not be satisfied, to devote efforts to "after-satori" practice. Hakuin Zenji would face body-mind habits arising over and over. More than ten years after the initial opening, after many more openings, Hakuin could say that "the understanding I had obtained up to then was greatly in error." Ongoing practice is certainly life practice. In fact, after-satori practice is ongoing practice of original nature. From the beginning our life is this original nature, therefore from the beginning our practice is after-satori practice. Practice is in Realization, as Dogen Zenji states. Nevertheless, seeing this for our self, awakening of satori, is valuable. And this ongoing practice continues. As Dogen Zenji states in Genjokoan, "To be enlightened by the myriad dharmas is to cast off one's own body and mind and the body and mind of others as well. All traces of enlightenment disappear, and this traceless enlightenment is continued on and on endlessly."

Ongoing practice deepens and actualizes insight. Habits of body-mind are opportunities of ongoing practice. Insight feeds and supports ongoing practice. Being Mu naturally manifests seeing Mu. At appropriate circumstances, being Mu manifests as seeing, as serving, as receiving, as our daily life.

Step by step, ongoing practice is straightforward and ordinary.

GIVE YOURSELF AWAY TO MU

Gerry Shishin Wick

THIS KOAN is designed to help you experience your true self, which is beyond dualities. It does not dwell in right and wrong, gain and loss. It does not cling to ideas and thoughts. We call that true self "no-self," because it doesn't depend on anything. In Master Hakuin's "Song of Zazen," it says that "the true self is no-self" and "our own self is no-self." To realize the true self, you must "go beyond ego and past clever words." So, what is this self that we cling to? This practice is to realize the unity of everything, but somehow we get attached to our thoughts and use them to create our self-identity. We assign all kinds of reality to them.

Master Dogen says, "To study the self is to forget the self." If you carefully examine this thing we call a self, you'll never find it. So you might as well forget about it! If you forget it, then you'll be enlightened by everything. As long as we cling to that notion of self, we're conditioning our life and causing suffering to ourselves and others. When we finally let go of our ideas of self, we can move freely in the world of samsara, the world of suffering. The very essence of Zen is to experience, reveal, realize, and manifest "no self." Joshu was pointing the way in this koan. He is expressing the essence of our practice, but you can't figure it out with your conceptual mind. You have to release whatever it is that you're holding on to. In order to do that, you have to be consistent in your practice.

In the Lotus Sutra, the Buddha gave an analogy of our practice. He said it was like rubbing two sticks together to create a fire. When you start creating the heat from the friction of the sticks, if you stop rubbing them together you'll never create the fire. Notice if you're doing that in your practice. Whenever that uncomfortable heat starts coming up, do you do something to cool it down? Even shifting your position can do it. When you let your mind wander or fantasize about something, or say, "Wow!

Here it is! I'm getting enlightened!" it is like dousing the heat of your zazen with water. You just have to stay steady.

Because of his facility with verbal expression, Master Joshu was said to be a master of "tongue and lips Zen." When he lived, during the Golden Age of Zen in China, he was a contemporary of Rinzai, who would shout and beat his students with sticks in order to bring them to enlightenment. But Joshu didn't do any of that. He used his cutting words. His cutting words were like an unsheathed sword that cuts off all delusions.

Joshu became a monk when he was only seventeen years old. He remained with his teacher, Nansen, studying with him and serving him for forty years until Nansen died. At the age of sixty, Joshu went on a pilgrimage for twenty years to further refine his understanding. When he was eighty, he finally decided that he was ripe. He took on students of his own and taught for forty more years. He lived to the age of 120.

This case takes place during that time when Joshu was teaching. This monk came, and asked him, "Does a dog have buddha nature or not?" Every student of Zen who studies koans has to pass through the gateless gate of Joshu's Mu. Let's appreciate what Joshu's really trying to convey with that Mu.

First of all, ask yourself, "What is the monk really asking?" He is a Zen monk. He knows that everything is buddha nature, not only people, but all things, including the animate and the inanimate. Joshu's Mu might have shocked him. When the Buddha was enlightened, he said, "Everyone without exception has the wisdom and virtue of the Buddha." Everyone without exception is the enlightened being. It is intrinsically true and there are no exceptions. When we practice, we need to have unshakable faith in that fact. But, somehow we can't take it. We can't just swallow it down and digest it. We're still clinging to notions of "self" that prevent us from doing it.

So what is this monk doing? Some have suggested that the monk is asking Joshu to show his own buddha nature, and of course, that's what Joshu does. But why not be more direct? I don't think the monk wants to know about a dog's buddha nature. He wants to know about his own! I can appreciate his dilemma. I struggled with this koan for several years. At the height of my frustration, I went to Maezumi Roshi and said, "Are you sure that everybody is capable of realizing their buddha nature?" He said, "Sure! Sure! Sure!" Okay! If you say so! I read somewhere that Mumon struggled with this koan too. That's why he put it as the very first case in this collection. If you struggle, know that you are in good company.

The point of this koan is to become one with Joshu's Mu and eliminate all separation. There isn't you over here and Mu over there! To realize Joshu's Mu you need to see eye to eye with Joshu and become one with him. There can't be any separation. When you're sitting with this koan, each breath is just Mu! When you're walking, it's just Mu! When you're standing, it's just Mu! It is the same when you're eating. First you notice an "I" that is concentrating on Mu. Then it becomes Mu concentrating on Mu. Then it's just Mu. Exhaust all your thoughts and ideas and projections. Like Master Dogen said, "Drop off body and mind!" To really see Mu clearly, you need to drop off all your attachments. Concentrate on Mu when you go to sleep and the first thing when you wake up in the morning.

Mu is a "no" that goes beyond yes and no. When Master Dogen was asked about life and death, he said, "Life and death are the life of the Buddha." In a similar way, "Yes and no are the Mu of Joshu." It covers every square inch of ground. Wherever you look, you cannot fail to see it. In a way, it's kind of a silly thing to say, "Become one with it." You already are one with it! But you just don't realize it. Don't be satisfied with conceptual understanding. Don't be satisfied even with a small insight. No matter how much we realize, how much we clarify, we can practice further.

When I first started sitting, I read a talk by Shaku Soyen. He was one of the first Japanese teachers to come to America in the last century. He said, "Zazen is not a difficult task. Just hold your mind against all incoming thoughts like a great iron mountain." Just stop all of your fanciful fantasies and all of your meandering thoughts. Hold your mind against them like a great iron mountain. When I read that verse of Shaku Soyen, I tried to cut off all my thoughts at the root. I worked real hard at it. In fact, I got so good at it, that even before a thought was formed, I could sense it with my whole body. Then I would put my attention back to my breathing or my koan.

It's similar to learning how to ride a bike. First, we're clumsy and we fall over. Then, as our skill improves, we don't even think about it. We just jump on the bike and start riding. Our whole body senses when we're starting to tip one way or the other, and it automatically adjusts in order to maintain the balance. When a seed is planted in the ground and watered, and the soil warms up, it starts to sprout. The earth over the young shoot begins to slightly bulge before the shoot breaks through to the sun. If you pay close attention, you can feel with your whole body a slight bulge that occurs when a thought starts to form. When you pay close attention, your whole body will tell you when your mind is starting to wander and to attach to a thought. Similar to when you ride a bike, when you discipline your mind, your whole body will adjust when your mind starts to tip off balance.

As you know, most of the people who developed Zen practice over the centuries are men, and cutting off thoughts is a very masculine way of doing zazen. One day I realized that I could just let everything come in. I could accept all thoughts, and not fight them. It is a more receptive way of practicing. If the masculine symbol for zazen is the iron mountain the feminine symbol would be the receptive ocean. All rivers flow to the ocean and become the one taste of the ocean. The ocean will accept everything. Animals live in it. They procreate in it. They defecate in it. The ocean doesn't complain. We dump our waste in it. Mud, silt, and sand are carried into it. Let everything come in and become the one taste of the Dharma. Since I have practiced in both ways, I've found value in both. Now I prefer to let everything come in. I find that Zen students, who primarily practice as an iron mountain, cut off their feelings and hide behind their zazen. They bypass dealing with their negative patterns of behavior and it comes back to haunt them in life.

When you breathe in, put everything into your lower abdomen, into your hara. The hara is like a boundless ocean. Put all of your thoughts and sensations and perceptions and conceptions and judgments and projections and opinions and ideas in your hara when you breathe in. Your breath will handle everything. Your hara will handle everything. Don't exclude anything at all. Put it all in there! There's nothing to hold back. There's nothing that's sacred. Then all of your thoughts and ideas and projections and conceptions and feelings and emotions become the one taste of Mu. Breathe in everything, and breathe out Mu. That Mu is so large that nothing is excluded. It covers everything. Just *Muuuuuuuuuuuuuuuuuuu!*

There are other koans that we sometimes use as the initial koan other than Mu. Sometimes at the Great Mountain Zen Center we will ask students to work on "Who am I?" For some students that's more effective. Master Hakuin, who lived in the eighteenth century in Japan, developed the koan, "What is the sound of one hand?" He found that koan to be effective with his students. But with these two koans, "Who am I?" and "What is the sound of one hand?" it is possible to conceptualize them. However, if you study them with a teacher, every concept you have about them will be snatched away. With Mu, what do you conceptualize? What do you grab on to? There's not even a toehold or a fingerhold. So you just have to let go. When you totally let go, then you become Mu itself. If you clearly see Mu, when you come into dokusan and your teacher asks you "What's Mu?" you'll know how to present it without hesitation.

There are a number of testing questions about Mu. When you clearly see Mu, you should be able to answer without hesitation. Master Hakuin said, "From the beginning, all beings are Buddha. Just like water and ice, without water, no ice. Outside us, no Buddha." The life of each one of us is the wisdom and compassion of the Tathagata Buddha. It doesn't matter whether you accept it or not. It's a fact! So just melt yourself into Mu until there's not a single trace of your ego-grasping self or your habit-ridden consciousness. Then you will understand Hakuin with your whole body and mind.

Give yourself away to Mu. There's no half-way to do it. So how do you express this Mu, without hesitation? There's no place to stick. In this Mu, there's no dwelling place. There's not even a square inch of ground on which to stand. When you point and say, "This is it!" then you've missed it. Mu defies explanation and excludes nothing. There's nothing extra. Just everything as it is. Your understanding has to come from your whole body and mind, not just from your conceptual thinking. So, what is it?

Keep putting energy into your zazen. The more you put in, the more it will give back to you. Your mind will keep trying to subvert you. The mind doesn't want to be controlled. But the truth is, if you let go of that small mind, then it will become boundless mind. Exhaust your conceptual mind, so you can get in touch with the boundless self that we call "no-self" because it's not fixed. Not being fixed, according to the circumstances, no-self can be anything.

Without disciplining yourself, you won't experience that freedom.

So please, do your best.

THE BABY AND THE BATH WATER

Barry Magid

THE PRACTICE OF MU is introduced to us in "Chao-chou's Dog," the first of forty-eight cases in the Wu-men Kuan, a thirteenth-century collection of koans. Aitken Roshi translates "Wu-men Kuan" as *The Gateless Barrier*. Earlier translators have called it *The Gateless Gate*. So much of our practice, and especially our practice of Mu, is contained in correctly understanding that very title.

What is the title telling us?

When we first hear of a gateless barrier, we may imagine that it means an impenetrable barrier, one with no opening or gate anywhere. Wu-men calls it the "barrier of ancestral teachers" and challenges us to pass through. It is as if the old teachers set up this barrier to their elite club of realization and no one who doesn't know the secret password is allowed to enter. Over and over the teacher challenges us, "What is Mu?" We try every spell we can think of, from Abracadabra to Zen, but nothing works, every answer is rejected. As long as we are convinced the gate is locked we can never open it.

But actually the gatelessness of Mu means just the opposite of impenetrable: the gate, and life itself, is wide open to us just as it is—in fact there really is no barrier anywhere. So why is there a problem? Why is Mu so difficult to pass through? Simply because we don't experience that openness in our lives at all. We feel that there are barriers everywhere, inside and out—barriers that we don't want to face or cross, barriers of fear, anger, pain, old age, and death. We think that all these forms of suffering block our path. We don't see or trust that they themselves are gates. Everything is a gate and we can enter anywhere.

The hard work of our practice consists of learning to recognize and acknowledge that we ourselves have imagined and set up these barriers.

Only when we are really willing to enter the territory they have shut off from us will we find ourselves in that wide-open, barrierless life that Wu-men wanted to help us discover through Mu.

At the most basic level then, this old story about Chao-chou, a monk, and a dog is all about the problem of separation, about the artificial barriers we experience within ourselves and between one another, cutting us off from life as it is. And Wu-men offers us the technique of concentrating on this one word, "Mu," as a way of breaking down these barriers. By becoming completely absorbed in Mu, the student, then as now, will first bump up against his own barriers, and then, by filling his whole consciousness with Mu, his whole world with Mu, the barriers themselves will disappear, along with everything else, into this one word. Wu-men summarizes these different kinds of barriers with the simple phrase "has or has not," making this the paradigm of our dualistic thoughts and concepts. When Wu-men speaks of "great doubt," at one level we can feel the overwhelming confusion and perplexity of the monk trying to reach an intellectual understanding of Chao-chou's truly incomprehensible answer. Why does Chao-chou answer "Mu," which means "no" in Chinese, when every novice Buddhist knows that the answer should be "yes," that every sentient being has buddha nature?

The paradox of Chao-chou's answer arises out of a conflict between what the monk knows intellectually to be the right answer and his own deeply ingrained feeling that there is an unbridgeable gap between the rarified spiritual world of "buddha nature," which seems to exist millions of miles away from the real world of dogs and miserable, ordinary monks like himself. The gap, seemingly so real, is nonetheless a creation of his own thoughts, his own preoccupation with "have and have not."

Today, we are more prepared to see the emotional underpinnings of our barriers. Wu-men's "red-hot iron ball" that we can neither swallow nor spit up is a picture of how it feels to come to grips with that painful sense of separation we don't know how to escape. We practice by focusing on our own inner barriers, one by one, especially the emotional barriers of fear, pain, emptiness, and anger that manifest as hard knots of bodily tension. These are truly red-hot iron balls. These are feelings we've tried to stay separate from, and to keep them at bay we have erected barriers between ourselves and life. Moment after moment in the zendo, these barriers take the form of "*This* isn't it." *This* moment is not what I want, what I'm trying to achieve or become. Mu is emotional flypaper. All our issues begin to buzz around it and eventual get stuck to it. I know a strand of sticky flypaper covered with dead or half alive struggling flies is a less grand image than a red-hot iron ball stuck in your gullet. But there's something to be said for taking the drama out of our struggles, seeing them more as pathetic and mundane rather than heroic. One of those flies is the macho fly—a swaggering noisy horsefly that is tougher than anybody, ready to endure anything, impervious to pain and eager for any challenge, the harder the better. The traditional language of struggling with Mu always brings this fly out. Then there's a fragile little mayfly, weak and afraid "I can't do it," or "I'll never be good enough." Maybe there's certain benefit to the kind of training that transforms weak mayflies into swaggering horseflies, but they both end up on the flypaper.

The fundamental dualism we face on the cushion is not some metaphysical abstraction like self and object, it is the dualism of a person divided against herself in the form of self-hate. All too often, or perhaps I should say, inevitably, one side of a person takes up arms against another side and enlists practice itself as the weapon of choice. We do this, of course, in very high-minded terms, telling ourselves we want to be spiritual not materialistic, compassionate not self-centered, self-contained instead of needy, calm instead of anxious, and so on. And while these are seemingly worthy goals, our so-called aspiration is a mask our self-hate wears for the world, putting a spiritual face on our inner conflict. Over and over again, I see students whose secret goal in practice is the extirpation of some hated part of themselves, sometimes their anger, sometimes their sexuality, their emotional vulnerability, their bodies, their very minds, which are blamed as the source of their suffering. "If only I could just once and for all get rid of _____." Try filling in the blank yourself. This attitude toward practice, if unchallenged, turns students into spiritual (and sometimes literal) anorexics. Practice becomes a high-minded way of purging ourselves of aspects of ourselves that we hate. Our hate for our own physical mortality and imperfection fuels a war against our own bodies, a war in which we strive to turn them into invulnerable machines that can endure anything, or discard them as irrelevant husks that merely clothe some fantasized true, inner idealized self. We go to war against our own minds, trying to cut off emotion or thought altogether as if we could rest once and for all in an untroubled blankness. We want practice to be a kind of mental lobotomy, cutting out everything that scares or shames us, cutting out thinking itself.

We are caught in the grip of our grim unconscious beliefs: beliefs that have arisen as our own curative fantasies about what can end our suffering. "If only I was free of...If only I could achieve..." These beliefs may reside for years outside of our conscious awareness, masquerading as common sense. I've often said that psychoanalysis, paradoxically, is a process in which we must come to distrust our deepest feelings—to question all that we are so sure is at stake when we keep parts of ourselves and our life at bay. In analysis, we may have to get worse to get better: what is called a therapeutic regression may entail the patient allowing warded off feelings of vulnerability, dependency, and neediness to emerge. The façade of compliance and accommodation we show to the world may begin to crumble and we may feel increasingly naked and exposed. "Great doubt" is Wu-men's name for the process of deconstructing all these inner barriers. And while for a long time we may merely feel that Mu—and our failure to "answer" it—is progressively stripping away all that we know and have relied on in the past, paradoxically, it is in the midst of doubt and not knowing, our habitual ways of thinking and separating ourselves from the world lose their grip. We can truly become Mu only when we have finally ceased to try to understand it.

The teacher demands you show him, "What is Mu?"

This is precisely like asking, "What is life?"

You can't answer by somehow standing outside of life, examining it, and offering your description. You yourself must become the answer.

Our practice, like our life, is both simple and difficult. The difficulties, as we all know, are multiple and endless; Buddha included them all under the general rubric of "suffering." In therapy we can achieve a measure of comfort and relief by having someone explore and understand what we're going through in our suffering. We have a natural human desire to be understood, and feeling understood in itself gives us a kind of strength to face the difficulties that life brings. We have an equally human desire to escape our suffering. Feeling understood also provides a supportive context within which we are able to face and experience the reality of suffering, rather than divert ourselves with one of our habitual tactics of denial or avoidance. While therapy may be good at exploring the difficulty in our lives, it traditionally has not provided a way to deeply experience the essential simplicity of our life.

Whether practicing Mu or just sitting, we settle into the simplicity of the moment, this moment's completeness and immediacy. This moment, just as it is, is all there is. This moment, just as it is, is exactly, perfectly just what it is. This moment, just as it is, is not happening inside me, or in my mind; the whole world, of which I am an inseparable part, is what's happening, right here, right now. There is no place to stand outside of this moment, outside of myself, outside of the world. This moment, this self, this world: all one thing, all Mu.

So often we imagine that we need an explanation of why things are the way they are. We want to know why we suffer, why we grow old, why we die. We look at our practice and we may ask why do we sit, why do we bow? All these questions, at every level, are dissolved in the experience of Mu. We find there is nothing whatsoever *behind* our experience, explaining or justifying it. Why are we alive? We are alive! Why do we suffer? We suffer. Why do we die? We die. It is like asking: Why do fish swim? They're fish! Why does the bear shit in the woods? And why is the Pope Catholic?

Although the basic practice at our zendo is shikantaza or "just sitting" I sometimes offer students the opportunity to sit with Mu. However, I don't treat it as a beginning koan or one to give indiscriminately to one and all. I don't treat it as a barrier to be broken through or passed. I want students to sit with Mu only when they're more practiced observers of their own process, whether through sitting or therapy practice. I want them to be able to experience all of the emotional dualisms that Mu evokes and actively engage their conflicts and self-hate through the koan. We practice with Mu in a way that Mu absorbs everything into itself. We use Mu to enter more deeply into our bodies and our feelings, not to push our feelings away. It's like breaking up with your boyfriend, and while feeling all of that pain and heartache, you break into a wailing, heartfelt version of an old Patsy Kline song. The more you feel your loss, the more urgently you sing it, and the more the song contains and intensifies everything you're feeling. Any difference between you, your pain, and the song vanishes. So it is with Mu. All our pain and frustration and judgment become Mu. Mu becomes everything and at the same time, Mu is just Mu. All our pain and emotion and thought are just pain, emotion, and thought. Each moment is just what it is. There is nothing to do, nowhere to go. No question and no answer. No barrier and nothing beyond the barrier.

We see for ourselves that the "no" of Mu isn't the opposite of "yes." It is the negation of distinction, the negation of opposites; Mu negates the difference between "has" and "has not." Mu denies that there is any difference between "dog" and "buddha nature." By undercutting our instinctive tendency to frame our experience into likes and dislikes, into self and other, and into the admirable and the shameful, what we want to be and what we are afraid we are, Mu dissolves all boundaries, drawing everything into an undifferentiated immediacy.

Mu is a powerful practice that has indeed entangled the eyebrows of successive generations of Zen students. That power however does not come without a price or without pitfalls. There is a very real danger that Mu itself can be used to avoid or bypass emotional reality rather than to engage it directly. Used as a one-pointed focus of concentration, a student can spend years trying to push everything out of awareness except Mu. Rather than everything coming in and becoming part of Mu, Mu forces itself out into the world, pushing aside everything, filling everything with Mu. We should remember, in Dogen's words, that "carrying the self forward to confirm the myriad dharmas is delusion, the myriad dharmas advancing to confirm the self is realization."

Mu is a powerful samadhi generator—a way to enter into a special state of consciousness that temporarily banishes the pain and confusion of daily life. It is indeed glorious to enter into a state that banishes pain— but like all painkillers it can become addictive. We become proud of our effort and energy in entering samadhi. We relish the joy it brings, and more and more the point of practice becomes to return to this blissful oasis. Although Mu unlocks a world without separation or difference, the subjective experience of kensho, the moment of falling away of all separation, can be intoxicating and even dangerous. Because of the intensity of the experience itself, students almost inevitably take the experience of opening itself as an "experience" they've "had." Paradoxically, a moment's experience of nonseparation can become immediately incorporated into a person's system of distinctions, and the fuel for the ultimate dualism: the dualism of delusion and enlightenment.

Suddenly we have a new model of how we want our mind to be, a new picture of freedom from all those aspects of ourselves we've been fleeing. Even though the moment of realization may have come about precisely when all our efforts and hopes of attainment failed us and left us wide open and vulnerable, our ingrained systems of self-hate and self-improvement stand all too ready to incorporate this new experience into their compulsive quests. We may become trapped in a new dualism of our own making, one that starkly contrasts the confusion we feel off the cushion with the empowerment we feel while sitting. Our initial attempts to bring that sense of empowerment off the cushion into our own lives however may risk becoming a function of our pre-existing egotism. We may have come to think of ourselves as a special sort of person, with a powerful and esoteric practice accessible only to a small elite. At last, we imagine we have entered into the select coterie of the ancient teachers. Arrogance and narcissism (in the form a preoccupation with our own condition and attainment) are the all-too-common byproducts of a practice gone astray. Mu is powerful medicine for the disease of self-centeredness, but as with all medicine it's good to be aware of the possible side effects. A good teacher and a steady and emotionally honest practice are necessary to steer us around these pitfalls.

This misuse of Mu, I'm afraid, has been all too common in the past, with emotional problems compartmentalized and so-called breakthroughs offering justification for bypassing emotional conflict in favor of cultivating a powerful but narrowly focused wholeheartedness. The scandals and misconduct that have rocked Zen communities for the past three decades should be seen as important data as to the nature and limitation of so-called enlightenment. Too often I have heard students and teachers alike try to attribute these repeated problems to a variety of related causes: the teacher in question had not "really" been enlightened or hadn't fully completed his training or there was some other irregularity that could be used to cast doubt on the legitimacy of their authorization. The implication is always that when the traditional system is rigorously followed and the prescribed course of training under an acknowledged master is properly completed, these sorts of problems would be weeded out. Yet anyone who knows the intimate history of Zen in America must know it has not been a handful of rogue or self-appointed teachers who caused most of the problems, rather misconduct has been committed by the most eminent, impeccably trained, and officially authorized masters.

I can only conclude traditional Zen training has never in and of itself been an adequate treatment for emotional conflict, character pathology, or substance abuse. Too often we want to have it both ways: no teacher claims zazen is a cure-all and at the same time many will blithely proceed as if sufficient sitting or sufficient koan study will eventually take care of everything. Many personal problems are indeed eliminated or ameliorated in the course of training but many others are clearly able to be split off, compartmentalized, or denied at every level of attainment. It is of no use to fantasize about enlightenment experiences so profound and thoroughgoing that all traces of such problems are wiped out once and for all—let alone imagine that they are the norm among teachers and students. The Dharma has not been transmitted for the last twenty-five hundred years from one perfectly realized buddha to another no matter how much we like to believe such fantasies. Transmission is from human being to human being and we better get used to it.

Perfectly realized buddha or human being? What is it to be a buddha? Or be a human being? What's the difference? It has been dissolved in Mu along with the dog and buddha nature. The world opened up to us by Mu is simultaneously extraordinary and everyday. Initially, inevitably, we are captivated by the side that is extraordinary. Yet over and over again we return to the realization that any one side, no matter how extraordinary, is never the whole story. What is it that is so extraordinary anyway?

It is as if we live in a world where everyone has some sort of stomach ailment. This one has indigestion, that one acid reflux, another bloating and gas. Everywhere we turn, doctors, healers, charlatans of every stripe offer remedies for a thousand stomach ills. (Now that I think of it, this isn't a parable; the world is really like this!) One way or another we find our way to a practice that after years of effort pays off by eliminating all our stomach problems. How wonderful! We've found what everyone is looking for. So now what? We can join the marketplace of people hawking their particular cure—and hey!—ours really works! But there are a couple of problems with this.

First our method is difficult and time consuming. Very few people will want or be able to stick to it. Second, although our practice gives relief, the kind of relief is unpredictable. For some, all their symptoms really do disappear; for others the symptoms recede into the background, still there, but no longer very troublesome. And for still others nothing seems to change in their stomachs, but they just don't let it get to them the way it used to. But in the end, regardless of how well our new method works, do we really want to spend all our time and effort being one more person preoccupied by our stomachs? Isn't the real goal to be able to forget about our stomach once and for all and pay attention to something else? And not just to the next "problem" organ, the liver, brain, or kidney— but to the food itself, its origins and preparation, the lives of the farmers, to meals eaten with friends, or to whetting of the appetite during the anticipation of a meal, during a morning's work.

Maybe, having had the luxury of not having to worry about our stomach for a while, our real insight is that it's all the rest of life that really matters and that being preoccupied all the time with how our stomach feels is a far worse symptom than indigestion. Maybe you don't even have to remove the stomach pain once and for all to get the idea that there are other things in life that are more important.

Our mental health or spiritual condition are really not so different. The real suffering arises not only from the content of our minds, but from our preoccupation with the state of our minds. To be endlessly monitoring or fine-tuning our inner life is not much more appealing than being on one diet after another. Yet here too we have to be very careful. There may be a fine line between accepting one's foibles and denying one's addictions. We all need the continual feedback of those around us to keep ourselves honest about this one.

Zen practice and the samadhi and insights associated with Mu can give us the extraordinary feeling that we finally found what works— but this is only a first step in dropping self-centered preoccupation altogether. The fact is that if we want to get rid of suffering, craving, and delusion, we can't *replace* them with enlightenment, we have to throw out the entire package of delusion *and* enlightenment. "Dog" and "buddha nature" go out into the trash together. It's the one case where we must throw out the baby with the bath water.

Mu gives us the wonderful experience of eliminating distinctions. My life, the whole world, everything is nothing but this moment, with nowhere to insert the slightest trace of have or have not. But this seemingly extraordinary achievement is in itself nothing special. We are just experiencing what it is not to separate ourselves from life as it is. Nothing has been added to life, it is the same as it always has been. The next step is...just to take the next step, one foot in front of the other, back out into the world where all those distinctions continue to matter.

Mu is the first koan, not the last.

No. Nay. Never. *Nyet.* Iie.

John Tarrant

Koans are purpose-built to transform consciousness. The usual pitch for using a koan is that it will open a gate into joy and freedom. As far as I know a koan isn't useful for any other purpose. Koans imply a universe that is in motion; they help us to sympathize and harmonize with the way of things and to find the knack of letting ourselves be carried by it. In other words koans imply that some crucial features of our consciousness can change.

You can think of koans as vials full of the light that the ancestors walked through, and if you can get these vials open you share that light. By getting them open I mean you get at the light any way you can—you find the key and open the vials with a click, break them, drop them from a height, sing to them, step inside them, shake them so that some of the light spills out. Then that light is available to you, which might be handy if you're ever in a dark and twisty passage.

The koan No has been used a great deal as a lantern. You sometimes have special discoveries associated with your first koan, so some people find it reassuring that many, many people have used this koan for over a thousand years.

The setup for the koan No is that a student asks, "Does a dog have buddha nature or not?" and the teacher says, "No."

I think that the key point, and the sweetness in the koan, is that we can change. If it really is possible, in this life, to have a shift in the way you come at things, well that's an amazing idea to consider. If you understand that a shift really is possible, then the rest comes down merely to questions of method. And that's the kindness of the path: the old master says, "Well sometimes it seems crazy to think it, but transformation really does happen. So try it out. Go at it. And here's a method for you."

I did actually work for some years with this koan. Since I began without teachers and just had to grab whatever was handy, it wasn't the first koan I worked with. And it wasn't the first koan I understood or with which I had an amusing time with a teacher. Yet when this koan opened up for me it was dazzling.

I tried to carry it with me every second of the day and even while asleep, and to merge with it, and I was slow at that. There wasn't a lot of becoming-one-with-things floating around in my universe. There was a lot of, "Where's the koan?" It seemed I had to learn to be patient with everything I didn't know. But my clumsy meditation turned out to be good enough. So you don't need a perfect technique, you just need a good enough one, a good enough path. Perfection is the enemy of results.

There is a tradition behind this inquiry into the nature of the dog. The question about whether human consciousness can be reconciled with the natural world is usually urgent, and making peace with the natural world, feeling ourselves to be part of that living matrix, is one way to understand the purpose of koan work.

In the first place, what I take from the question about the dog, though, is that sometimes, when you begin a quest, you are just groping in the dark. The questioner, along with you and me, doesn't even know what to ask, or what to explore, or how to get a grip on what's primarily important, and that such cluelessness is traditional and even necessary. So there's no such thing as a bad question. If you don't have a clue, you might be starting in a good place. Not asking, when you're puzzled, is probably not smart. And I've found that it's good not to be snobbish about other people's questions because my questions are just as silly as everyone else's. Other people's naivety might seem apparent to me but that's nothing to do with me. My own innocence and naivety is opaque to me, and my questions move into that unknown territory. So asking a dopey question might be helpful.

And it's good to know that any question contains the whole of our inquiry into the nature of mind and the universe. Any question you ask will be good enough as a place to begin. You begin where you can. In the Zen tradition you have to inquire for the sake of the exploration itself. A spiritual quest is always an inquiry and there's a temptation to go into any discovery process with various agendas—alleviating our suffering, impressing others, or improving our opinion of ourselves. But such motives don't work as a guide. Koan inquiry carries a true risk; you have to just want to find out what's really happening. You have to really ask your question, to do the exploration into reality for its own sake.

Zhaozhou's koan takes away what you think. He doesn't value your opinions and you might find that you don't either, which is good because they are a weight to carry around. There are two versions of this koan and the question, "Does a dog have buddha nature or not?" occurs in both. In one case the response is "Yes" and in the other "No." "No" is more famous because it goes against what the sutras say, and if you are inclined to believe sutras, that makes it more interesting. But if you were to work with "Yes" it would be just as effective. "Does a dog have buddha nature?" "*Yes!*" "Does a dog have buddha nature?" "*No!*" You can tell that Zhaozhou doesn't care about your views because he is not interested in his own.

Michael Katz related to me a conversation with Gregory Bateson, the thinker and anthropologist. Michael was driving him to a conference at Lindisfarne on Long Island and Bateson said he dreaded something about conferences.

"What is that?" asked Michael.

"Well, people don't have a sense of humor."

"What do you mean? What does that mean to you?"

Bateson thought about it and said, "A sense of humor depends on knowing that what you think doesn't really matter, or even that you don't really matter."

So life is not about how much you matter, and if you don't start thinking that you matter, perhaps you matter more.

If you can go into the inquiry without prejudice, without prejudging the outcome, you'll be likely to find that every difficulty you have is about your prejudices. The fundamental prejudice is some form of, "This shouldn't be happening." This rejection of circumstances can be anything from "He shouldn't have left me" to "Nobody loves me" to "I'm doomed. Even meditation doesn't work for me." And what rises might be a trivial thought or it might be a tremendous and traumatic thought—"Why did she have to die?"—but the solution is the same. You can bear it. Or rather you don't need to bear it; that's the koan's job. Bearing things is usually to do with finding an explanation or a meaning, and life is truly beyond that. So there's no need to bear things, and there's no need to have a handle on them.

Eventually we just start to accept. Not only do we not dislike our circumstances, we do not dislike our own states of mind, which is the key thing. We begin to think, "Fortunately I don't get it yet." And if we forgive life for not being what we told it to be, or expected, or wished, or longed for it to be, we forgive ourselves for not being what we might have been also. And then we can be what we are, which is boundless.

We start off into the spiritual work hoping to change, hoping to become different, and we notice that there is a trick of the mind going on, and that actually we don't want to let go of who we think we are. The Buddha found that he was prepared to starve himself and do all sorts of strange, ascetic practices, as long as he didn't fundamentally change. So there's an ambivalence in the human quest, which means that we have to muster more than reason on our side if it's all going to work. That is why the koan doesn't make sense. If it made sense our reasonableness and ambivalence would be able to block it. The koan embraces the whole of your experience, not just the noble bits.

My own experience was that sometimes I worked with this koan very hard, in a way that took me further away from it. The effort assumed, "What I have is not what I want. When I understand, when I awaken, that will be what I want." And so anything that came into my life was automatically rejected, and any little piece of awakening that came along got rejected too, because it was in my life and therefore couldn't be what I was seeking.

I knew that some weird game was going on in the mind, a game that seemed close to the core of the problem of the nature of the mind. Then I noticed that the impatience and critique was diminishing and there was a tiny bit of kindness for my own condition, a blessing on the moment. I had a lot of physical pain, so I would get distracted. I would sit up all night and the predominant thought would be, "I hope I can last till the end of this period." And I had to accept that about myself. It's unique for everyone—what we have to embrace is the very thing we don't want to embrace. Our incompetence, our distractibility, our greed, our fear—that makes us fall apart at little things—our detachment that makes us indifferent to big things.

At a certain stage I stopped whipping the dog. Whipping the dog doesn't make it not a dog. First it's good to accept that it's a dog. And in my case I noticed that no matter how perfectly I did everything according to Wumen's famous recipe about becoming one with the koan "No," I wasn't one with the koan. I was hanging on to its tail, or being driven by it, or trying too hard. Sometimes I would fall into a deep meditation state and disappear and then I couldn't find the koan because there was no one there to find the koan. By that stage it was becoming interesting.

I just started being there, keeping company with the koan in all weathers, and things changed then for me. I stopped trying for those recommended states of being. It became clear that even with the mind I had, I was free. I'd done everything in the prescribed way and still my mind was often chaotic and busy. The freedom was that I found this immensely funny instead of a problem to be solved. The thoughts were things like, "I have the wrong mind for meditation; Australians can *not* get enlightened." What was hilarious was watching the way the mind produced nonsense and then believed itself. Then everything started unfolding, awkward and inevitable, like a crane preparing to take off, and my mind did clear. And the koan became clear too, and the laughter became involuntary and lasted silently for months and months, but it wasn't something I did. I didn't manipulate reality. I just paid attention to reality instead of trying to change it, or having reservations about it. And I think that's where the kindness of the koan is.

Zhaozhou's koan is gesturing toward embracing your current state—that's why the dog is important, because in many cultures Rover is not greatly appreciated. Rover may even be served for breakfast, and so to be a dog is not a high state of existence. And when we're unacceptable to ourselves, we regard ourselves as despised creatures. And that's how it is until we stop building the prison and the inner conflict ends. I think that this No koan is very deeply about the ways we reject experience as not being correct or appropriate. And if you are making a fundamental judgment that this moment isn't right, and if you go into the heart of that refusal, it becomes a gate. Go toward the frightening thing and you find that it holds a blessing. Then No then becomes "No" to your critique, "No" to your "I can't do this." It's a recognition that thoughts are just thoughts and the koan rises to explode them. "I'll never get there, I'm in the wrong company, I'm unhappy," all just thoughts. This is a way in which the koan starts to serve the inquiry at a cognitive level. This has a certain deconstructive power.

At the deepest level the koan takes away not only your judgments and your criticisms, but the point of reference that they depend on, the point of reference that makes a problem a problem. And it's never anybody else who's causing the problem, and also, not only is it not anybody else, it's not even you. Even you are not a problem. It becomes clear that the problem of existence is an apparent problem, that existence is existence, full of richness, shimmer, and intimacy. Everything is beautiful when seen in that dimension.

The blessing is there, even when it's not the outcome you intended—you know if you're sad about something and you just accept it, you don't have to not be sad, as evidence that you're accepting it. You can accept that you're sad and then it can be lovely. If your meditation sucks, you accept that you have miserable meditation. It's all right, and so the kindness comes in somewhere on the chain of harshness, and everything moves. There's nothing wrong with being a dog and barking and being frustrated. And what's wrong with throwing yourself at your life?

At the same time, the experience we have when all that just stops is a wonderful thing. When you open up and—how can I say it—things are friendly. Part of freedom is about not thinking, "It's not here." When you stop thinking, "It's not here," you start noticing all the ways it's here. And the more you notice how much it's here, the more what the old teachers speak about as accumulated karma—the stacked up disappointments of your life—starts falling from you. If you only ever do things for strategic reasons, in order to manipulate people, that might fall off you. In this case you might want the dog to change or receive your kindness, yet the dog's world is already complete. If you're stingy, that might fall off you. If you try to buy other people's favors and love, that might fall off you. So in other words, you're not treating your self like an object, so you will start noticing those times when you're not creating the walls of a prison. Life is not as hard, and more and more space surrounds that discovery.

What follows are some thoughts about method. These are suggestions about ways to line up to the koan and to manage your mind once you are on board the koan.

Hacks for Consciousness

First a new metaphor: A koan is a kind of technology, a hack for the mind. It strips our opinions and views away. Unlike some other technologies, koans don't work in a linear fashion. They surprise you by transcending the terms on which you took them up. They draw you into a different way of seeing and experiencing your world.

Teachers

When the fit is good with a teacher it is one of the most intimate relationships possible, and humans like intimacy. But the fit is not always good and people being people, your relationship with your teacher might turn out to be important or trivial. Also, your teacher could be someone you met for one retreat, or the master who initiated the koan a thousand years ago, or someone who visits you in a dream. In the end the koan is your absolute, fallback, rock-bottom teacher.

Because it is a technology, not a set of answers, a koan allows certain insights to be passed on through someone who doesn't have a deep understanding of them—an obvious advantage if you are interested in handing the light down over thousands of years or ferrying it across cultures.

Choosing a First Koan

It can't possibly matter which koan you use first. I've noticed that people succeed with a wide variety of them—for example, "Quickly, without thinking good or evil, before your parents were born, at this exact moment, what is your original face?" Or, "In the sea, 10,000 feet down there's a single stone. I'll pick it up without getting my hands wet." There are probably a thousand of these that work well. Zhaozhou's dog is famous though no one knows why—perhaps its simplicity and the fact that many of the Japanese schools had a rigid order to their curriculum and this one came first. Hakuin used this as a first koan so it went more or less at the beginning of his curriculum, though as a teacher he was inclined to experiment. In spite of its popularity, it's a fine koan.

A rigid curriculum has the virtue of introducing a predictability and impartiality to the process. On the other hand, there are advantages for a master who is confident or foolish enough to move around in a curriculum according the needs of the student. So some Japanese schools (as well as Korean and Chinese ones) don't use a rigid sequence to their curriculum. Pacific Zen School, which includes Open Source, feels itself to be in sympathy with those traditions, so we use many different first koans.

If you dream of a koan, if it sticks in your mind like an ear worm, if you find yourself humming it, if it gives you vertigo or nausea, if you feel as if you have come home from a long journey when you hear it, if a koan grabs your attention, if it follows you home—then that's a good reason to keep it. It chose you. You might as well trust being grabbed; a force bigger than your usual awareness is at work.

The Method of Working with a Koan

The method is simply to keep company with the koan, adhere to it day and night. That's it, the whole method. And don't think that it's not there when you sleep or forget about it for a while.

Strategies for Working with the Koan

1. First find the koan. If your mind is somewhere, find the koan. If your mind isn't anywhere, there's not a problem.

2. Any part of the koan is the koan. In this case, *No, dog, buddha nature, does?* could stick in your mind—or the koan might consolidate to a sense of being on a quest, of traveling through the mind. Quirks occur; one person had an interesting experience when a cat exchanged itself for the dog in his mind. There is an autonomy to any real process in consciousness and working with a koan is something you do your best to guide without entirely controlling. It's a creative act and you attend to what appears more than you impose your will on the universe.

3. Accept your mind and its states. If you are being reasonably accepting of your mind states that's probably a good direction. Mind states are, after all, what we have as humans, they are what we have to embrace and for-give and love, as they are.

4. *Relax.* Trying to achieve a certain state implies reaching for something not present, living in a projected future world. So, no need to try. I know that some of the old teachers said to try hard, but what did they know? You have to truly appear in your *own* life. Then there is no question of effort or trying, there is just the koan.

5. *Mind your own business.* Making a critique of your colleagues and peers and their progress is, well, useless and somehow ungrateful. In fact even an assessment of your own progress is probably useless and some-how ungrateful. Don't mind even your own business. Just keep company with the koan.

6. *Timing.* It takes us years to build a prison in the mind. It's OK if it takes some years to deconstruct that prison. Freedom is worth it. Being on a quest is what life is about.

Membership in a Community

One thing we are doing is making a culture for awakening, making awak-ening a feature of the landscape of modern intellectual life. The medita-tor isn't a *ronin*, a masterless samurai, wandering around alone, looking for personal survival at any cost. Koans make you a participant in the drama of discovery, a member of a community of those who care about consciousness. The deeper the journey goes the more you are likely to notice your love for this community.

The Koan and Your Life

The link between the koan and the transformation of your life is real but since the process isn't linear you might not notice it at first. The link might seem to be in a black box—invisible. There will be times when the koan shows you your most painful mind states and your most confining thoughts. It doesn't invite you to identify with them. Nonetheless, you might think that the koan doesn't seem to be working during your official meditation times, but your life might be opening up greatly. Well, that's not really a problem.

Gradual and Sudden

The process is always both gradual and sudden because there is some development and then a jump. An example of the gradual side of things is that for some people the koan opens a space in which the mind is not building its prison. In that space, you will notice joy and aliveness and a sense of having a link to eternity. This is in the neighborhood of awakening. Then the space will close up, perhaps leaving a sense of loss. You can just notice these things without grabbing them. Over time you will get more and more space till the spaces start joining up.

Sometimes your longing and impatience and harshness appear in front of you. It doesn't seem to work to force your way through. You just have to know that the obstacle is somehow you and keep going as best you can and when you acknowledge this and don't chew your leg off, the trap will disappear.

On the sudden side of things, some people have epiphanies. They plod along for a period and then there is a bang and a large shift happens all at once. This can happen completely outside of a training context also. Whichever way you come to it, freedom is freedom.

The Basic Nature of Consciousness Is Empathy

If it's heartless that's not the koan, either as a method or as a result of the method. When consciousness is stripped down there is a velvety, vibrant quality to it—everything is alive and sparkling and also I am you. It's unlikely that you can get to this by a harsh method. As far as we can say that a dream has a basic nature, the basic nature of consciousness is something like empathy and a boundary-less love.

Experiences with Joshu's Mu

Jules Shuzen Harris

WHAT IS IT? What is this burning question? What do we encounter when we seek this Mu, when we go round and round in our minds trying to understand it, trying to make sense of it, trying to find it, trying to break through to that elusive realization. What is it? And what do we meet when we confront that which seems utterly impossible? What is the resistance we are holding on to? It certainly is not easy, this letting go, but after all the tense holding, pulling, and struggling, out of somewhere, finally, something begins to relax. Maybe it is out of sheer exhaustion, but our grip loosens. The tail slips from our hand, the animal vanishes in the air, and there we are, empty handed and singing to ourselves.

In a short series of interviews with students who have worked on the koan Mu, we inquired into the nature of what came up along the way, what we met in our own lives while working with Mu. What we heard were the ways that the koan Mu focused us on our stuck places, how it began to shine a light on our daily lives in a way that slowly or suddenly illuminated something that was coming between us and our own true nature. As we are digging in to Mu, going deeper in our work with the koan, we are also digging in to our lives and looking at what obstacles are keeping us from waking up to ourselves. Though the experience of working with Mu was different for each student, all of those who worked with this koan spoke about the ways it awakened something about the ways we live, the ways we are with ourselves, our family, our friends, our work, and our lives.

Here follows some of what a number of students of this koan observed and said:

One student spoke principally of experiencing just frustration, despair, self-doubt, discouragement, uncertainty, more frustration—he said nearly anything that you can think of that was negative—there it was in this endlessly frustrating attempt to come to know what is Mu.

Another had practiced shikantaza for nearly ten years before taking up koan study and sitting formally with Mu. Sitting with Mu, he had a sense that it was already there, it was already seen, but there remained the task of wiping away the veil obscuring the full clarity of realization. Mu took him right to a stuck point, a place where he didn't even realize he was stuck, and gave an extra push to see through it. The koan offered the seed around which something new could crystallize.

Another student spoke of her lifetime of depending on the brain, of expecting the brain to give her answers, give her right answers. And here was something that the brain could not solve—she said her first experience was one of a sort of subtle disbelief—how can I not be getting this? It took time to stop fighting, to stop struggling, to give up the struggle to get it, to see it—then real doubt arose, and finally a complete surrender to simply realizing "I can't think through this." Along the way, she felt she moved away from using words, mind words, idea words, finding that whatever she could say or explain, that was not it. In reading Dogen, she came to a sense that this Mu was not something outside, not something external, but something internal and beyond concepts. The fullness of meditating on Mu, especially the actual sound of the syllable Mu, seemed to open a space to seeing the oneness of buddha nature. She recalled that it was very hard, and certainly required deep perseverance, and also required her to move through some sense of "Why is this being done to me?"

One person noted that while he jumped right into Mu, he immediately saw and realized the obvious nature of Mu, that he found it interesting that realizing it again and again, or realizing it more fully and with greater clarity, continues to take ongoing effort and inquiry. Even after "seeing" Mu, there remains much more deepening. He still sometimes found himself "thinking about" it, or explaining it, rather than living it, realizing it. When he feels clear on Mu, he feels clear on all the koans.

Another spoke of nine months of work, walking her dogs repeating Mu, while all alongside her work with this koan, she was also gaining a sense of unity, of seeing someone else and saying "Oh, that's me, too," so that over these months there was a gradual sinking in of Mu, there was Mu creeping into awareness, not in a flash but in a steady, slow opening and recognition. In that sense, she felt all the pieces were in place, and she felt she perhaps should have seen it sooner, but there was still some hesitation, some sense of not completely trusting that this is really it.

And one person expressed his experience as an intensity of focus, an intensity of inquiry, and found the very clear, repeated sound of the voice of asking "Mu: What is it?" to be quite important—the voice itself was a central part of the experience. Who is asking? What is this Mu? And who is being asked? If any insight ever comes, who is going to provide it? Who recites the koan? Where does it go? Many, many years ago, he read Alan Watts' little paperback *The Book: On the Taboo Against Knowing Who You Are* and it really resonated for him and he thought inquiring into Mu really began then and there. He likes to imagine Mu as the last syllable before he goes to sleep, and the first syllable he wakes up to, and sometimes it is.

The koan of Mu certainly never leaves us. Seeing it and tasting it as the fundamental truth of our nature seems to be just a beginning. *Being* it with a clear and ever present fullness, manifesting Mu as this truth, is always awaiting in another moment of waking up.

It is perhaps in the very process of inquiring that we are brought to examine and realize the ground in which the inquiry takes place. Even more than seeing the koan, it is in sitting with it, being stuck with it, and *not* seeing it that we might be led to recognize more fully the habits, the fears, or the uncertainties that hamper us. While we work with dedication and purpose at becoming the koan, we may surprise ourselves in noticing all the other pieces of our life that come into the light and share the space of insight.

Mu contains all that needs to be known about Zen, about Buddhism and in the Buddhist context about everything. Thus, it is fitting that the koan Mu is usually the first koan given to a student who engages in koan study. For it brings the student into contact with the first barrier to living a liberated life him/herself.

Thomas Merton writes: "The heart of the koan (Mu) is reached; its kernel is attained and tasted when one breaks through into the heart of life itself, as the ground of one's own consciousness."—I'm working through Mu, one expresses oneself as the question answered, and *I* and *other* disappear and one is simply aware.

But before this happens, as noted in the comments above, one struggles, one often becomes frustrated as one extricates himself from himself, herself from herself.

Mu drives us to dissolve our limited subjectivity to go beyond yes and no and all affirmations and negatives. Mu brings us to a state of pure consciousness: a state beyond a consciousness "of."

Enjoying Mu

Kurt Spellmeyer

For a moment—if "a moment" actually exists—let's imagine ourselves sitting once again in a darkened theater. We're watching the movie and having a great time. The hero is just about to kiss the leading lady. Their eyes meet, their faces are drawing near, but just then the spectacle on the screen begins flickering and breaking up. Now the beautiful illusion is gone. Instead of one continuous flow, what we see are discrete images, like a series of still photographs rather than a moving picture. Finally the images come to a stop and somebody turns on the lights. Something's gone wrong with the projector, they announce.

The truth is that all we ever see on the screen are individual images. But our minds supply a continuity that the images don't possess. Between each image and the next, there is really an empty space that our minds want us to ignore, and the projector helps us out by firing the images very rapidly. Except on those occasions when things go wrong, we only notice the continuity, the seamless flow that we help to create. But when the projector gets out of sync, we can plainly see the static images, and we can observe the empty spaces in between.

If you do zazen long enough, you will experience this empty space between the moments when the world seems to exist in a timeless, changeless way. The Japanese word for this space is "Mu," which means, quite simply, "nothing." Finding Mu might take you a few months or it could require several years, but if you focus your attention on anything, you'll eventually bump into Mu. The object of attention might be your breath, gently going in and out, or the rhythmic sound of the crickets outside, or a candle on the floor in front of you, or an image that you visualize. But no matter what you focus on, sooner or later it will lead you to the space where absolutely nothing exists. The first time you become aware of this space, it might seem to pass by in a flash. You might even wonder if anything occurred. But gradually the empty spaces will acquire a longer duration and a kind of depth, like an ocean you are swimming in at night.

Zen teachers have a penchant for the dramatic. Over the centuries when they've tried to describe what Mu or emptiness is like, they've spoken of it as a kind of death. "Die on the cushion!" they frequently shout. The death they have in mind might be just a metaphor, but they could mean it quite literally. Maybe those empty moments are indeed where we'll wind up when our lives reach the end. Or maybe they're just a trick played by our minds, an odd defect of human consciousness.

But that wouldn't be what most Buddhists think. The bodhisattva Avalokiteshvara—the one known in Chinese as Kwan-yin—describes Mu this way in the Heart Sutra, probably the most important sutra in Zen:

> In emptiness there is no form, no feelings, perceptions, impulses, consciousness. No eyes, no ears, no nose, no tongue, no body, no mind; no color, no sound, no smell, no taste, no touch, no object of mind; no realm of eyes and so forth until no realm of mind consciousness. No ignorance and also no extinction of it, and so forth until no old age and death and also no extinction of them. No suffering, no origination, no stopping, no path, no cognition, also no attainment with nothing to attain.

Avalokiteshvara doesn't say that nothingness is just an illusion or a fluke in the design of the human brain. He, or she—the bodhisattva can be both—says it's the basic reality.

If you're willing to concede that this might indeed be possible, the implications could seem rather frightening. In the West, we often think of nothingness as the occasion for deep despair. If life really is One Big Nothingness, then why should we take the trouble to go on? Total nothingness could sound even worse than an eternity in the Christian hell, since you would at least still exist, and possibly God might change his mind. Nothingness could be worse than hell itself!

But the sutra goes on to say something else: the experience of emptiness ends all suffering. Emptiness is a sure way out of hell. And this is indeed what Zen students learn. Even if this emptiness looks a lot like death, or like the world coming to an end, its effect on our lives is astonishing. It can free you from every fear. There's no memory, habit, or buried trauma—no obstacle of any kind—that it can't dissolve like water wearing down a stone.

Mu doesn't liberate by transforming what exists through some special kind of alchemy. The nature of things doesn't change at all. What has changed is our perception of them. We discover that everything is Mu, and that Mu is everything. "Form is emptiness," the sutra declares, "emptiness is form." And when we see our obstacles for what they are—fundamentally nothingness—their hold over us gradually erodes.

Form and emptiness are believed to be different aspects of the same reality. They're not even different sides of the same coin. They're like different views of the same thing. The seventeenth-century master Hakuin wrote that the difference between enlightened mind and our ordinary consciousness is like the difference between water and ice. Ice is always water fundamentally, but it seems like another substance when the temperature drops below the freezing point.

The *thingness* of things shouldn't be ignored—the rockness of rocks, the treeness of trees—even if the rocks and trees are always more than words and ideas can encapsulate. If we simply dismiss it all as an illusion, we aren't doing justice to reality. The sutra doesn't teach that there's no form at all. Hakuin didn't tell us that ice doesn't exist. But in a way the conscious mind can't quite understand, Mu—nothingness—is also everything.

How can everything and nothing coexist? That's pretty hard to wrap your mind around.

There's a koan that might help to clarify the matter. On one occasion when he was young, a Chinese master of long ago had the chance to meet the great Joshu, who was then many years his senior. And when they met, Joshu asked him this: "What if a person of the Great Death comes back to life again?"

The phrase Great Death might be understood as nothingness itself. And so the koan could be taken to mean, "Once everything has completely disappeared, once you yourself are only emptiness, what will happen then, if anything?"

In response the younger master gave this reply: "Don't go by night; wait for the light of day to come." As usual with koans, this answer might seem to make very little sense. But if you've spent a lot of time in Mu, sooner or later you will observe that you can't stay forever in that empty space even though it's so profoundly liberating. No matter how deeply you concentrate, something is going to interrupt your beautiful, untrammeled emptiness.

The universe always comes back again. No matter how skillfully we meditate, emptiness won't stay empty for very long. Something always seems to keep popping up.

If your goal is to stay in Mu without breaks or interruptions, this oscillation will appear to pose an enormous problem. But if you stop assuming there's something wrong, you can sit back and enjoy the show, knowing it's the way things have to be. The oscillation is the natural order of things.

In fact, it can't be stopped no matter what we do.

Becoming Mu

Grace Schireson

AFTER THIRTY YEARS of American Soto Zen practice I finally caught up with Mu on a trip to Japan—or maybe Mu finally caught up with me. For several years I had been vacationing in Japan; wandering around exploring temples and unconsciously looking for a way inside monastic practice. I thought I was looking for a Japanese Soto Zen teacher, but people kept referring me to Kyoto's "great Rinzai resource," Keido Fukushima Roshi. It was a little annoying, but after the third referral I figured I might as well face up to my karma and meet this teacher. I called him and scheduled a meeting for myself to be accompanied by my husband. What harm can there be in meeting a teacher anyway? I was soon to find out.

Within the first few minutes I realized that I had landed in deep water, and that my skills might not be up to these waves. The roshi quickly dispensed with the niceties and set me in the middle of the Zen conundrum: "After all these years of Soto Zen practice, what brings you to Rinzai practice?" he asked bluntly. A simple enough question, but right to the point. In classic Zen master style, he took control. Breaking all rules of politesse and Japanese circumspection, he let me know I would not be wasting his time, and he would not waste mine. *What are you doing here?*

Too bad for me that I answered from my intellect. We Zen students know that relying on thinking mind only makes it worse, but habits are tenacious and we keep reaching for the intellect. "Rinzai and Soto practice are one at the root, it is the teacher that matters," I said confidently. He acknowledged my effort to right the boat and sent another wave my way: "Are you asking me to be your teacher right now?" His meaning was, *OK, smarty-pants, we all know about Zen history in China, but what about right here and now, what will you say now?* Uh-oh, I thought, when did I enter this water and where the hell is my paddle?

I didn't realize it, but my active engagement with Mu had begun. What do you do when you don't know what to do? What do you do when neither your intellect, influence, willpower, nor your bravado, begging, or temper tantrums will get you out of a jam? When you are up the creek with no paddle, what will you use to guide your boat? I was stunned and speechless; indeed, a rare occasion. I stammered through "I don't know," because I couldn't speak. But the fact is I did know. I had found a teacher and Mu. To save face I tried another tack as soon as my brain started whirring again, "I won't ask you to be my teacher until I know you better. How do I get to practice with you?" There it was: both attraction and protection in one seemingly reasonable remark. Out of the water now, thinking I might be safe on land, I had entered the lion's den. Whether protesting or walking straight through, there is only one exit from this cave.

Fukushima Roshi invited me to train with him and Mu by doing sesshin at Tofukuji, a Rinzai training temple. Their monastic idea of a good time was to sit one hour (or longer) meditation periods from 3 a.m. to 11:00 p.m. for seven days. He explained Tofukuji's eight sesshin-per-year pattern and told me I could stay at the temple and try one. After the nature of our engagement had been settled, my husband and I were quickly escorted out of the temple. As if falling from a cloud, we hit the street with a thud. "What just happened?" we asked each other.

I felt like someone had socked me and knocked me senseless. I felt like I'd run full speed into a brick wall. When had it happened? How did he do it? We both felt like Roshi's spiritual force had hit like a physical blast. While we both felt the power of meeting Roshi, my husband suggested that since this had been my idea, I ought to try if first. If I lived through it, he might join me some time later, much later. Whatever it was, I knew I would have to come back for more, and I also knew I would be on my own.

I had met Fukushima Roshi's Mu through the roshi's living expression of it. Later in dokusan, in private interview, with the roshi I understood more. *When Joshu answered Mu, he expressed his buddha nature, when you express your buddha nature, what is it?* When Roshi meets you, you know his Mu, but what is yours? Becoming Mu means becoming your essential self, becoming the Self that precedes the mind's division. Roshi embodied the power of Mu. Through his embodiment, Mu had become tangible to me. Rather than an abstract absence of something, Mu showed itself as a vibrant, dynamic, thrilling life force. But the task was for me to find it for myself not just to admire it in the roshi.

Becoming Mu with Fukushima Roshi meant meeting him in dokusan five times a day in the midst of seven days of bone-crunching sesshin. Sometimes meditation periods went on for ninety minutes, and each session had its own special terror. Novice monks were repeatedly whacked with a kyosaku that looked more like a long baseball bat. Monitors patrolled the room menacingly, taunting and poking with the stick to see if your attention would wander from Mu. But Zendo drama paled in comparison to meeting Mu in the dokusan room. *"What is it?"* Roshi would roar inches from your face. Periods of zazen were a quest to find something essential, something that would make the utterly exposed humiliation of dokusan less devastating. I was warned when training to do dokusan, "If he doesn't absolutely hate your answer, he will pause just a second before he rings the bell that ends the interview." It was worse than that; sometimes your best answer, wrought from hours of painful sitting, just made him shake his head as if to say, *"My God, just how dull are you?"*

There are more than three thousand koans in Tofukuji's curriculum. There are more than one hundred that involve Mu; these come first. Each individual Mu koan is designed to bring forth new understanding about the nature of reality—the nature of the absolute and the relative. Each koan brings up a separate aspect of Mu: What is Mu beyond form and, then again, how does Mu express itself in this phenomenal world? Despite the impossibility of ever completing the koan curriculum and the physical difficulties of the training, something in me knew for certain that what I was doing mattered. While I had no idea how to become Mu, I knew other people had done so and figured that my body would find the way. Just like I trusted my body to find its way to the next breath after I was knocked over by a wave in the ocean, I trusted my body to become Mu if I gave it a chance.

Through bodily sense I practiced becoming Mu, and through interactions in the world, I realized I was finding my way to deeper experiences of nondiscrimination than I had previously in practice. Mostly, I just became Mu without knowing what was happening, but sometimes

I realized I had changed. For example, during one intense experience of becoming Mu, I discovered that I had become freed of language and self-reference. This realization only occurred because I had left the temple during the retreat to take a bath, otherwise there was nothing to think about and no way to know what Mu was doing with me.

I raced down the small streets neighboring the Tofukuji complex between periods of zazen to take a bath a few blocks from the temple. I hurried to enter the local neighborhood bathhouse in my Zen robes so I would not be late for the next session. Having used public baths and mastered enough Japanese to get around I had no concerns about the venture. I just wasn't taking the power of Mu into consideration. The local Higashiyama bath lady had undoubtedly spent her life in Kyoto at this family bathhouse and knew a Tofukuji monk when she saw one. With a shaved head, and my American height of 5'10" inches, to her I was a man. She took my money and motioned me to the men's side of the bathhouse. When I entered and saw the naked men, I knew something was wrong, but I just couldn't figure out what it was.

Without my understanding conceptually what was going on, Mu had moved me beyond the discrimination of man and woman. While the concept of gender eluded me, a glimmer of intelligence remained to warn me that this bath situation was not going well. Even though I couldn't quite understand what was wrong with being in the room with naked men bathing, I sensed that the situation was somewhat problematic. I went back out to the bath lady to express my question, but I was unable to say any words. Nothing came out of my mouth, so she just sent me in to the men's bath again with an impatient wave of her hand. This time I knew what the problem was straight away when I went in again to the room with the already naked men. Without speaking, I came right back out to face her squarely.

The problem now showed up on my face, even though I still had no words for my dilemma. This time, she read my strong intention and inquired, *"Onna desu ka?"* she asked in a shocked voice—Are you a woman? Still I had no words, but I was able to nod vigorously, YES! She motioned me over to the woman's side of the bath, and then followed me in to make sure that I had the requisite body parts to join the bathing women. She told the other women the story as I undressed. There was much laughter and some nervousness while I took off all my clothes. "*Ah soo desu ka,*" they all agreed, "*sugoi ama-san!*" Wow, this is, indeed, one awesome (huge) nun! I laughed along with them, completed my bath and smiled when I heard them on the streets later refer to the sugoi Ama-san as I passed. Thanks to becoming Mu I had been publically humiliated, but thanks to becoming Mu I experienced no residue of embarrassment or self-consciousness.

I was learning that it was one thing to become Mu, and it was quite another to be able to express it. The first step was trusting my body to find the reality free from discriminating mind. The experience of freedom through becoming the One Self occurred with repeated and faithful aim. But there was still more to becoming Mu. Once I had become Mu, how did I express it? Clearly, this had been a particular problem at the bathhouse, but it was also the essential task of dokusan. Once I had become Mu, in the context of any particular koan, what was my real life embodiment that expressed it? How do I express Mu so that the delusions brought to light by this particular koan are both revealed and smashed? In one act, understanding was meant to reveal and dispel delusion.

The thrill of becoming Mu and encountering my own personal freedom buoyed me through many physical hardships. One Tofukuji winter sesshin I sat with snow blowing in the open windows across my shoulders. There was no heat anywhere in the temple; I would have sold my soul for a flick of someone's Bic cigarette lighter. Fortunately for me, no one offered me the slightest warmth in exchange for anything. The only permanent injury I sustained during that sesshin was a chipped tooth. I had tried to bite into a PowerBar that had frozen solid in my room. My room was so cold that it took twenty minutes of shivering to warm my futon bed to body temperature. I don't think I undressed once during that particular week in the temple. I had so overdrawn my body's physical reserves that on the fifth night of sesshin, I fainted during the 6:00 p.m. period of meditation.

Just before passing out, I remember thinking that there was something wrong. There was too much pain, too much nausea, and then along with all of this, some other weird feeling I couldn't name. At that point the lights started to go out as if a curtain were dropping from the top of my head across my field of vision. I knew I was about to faint. My last thought was, *"Uh-oh I don't want to fall head first onto this slate floor..."* I put my weight back on my elbows and fainted straight over backward onto the tatami platform where I had been sitting. It was a brief, deep, and restful sleep, too soon awakened by the Zendo monitor's almost hysterical demands, *"Dai joobu desu ka, dai joobu desu ka?"* *"Are you all right, are you all right?"* I excused myself to use the bathroom, looked up the Japanese word for fainting, and returned ten minutes later to becoming Mu.

I realized soon thereafter that even though becoming Mu was urgent, it would be better for all concerned if I didn't die in the process. Imagine the international incident created by the large gaijin (foreign) woman dying while meditating at Tofukuji! In order to live through becoming Mu, I had better make use of a nearby inn to eat and get warm during future attempts. From then on, I arranged to stay outside of the temple and to follow a modified schedule during the sesshin. If I had nine lives I had already spent three of them staying at Tofukuji, and I was so hoping to have a chance to enjoy the fruit of becoming Mu. Now that I had found a moderate approach, my husband, and occasionally another friend or student, would join with me for sesshin.

My pattern of working with Mu was to go to Japan for sesshin, return home with my koan, and then to visit Japan some months later. During meditation at home, I would wrestle alone with whatever aspect of Mu had stopped me in my tracks in my last dokusan with Roshi. Six months later I would return to Tofukuji and Roshi. I knew I had developed some understanding of the koan, but I was not yet clear on how to express it. Presenting my understanding to Roshi would result in his hair-raising roar: *"You have explained the meaning, but now SHOW ME!"* Shocked out of complacency, I would have to abandon my mind's neat little explanations and throw my body into the fray. I didn't know where the answer would come from or what the enactment would be, but I had faith that Mu would continue to find me.

One thing I learned was that being in the roshi's physical presence transmitted the necessary energy and clarity. I would approach dokusan with what I thought might be a perfectly respectable answer, and Roshi would reject it with a simple shaking of his head, an unspoken "No." As

I left the dokusan room I was then able to see what had previously been hidden from my view—the limitations of my answer and ultimately my own understanding. Without saying a word, meeting Roshi had opened my mind. Mind-to-mind transmission began to make sense while becoming Mu. My becoming Mu depended initially on encountering the roshi's Mu. His presence with the koan seemed to be like the necessary role of light, water, and soil for sprouting a seed. For the seed to sprout there must be beneficial conditions. For Mu to become me, Roshi needed to beam. The encounters we shared in becoming Mu continue to sprout and blossom as insight for me many months and years later.

Over time becoming Mu has unfolded in my daily life as personal freedom and clarity. In difficult personal interactions I find that sometimes I can let go of my ideas about the problem and *become* the actual situation or *become* (one with) the other person. Becoming Mu seemed to translate into letting go of self-clinging and deepening my engagement with whatever I was encountering. I was taking down long-forgotten barricades that I had constructed between myself and others, between myself and reality.

You may wonder how my adventures in becoming Mu continue as I approach my sixtieth birthday? Roshi has instructed his students to answer any questions about progress in koan study with a simple "I am almost finished." This is a wonderfully humorous approach to our never-ending work of self-realization.

In the words of my early Soto Zen teacher, Shunryu Suzuki Roshi, "Everyone is perfect and we can all use a little improvement."

I am almost finished.

Joshu's Dog

Elaine MacInnes

Teisho on the Case

The case is very concise. The koan involves two people only, a monk and his teacher. We are not told anything more about the monk except that he is a monk. He could be a very green monk; he could be a half-done monk; he could be well on toward becoming ripe. But let's suppose he was like the people in our zendo who are working on Mu, people who are usually rather new to Zen. The monk had doubtless read many of the sutras, and he had probably, to some degree or other, become convinced of and enamored by this beautiful Inner Life, the essence of all creation that Shakyamuni spoke about following his great enlightenment. And perhaps, while reflecting on this wonderful Essential Nature, he happened to see a dog, a dreadful-looking dog, running across the temple floor. So he started to wonder: "Can that miserable-looking dog have this beautiful Essential Nature that Lord Buddha told us about?" His wonderment obviously led to doubt. Finally, he did what a good student should do: he took his doubts to his teacher. And we must also not overlook the other possibility that the monk was, even at that point, asking Joshu to show him the real buddha nature, and was not asking for its *interpretation* or meaning at all.

[...] Dogen Zenji, like most Zen masters, never handed out bouquets— but he did admire Joshu and called him the old Buddha. Joshu is also famous for the rules he wrote for monastic observance, and I understand that the contemporary monastic schedule is still based on Joshu's guidelines. They are the legacy of a very great Zen master indeed.

Now I'd like to say something about the temperament of this Zen master Joshu. In so many of our koans, the master is a kind of bumptious person. Perhaps Rinzai comes to mind first—General Rinzai with his dynamically sharp spirit and thunderous cry, *"Katsu!"* Or there is Bokushu who, as soon as a student entered the dokusan room, would grab him roughly by the collar and shout, "Say it!" There was Unmon, who was very famous for the strict and severe way he guided his disciples.

But Joshu wasn't like that. In fact, they say his ordinary speaking voice was soft and low, not much more than a gentle whisper. His Zen was quiet, as was that of Dogen Zenji and Shakyamuni. When the monk asked him if the dog had buddha nature or not, Joshu probably gently replied, "Mu."

I am reminded of an incident I saw in Japan some years ago. I was in *sesshin* (meditation retreat) at Takatsuki in Kansai, and one day Yamada Roshi's assistant changed the room where we went to write after dokusan. That evening after dokusan, I entered this room and sat down and began to write. I heard a very loud voice, which was indeed a shout, calling out *"Muji ni sanjite orimasu!"* ("I am working on Mu!") I looked up, and a short distance away at a kind of angle was the dokusan room; there beside the open window was Yamada Roshi. In front of him was a disciple. The roshi was rubbing his face and eyes in that vigorous way he did when he was tired, and the disciple, who was obviously in desperation shouted again, *"Sanjite orimasu!"* The roshi finished his massaging, took his hands away from his face, looked at the disciple directly and kindly, and said very gently, "What did you say?"

Now about this word Mu. One student working on Mu said recently that he is a little disturbed by Mu because he knows it is a negation, that it means "No." I should like to point out that there is another koan: "A monk asked Joshu, 'Does a dog have buddha nature or not?' Joshu answered, 'U.'"—which is positive. In Case 30 of the Gateless Gate, Taibai asked Baso in earnestness, "What is Buddha?" Baso answered, "The very mind is Buddha." And then in Case 33, a monk asked Baso in all earnestness, "What is Buddha?" Baso replied, "No mind, no Buddha." Whether it's yes or no, mind or not-mind, it doesn't make any difference. So don't give any thought to yes or no. Don't give any thought to anything.

I think we are very fortunate that when studying this koan in English we simply leave it as Mu and do not translate it as "no" or "not" or "not-being." In English, Mu is harmless. It is just something a cow says and has little appeal to the intellect. It is relatively easy to stop thinking about Mu. (Though there might be a problem for those well-versed in Greek and contemporary physics. In that language, we are told there is hidden a whole world of Mu. In one case, the Greek letter Mu symbolizes the coefficient of friction and is used as a symbol in thermodynamics and electromagnetism. But I'm sure we sitters can discard the Greek approach to Mu with no difficulty at all.)

Remember, for most of us our intellect is overworked. It's a wonderful faculty, but just because it's wonderful doesn't mean we have to use it for all occasions. I am reminded of a story told by Bishop Tudtud from Mindanao in the southern Philippines. He said one of their seminarians had been ordained a deacon just before Christmas. The bishop gave him a watch to mark the occasion. He asked the new deacon to preach at Midnight Mass, and the young priest-to-be told the congregation four times during the sermon what time it was! How wonderful a watch is for telling time! In another area our intellect is wonderful, too, and it helps us in so many of our problems and enterprises. It is unsurpassed at analyzing and investigating and breaking down complexities. But when we are trying to meet Reality, or what Yamada Roshi calls the Empty-Infinite, the intellect is useless because we can't break IT down.

Now let us take another look at the question in this koan. When a monk or any Zen disciple asks a teacher if a dog has buddha nature or not, the answer has to be "yes," "no," or "maybe." And these are all intellectual answers. When a student asks a Zen master an intellectual question, it's the business of the teacher to get the repartee out of the field of intellectual responses, the field of "yes," "no," and "maybe." A good teacher would never answer like that. Those answers feed the very faculty that it is their business to stop functioning. That's the appropriateness of Mu in English. It's not very nourishing intellectually.

Mu is a wonderful broom to sweep away all the thoughts and ideas and concepts that keep the intellect fed and working. That's its proper activity, to sweep and to empty. When people come to dokusan right after *shoken* (formally becoming a student) they usually have a lot to say. This is an easy time for a roshi, and interesting too, because we hear all kinds of stories about dogs and buddhas and monks and temples and such things. But after the Mu has been sweeping for a while, these stories gradually come to an end. To the teacher, this speechlessness of the student is a good sign. When all words are exhausted and there is nothing to say, then the teacher takes the initiative.

After one's sitting deepens, something happens to Mu, and in teaching we use it as a handle. It is the subject of what is called *mondo*, repartee. The thrusts of mondo are best when they arise from silence. Together, teacher and disciples will investigate Mu, its rises and falls.

This stage of becoming intimate with Mu is the stage of building *joriki*, the power that arises from sitting. The kanji for *jo* means "to be settled or quiet," and has overtones of foundation; *riki* is power. Lao Tzu tells us that silence is the great revelation. As silence deepens, we experience change, and we discover to our delight that revelation is not knowledge; revelation is power, a power that brings transformation and insight and, as you may have noticed, in the mondo at the beginning of the teisho, the time and place are always here and now.

Teisho on Mumon's Commentary

Let us now look at Mumon's commentary. Mumon himself came to the second stage of Zen practice, satori, after working on Mu for six years. This commentary is his *ken sho-ki* (a written account of the kensho experience). He says, "*For the practice of Zen, you must pass the barrier set up by the ancient masters of Zen.*" The barrier is the koan Mu. "*To attain marvelous enlightenment, you must completely extinguish all the delusive thoughts of the ordinary mind.*" As long as you are using the intellect, you will not come to know intuitively. "*If you have not passed the barrier and have not extinguished delusive thoughts, you are a phantom haunting the weeds and trees.*" Those are the bad names he is throwing out at Muji people (i.e., people working on Mu): you are phantoms, haunting weeds and trees! You are *wak-wak* (a ghost), as they say in Leyte. "*Now, just tell me, what is the barrier set up by the Zen masters of old? Merely this: Mu—the one barrier of our sect.*" Muji (the written character of "mu") is true Soto, but many Rinzai temples now also use this koan for pre-kensho study. "*It has come to be called 'The Gateless Barrier of the Zen Sect.'*" Yamada Roshi called his book on the Mumonkan *The Gateless Gate* because in the end, when you pass the gate, you discover there never was any gate there to begin with.

"Those who have passed the barrier are able not only to see Joshu face to face, but also to walk hand in hand with the whole descending line of Zen masters and be eyebrow to eyebrow with them." These are all the delightful people spoken of in the koans and teisho and it's not that you're so close that your eyebrow is pressed against their eyebrow! That expression is about as close as words can get to express Oneness. One with Joshu himself, and Shakyamuni and Unmon and Dogen Zenji and Harada Roshi and Yamada Roshi!

"You will see with the same eye they see with, hear with the same ear they hear with. Wouldn't that be a wonderful joy?...Then concentrate your whole self, with its 360 bones and joints and 84,000 pores, into Mu, making your whole body a solid lump of doubt." I'd like to make a little observation here. Mumon lived almost five hundred years after Joshu. Now a few minutes ago we spoke about Joshu and his gentle spirit. We saw him coaxing his disciple out of the world of duality into Oneness by the gentle "peck" of Mu. We just can't imagine him thundering to get 84,000 pores into a great lump of doubt. Here we have two different personalities five hundred years apart. Time brings changes in pedagogy in all fields. In our lifetime, right in the Sanbo Kyodan, our stream of Zen, we have seen quite a bit of change. Yasutani Roshi was still alive when I first started to attend their *zazenkai* (day-long retreats), and he, like his teacher, Harada Roshi, ran a rather lively zendo during sesshin. Both of those teachers allowed one day of sesshin "open" to sound—that is, everyone working on Mu could say it out as loud as they wanted to. Can you imagine a more aggravating basis for sitting than being in a room all day with fifty people all pressing audibly on their practice! And not only that, there were usually four *godo* (well-seasoned students in charge of discipline), all brandishing a *kyosaku* (awakening stick) with great flourish—and not limited to two strokes on each shoulder! Accounts in *The Three Pillars of Zen* tell us that many sitters became exhausted and nervous just hearing other people being hit!

Yamada Roshi changed all that. It may be partly due to his temperament, but Yamada Roshi felt that Dogen Zenji and Joshu and Shakyamuni all fostered quiet Zen. And he had acquired a lot of experience in working with people from many countries all over the world. I well remember one North American saying, "I will not be hit into kensho!"

All this leads me to believe that we do not have to take Mumon's advice literally. Not only that, but I strongly advise you not to. I don't want anyone coming into the dokusan room to me with a built-up solid lump of doubt. I'm not saying that nothing will happen when you do Mu. Mu is abrasive and, sincerely done, will produce results. Something will happen. That is why a teacher is necessary, as guide during that descent to the depths of self. But I want to see that you go at a speed you can handle. This is another reason that Muji people should come to dokusan regularly, even if you have nothing to say. Remember, a blank consciousness is the best condition.

In the commentary on this koan, Mumon relates how he came to kensho. He says, "*Day and night, without ceasing, keep digging into it, but don't take it as 'nothingness' or as 'being' or 'non-being.'*" It must be like a red-hot iron ball that you have gulped down, which is that "leap in the dark," referring to the moment when we have to "let go" and "leap." Unconsciously, some people resist. "*You must extinguish all delusive thoughts and feelings that you have cherished up to the present.*" He goes on to say, "*After a certain period of such efforts, Mu will come to fruition, and inside and out will become one naturally.*" You meet non-duality.

Here I follow Shibayama Roshi in inserting the sentence that appears a little later. "*Then all of a sudden, Mu will break open and astonish the heavens and shake the earth.*" When will this happen, you ask? Yamada Roshi says it will happen when all things are ready, to which Dogen Zenji would add, and a touch of help comes from beyond. Some people refer to their kensho as a mountain that in time may seem like a pimple on a great plain. But at the time, it is a Mount Fuji or Mount Mayon.

"*You will then be like a dumb person who has had a dream. You will know yourself, but for yourself only.*" The experience is essentially incommunicable. Even if you have considerable skill with words, you will not be able to relate the experience satisfactorily. You will, however, be able to speak of it relatively. You will be intimate with many of the words and phrases we use in dokusan and teisho. That is one of the advantages of hearing frequent teisho.

Sometimes the opening experience is not very forceful. Sitters usually have preconceived ideas about kensho, and unless the "happening" meets their expectations, they do not confirm themselves, so to speak.

Confirmation of kensho is the teacher's business. Leave that to her or him. The emptying in your sitting should get rid of the delusion of kensho or not. In our stream of Zen, the confirmation of kensho is dependent on answers to a prescribed set of questions. Of course, it goes without saying that there are other factors, and I will always help the person who has had an experience to come to some understanding of what happened. But that is the business of being a teacher. Your business, as Mumon says, is to concentrate on Mu and to use up your energy doing it. All of this is just on the periphery, however. The experience itself is incommunicable.

Mumon goes on to talk about the effects of the experience. "*It will be just as if you had snatched the great sword of General Kan. If you meet a buddha, you will kill him. If you meet an ancient Zen master, you will kill him.*" Notice they are *ancient* Zen masters—not extant ones!

These are all ideas. In sitting, things in the head have to be gotten rid of. Kensho is an experience quite apart from all this; and when it happens you are well aware of the fact. At least for a time after kensho, people are very sure of themselves. It is quite delightful, really. There's usually not a doubt, and an argument with Buddha would ensue if he came along and said something contrary to the experience.

"*Though you may stand on the brink of life and death, you will enjoy the great freedom. In the six realms and the four modes of birth, you will live in the samadhi of innocent play.*"

"*Now, how should you concentrate on Mu? Exhaust every ounce of energy you have in doing it.*" As I said above, we give that advice with qualifications. "*And if you do not give up on the way, you will be enlightened the way a candle in front of the Buddha is lit by one touch of fire.*" If you persevere, as surely as the coming of dawn or the rain of early spring—*BANG!*—the bottom of the barrel will disappear! As quick as a flash of lightning!

That is Mumon's story as he tells of his own six-year practice, and his ensuing enlightenment.

TEISHO ON THE VERSE

[...]"*A little 'has' or 'has not'*" is the concept of discrimination. Sitters who are this far along in their practice know that insight and freedom are not attained in the world of having or not having. Look at what is being presented by Joshu. There is no debate or complexity about the dog, or the buddha nature, or commanding and manifesting. They are simply dog, buddha nature, commanding, manifesting. We are being told that "a little" discrimination throws the whole Zen world out of whack. That shows how destructive mental and intellectual procedures can be to our sitting. Even a little, even a little.

We frequently come across that phrase, "a little," in our Zen studies, and eventually we come to understand that it has an absolute meaning. It absolutely says that there must be no intellection at all. This is rather difficult to swallow and can almost seem devastating when we have spent most of the waking hours during our life intellectualizing. And even into old age, when it seems that Zen meditators carry on with their work, there is a certain proclivity to approaching the next minute through the intellectual door.

So I want to say a word of encouragement to all. If you find yourself in the area of the dualistic world, not totally but rather "somewhat," then don't give up. Godos in our zendos frequently shout "*Gambatte!*" which means "persevere," "stick to it." In the verse of Case 39 in the Mumonkan we read, "Angling in a swift stream, those greedy for bait will be caught. If you open your mouth even a little bit, your life will be lost."

John of the Cross tells us that there is often just a thin thread holding back a bird from flying where it will, but it might as well be a steel cable! Sometimes, it is just a little bit of delusion that keeps us from being free. It so often means that we have only a little bit further to go to have true insight.

So be encouraged, especially if you are aware of this "little bit." Perhaps with just a little bit more sitting, a little bit of deepening, that little bit of duality will be swept away. I don't know if this is of any comfort to you, but Yamada Roshi used to counsel us to remember that when we are tired and discouraged, even a little bit, the "enemy" is also tired and discouraged, even a little bit.

It is important that meditators feel that as they advance in Zen they will not necessarily become great strong leaders. Perhaps they will, if they have the innate potential. But you will be who you were meant to be, which is the peace and comfort of the satori experience. So if you feel you are just an ordinary person, then that is the most appropriate, and consequently you may be the one to allow things to happen and unfold, when dust storms arise. The great South American teacher Paolo Freire used to tell his followers that the humanization of the world cannot be accomplished by the strong and powerful. He'd say it is going to be the little ones, the unarmed and the not powerful, who, when healed, will have the freedom to release the liberating spirit. Orthopedic doctors tell a similar tale about a broken body bone. Once it is set and healed, it is stronger than the original bone, and its greatest strength is the very point of the break itself.

So if we get discouraged sometimes with the "little" lingering delusion on the road to liberation, let us remember that the seeping away of the delusion, the healing of it, will be, in time, our greatest strength. Only then can we as individuals do something truly constructive about the social injustices in our world. Until we are free, we don't have much to give others, except further delusion.

What Is *Kongen*, the Origin of Mu?

Kongen is a kind of double-barrel word, which means both "root" and "source." Together they suggest the ultimate or root-source. So in English the koan could read, "What is the root-source of Mu?"

Because it comes right after the magnificent Muji koan, Kongen is especially profound. In the Sambo Kyodan, our stream of Zen, this one is almost not a koan. The Rinzai school treats it a little differently, and reaches a certain level, a level we also touch. But the Soto school takes it beyond that point. Unless you take it beyond and beyond, until it blows the mind, you have never tasted the koan nor allowed it to enrich you. Your contemplation, your spirituality, will not have true depth until you have experienced the root-source of Mu, until that root-source becomes the fabric of your Zen. As long as you find God reasonable and comprehensible and knowable, you are in touch with the eschatological and transcendent God only. The horizontal—the immanent God—is the way of Mu. To paraphrase Father Raimundo Panikkar, it is the other side of God's face that is shown to the Orient.

When you find Mu, you will easily discover its root. But what is the source of that root? Confucius has said, "To know what you know and what you don't know is the characteristic of one who knows." Having come to the knowing of the root, one comes to the not-knowing of the source.

Ultimately, there is a mystery at the core of the Void. In Zen, we must be careful of referring to mystery. Yamada Roshi says there is no mystery but the *fact* itself. This koan, however, is the one exception. It is also, among all the koans, the one most overtly religious. If a teacher were a trained theologian, this teisho could be called, "A theology for the Oriental contemplative." John of the Cross defines contemplation as the silencing or emptying of our sense and spiritual faculties. All our theological knowledge from this koan can be learned only by emptying our mind and senses.

As said above, ultimately there is a mystery at the core of the Void. *Muji no Kongen* is an invitation to that core. As Lao Tzu says in the Tao Te Ching, "Impenetrable is the darkness where the heart of Being dwells. From eternity to eternity It will never perish. Who saw the beginning of All?" Or to quote another ancient Chinese sage, Wang Wei (699–759):

> *When there is nothing to give up,*
> *One has indeed reached the source.*
> *When there is no void to abide in,*
> *One is indeed experiencing the void,*
> *Transcending quiescence is no action;*
> *Rather, it is Creation, which constantly acts.*

Once the third eye has been opened, no matter how tentatively, we must reach for Kongen. Although the world's beginning may naturally be considered, this is not a question of past and future. Kongen and nirvana are here, now. All of creation, whatever exists, is silently concentrated right here, right now—in my own creation, in my own being. Likewise, all of creation is a beginning and is pervaded by what I myself am. The beginning and nirvana are upon us. But if we seem apparently lost and wandering and seeking, we are already encompassed by infinite blessedness. As Mumon says so beautifully in the verse to Case 35 in the Gateless Gate, "All are blessed, ten thousand things, ten thousand blessings." Original Blessing indeed!

I propose that this approach is the Asian soul. Everything we learn from the root of Mu tells us we come from Original Blessing. Accordingly, the Federation of Asian Bishops' Conference in 1978, in India, stated, "The techniques developed in Asian religious traditions, for example, Yoga and Zen, are of great service to the prayer experience of immanence. The spirituality of immanence can lead us to newer insights into theology." I wonder if the root doesn't tell us that the newer insights are older insights after all. Long before original sin became the start of the Church's theology, the Asian sages had a deep, innate, positive, blessing-filled religious sense.

The Asian bishops went on to say that Asian Christians are to have an Asian spirituality. The root of Mu tells us this has to be based on Original Blessing. By then a further step is revealed, and in the ancients' unrelenting search and hunger for God, and their patient acceptance of the void in deep meditation and silence, they came to its source. Having come to the knowing of the root, they prostrated themselves before the non-knowing of the source.

Rinzai is root, and Soto is root-source. In root, we find we are of God. In root-source, we discover our limitation. And this experience has nothing to do with an elitist consciousness. Both Rinzai and Soto teach that we decline pronouncements on things we can never really know "in this world"; for instance, things before birth and after death. Let us keep within the limits of our experience. Kongen has a built-in curb to our morbid curiosity.

Kongen is the unutterable inconceivability of God.

Lao Tzu again:

> *The Tao that can be told of*
> *is not the Absolute Tao;*
> *The names that can be given*
> *are not the Absolute Names.*

If God is utterly inconceivable, then ultimately so am I. "Therefore I ask God to rid me of God. The nonbeing Being of God is beyond God, beyond all differentiation; there was I alone, wanting myself alone, and saw myself as the one who had made this man [this woman or myself]!

So I am the cause of myself and of all things. But if I were not, God were not." Aren't those the words of Meister Eckhart? Let us not slip up on the words (as Unmon tells the monk in Case 39 of the Gateless Gate).

In Zen there is a saying, "The truth that is as it is, has been continuous since antiquity, without ever having varied so much as a hair's breadth." Kongen is the family treasure. It does not come in through the gate. In the preface to his book, Mumon says: "Zen makes no-gate the gate of Dharma."

It is no-gate from the start. How can we pass through it? Haven't you heard the old saying, "Things that come in through the gate are not the family treasure!" Such remarks are just like raising heavy waves when there is no wind, or gouging a wound in healthy skin. How much more ridiculous to adhere to words and phrases or try to understand by means of the intellect. It is exactly like trying to strike the moon with a stick, or to scratch an itchy foot through the sole of your boot.

The mystery of the root-source of Mu is the contemplative's school. It can also be the point where the theologian becomes contemplative. The following is from the writing of the eminent theologian of the twentieth century, Karl Rahner. He seems to speak of the origin of Mu.

> Our beginning is hidden in God. It is decided. Only when
> we have arrived will we fully know what our origin is. For
> God is mystery as such, and what he posited when he
> established us in our beginning is still the mystery. With-
> out evacuating the mystery, we can say that there belongs
> to our beginning all that is there, everything whatsoever
> which exists, and is silently concentrated in the wellspring
> of our own existence. And is pervaded by what each is in
> himself, and herself, posited by God as a beginning
> uniquely and unrepeatedly. With what is hard and what is
> easy, delicate and harsh, with what belongs to the abyss
> and what is heavenly. All is encompassed by God's knowl-
> edge and love. All has to be accepted....The possibility of
> acceptance itself belongs to the might of the divinely
> posited beginning. And if we accept, we have accepted

sheer love and happiness. And the more that love and for-
giveness which encompasses and belongs to our beginning is accepted in the pain of life, and in the death which
gives life, the more this original element emerges and
manifests itself and pervades our history....When the
beginning has found itself in the fulfillment and has been
fulfilled in the freedom of accepting love, GOD WILL BE
ALL IN ALL.

So speaks an eminent theologian. Our final arrival is mystery and so
is our root-source; to face our infinite incomprehensibility is to be a
contemplative.

We meditators not only face the infinite incomprehensibility of the
Infinite, but also our own hiddenness. And when contemplation is born,
all objects die. Where God is concerned, contemplation is appropriate, for
God is utterly unknowable by reason, and no thought can give us an idea
of what he is.

The medieval Saint Richard of St. Victor says, "Contemplatives
who endeavor to think, only kill their incipient mystical life...they are
like mothers who strangle their children at birth." He continues, "Let
them be quiet, still, expectant, calm, lest they smother the tiny flame
which is their most precious possession." And so he goes on that all
thoughts, all desires and hopes, all fears, all images, and all ambitions—all must be trampled down under the cloud of forgetting. His
"forget, forget, forget" is like the *"nada, nada, nada"* of John of the
Cross. And it is the most natural thing in the world, to compare these
texts with the Zen masters: "Empty, empty, empty," "Mu, Mu, Mu."
Where there is nothing, there is everything. What is the root-source
of nothing?

In our Zen stream spirituality, we seek the return of our Original
Nature to its original spontaneity. For a while, perhaps when we begin,
we see this Original Nature as an object. But soon we have to give up the
attempt to make our nature an object of contemplation. We have to eliminate all symbols and all thoughts, and *allow this nature to be totally
itself, pure and spontaneous.* You will remember being told in the first
couple of years of sitting, "There is still a gap between you and Mu." The

closing of this gap is kensho, when we "see" in a flash. But enlightenment was not always seen this way.

The origin of *dhyana* (the Sanskrit word for meditation, which comes down to us as *zen*) is lost in history. Its root is found in the Vedic Books of India, completed by 1500 B.C.E. We know from our koan study that the Indians taught fifty-two steps to enlightenment. We read in some books that it was based on a process that caused the disciple to pass through a series of stages of progressive simplification of thought and an increasing sublimation of the "object" of contemplation. Obviously, enlightenment came when thought was simplified to nothing at all, and the object of contemplation was sublimated out of existence. For many people this could be a natural process.

Our friend, the late Father Yves Raguin, S.J., has clearly outlined the history of our Mu and the changes it underwent in China. The teaching of Bodhidharma, who was the first Zen ancestor in China, is contained in the Lankavatara Sutra. He taught a method of total concentration in order to free the mind from all false notions and all attachments. The fruit of his efforts was to be a revelation of the purity of the Original Nature. As Father Raguin says:

> The main idea of this scripture is that the true state of nirvana is total emptiness devoid of any characteristics, duality, or differentiation. It is inexpressible in words and inconceivable in thought. *Our emancipation consists in our intuition of this highest truth.* Every human being is capable of this because everyone has the buddha nature. But our minds are obscured by desires, erroneous thoughts, and attachments of all sorts. Therefore, Bodhidharma taught the method of undisturbed concentration as if one faced a wall (hence the legend of the nine-year meditation) to free the mind from erroneous thoughts and attachments. Eventually the mind must become free from everything even to the extent of abandoning both being and nonbeing. Bodhidharma also taught ascetic practices in order to reassert our originally pure nature.

Six generations after Bodhidharma, Zen in China became divided into the Northern and Southern Schools. The Sandokai ("Identity of Phenomena and Essential"), which we chant at Vespers, makes mention of the Northern and Southern Patriarch. The founders of both schools, Shen-hsui in the North and Hui-neng (Eno) in the South, originally had the same teacher, Hung-jen.

The Northern School was seen at the time as holding tradition, which D.T. Suzuki epitomized by their acceptance that "the seen and the seeing are two separate entities." The Southern School united these entities, and called it *chien-hsieng* (kensho in Japanese). To see the ultimate reality of all things, the original nature. It is no longer a matter of thought as intermediary to reality. There exists only one thing, one single reality, and since it is not separate, there are no stages to go through. The awakening to the reality of the Original Nature can only be sudden, for there is no possible intermediary.

In many ways, we can say Mu entered the Way at this point in history. The tag *Mu* was affixed to the Way in the Southern School of Zen in China (our lineage) and flourished. Its success was due to its radical nature. Historians tell us this marked a stage in the Sinocization of Buddhism. Eno, the Sixth Ancestor, assimilated something of the abrupt nature of Taoist contemplation by stressing the absolute spontaneity of the Original Nature. Taoism has instituted absence of thought as its doctrine. Absence of thought means not to be carried away by thought in the process of thought. But if one can cut all thought for one instant from all attachment to what exists, then the Original Nature is freed to act spontaneously and appropriately.

The Orient would have its beginning in the darkness of blessing, and freeing our Original Nature. Therefore, our journey is letting go and letting Be-ing be! This is our contemplation. As said before, when contemplation is born, all objects die, and we let them die. Where there is nothing, there is everything. We cannot find the root-source of nothing until we let go. We let go of the past. I am not alive if I cling to yesterday, because yesterday is just a memory. It's not real; it's a creation of the mind. To live in yesterday is to be dead. Let go of the past. Let us establish our own personal program of peace and reconciliation, and grant amnesty to all the people we resent and have grievances against. Let us free our prisoners. Let us also let go of our regrets, our losses and failures, our hang-ups and mistakes and handicaps, our bad luck and unfortunate experiences and lack of opportunities. We also have to let go of our successes and good experiences because they too become oppressive if they keep us dead in the past. We must continually say goodbye to people, occupations, things, and places that we have treasured in the past. We shall never meet again, because when we return we shall have changed. So: thank you and goodbye to the past.

Where there is nothing there is everything.

Let us also let go of our tomorrows, for, like the past, they are a construction of the mind. If we live in the future, we are dead to the present. Let us drop our desires and ambitions, which are our bondage to anxiety. "Creations are innumerable, I resolve to free them all." The root-source of nothing is Lao Tzu's "impenetrable is the darkness where the heart of Being dwells." And this is our other side of letting go, letting Be-ing be.

"I live now, not I, but Christ lives within me." The perfect communion of the saint and Absolute.

And all our exploring of the root-source of Mu is to arrive where we started and, as T.S. Eliot says, to know the place for the first time.

And meditation is not in time. Martin Buber tells us, rather, time is prayer. To reverse the relation is to abolish reality.

The koan of the root-source of Mu is a "journey-back" in time *and* space. It is an experiential journey of the utmost importance for a meditator. The presentation of this koan in the dokusan room must be unaligned wisdom. Our transformation must begin in the darkness and the letting-go and letting-be to the root-source of Mu.

These few words from "You Darkness," by Rainer Maria Rilke, speak beautifully of the cosmic womb of our origin:

> *fire makes*
> *a circle of light*
> *darkness pulls in everything...*
> *powers and people—*
> *and it is possible a great energy*

is moving near me.
I have faith in nights.

And this seems the night that John of the Cross speaks of, the night that cleanses memory.

—with special thanks to two Jesuits,
Karl Rahner and Yves Raguin

Melissa Myozen Blacker
and James Ishmael Ford

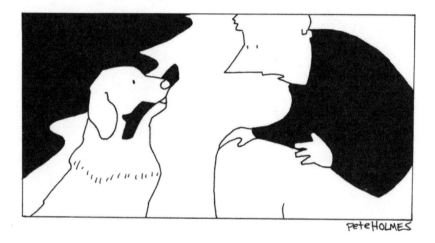

"Don't you get it? It was never about the stick—
I sent you there to find yourself."

LIKE THIS DOG'S MASTER, we compiled these texts so that you could find yourself. It was never really about Mu. It's always about this great matter, taking form now as a breeze, now as a bird song, now as a headache, a flower, a stick. We hope, while reading these texts by great teachers from many Zen traditions and lineages, all deeply engaged in the koan Mu, that you have found inspiration for your own Zen practice.

At this point, it's up to you. Sitting with Mu is best done in companionship with a teacher, who can act as a loving guide, someone who is both a sounding board and who directs you back, over and over again, to what

307

is true, right here and now. If you don't have a koan teacher, and you want to work with Mu, please find one.

As Wumen says, "What comes through the door is not the family treasure." What we have been searching for is already here, right beneath our feet. Never stop looking.

Mu!

"Mu" by John Daido Loori

About the Contributors

Robert Aitken (1917–2010) studied with Nyogen Senzaki, Soen Nakagawa, and Haku'un Yasutani. He received Dharma transmission from Koun Yamada. Together with Anne Aitken he was the founder of the Diamond Sangha network. He died in 2010 in Honolulu, Hawaii.

Jan Chozen Bays is a Dharma successor to Taizan Maezumi. She continues training with Shodo Harada. She is the co-abbot of the Great Vow Zen Monastery in Clatskanie, Oregon. She is also a medical doctor specializing in pediatrics.

Mitra Bishop is a Dharma successor of Philip Kapleau. She continues her studies with Shodo Harada. She is spiritual director at the Hidden Valley Zen Center in San Diego and abbot of the Mountain Gate in Ojo Sarco, New Mexico.

Roko Sherry Chayat studied with Haku'un Yasutani, Soen Nakagawa, and Maurine Stewart. She received Inka Shomei from Eido Shimano, making her the first Western woman to receive full authorization in a traditional Rinzai line. She is abbot of the Zen Center of Syracuse, in upstate New York.

Dae Gak (Robert Guenther, PhD) is a Dharma successor to Seung Sahn. He is guiding teacher at the Furnace Mountain Zen Retreat Center in Clay City, Kentucky.

Dahui Zonggao (1089–1163) was arguably the third most important figure in the evolution of koan introspection after Linji and Hakuin. His teaching style informed the mainstream of koan introspection practice after him and became the basis for Hakuin's curriculum system.

EIHEI DOGEN (1200–1253) is the founder of the Japanese Soto school and was also founding abbot of Eiheiji, one of the two principal monastery complexes in the lineage. A figure of incalculable importance in the development of Zen thought as well as practice.

YAMAMOTO GEMPO (1866–1961) was a leading figure in Japanese Rinzai Zen throughout the middle twentieth century.

RUBEN L.F. HABITO is a Dharma successor to Koun Yamada. He is a former Jesuit priest and one of the leaders of the Sanbo Kyodan in the United States. He is founding teacher at the Maria Kannon Zen Center in Dallas, Texas.

HAKUIN EKAKU (1685–1768) revitalized the Japanese Rinzai school, and is closely associated with the establishment of the curriculum style of koan introspection practice represented in this book. The two principal variations on the discipline, the Takuju and the Inzan, are named for two heirs of his successor Gasan Jito.

SHODO HARADA is a Dharma heir to Yamada Mumon, and a leading figure in teaching Rinzai Zen to Westerners. He serves as abbot of Sogenji monastery in Japan and frequently leads retreats at One Drop Zen Monastery on Whidbey Island, in Washington State.

HARADA SOGAKU (1871–1961) was a leading Soto master in the first half of the twentieth century, who also studied with several Rinzai teachers. He introduced a reform of the Takuju koan curriculum, which is widely taught in the West.

JULES SHUZEN HARRIS studied with Taizan Maezumi, John Daido Loori, and Bernie Glassman. He received precepts transmission, full ordination as a Soto priest, from Genpo Merzel and Dharma transmission from Enkyo O'Hara. He is the founding teacher of the Soji Zen Center.

RACHEL MANSFIELD-HOWLETT is a Dharma successor to John Tarrant. She conducts individual and small group koan work and holds retreats in California. She is an attorney practicing public-benefit environmental law in Santa Rosa, CA.

PHILIP KAPLEAU (1912–2004) studied with Soen Nakagawa and Harada Sogaku. He received permission to teach from Haku'un Yasutani, later establishing an independent Zen line in America. He was the founder of the Rochester Zen Center.

BODHIN KJOLHEDE is a Dharma heir of Philip Kapleau and succeeded Kapleau as the second abbot of the Rochester Zen Center.

JOHN DAIDO LOORI (1939–2009) studied with Soen Nakagawa, Haku'un Yasutani, and Eido Shimano before receiving Dharma transmission from Taizan Maezumi. He was the founding abbot of the Zen Mountain Monastery and the Mountain and Rivers Order.

TAIZAN MAEZUMI (1931–1995) was born into a Soto priestly family. He received Dharma transmission from Hakujun Kuroda, Koryu Osaka, and Haku'un Yasutani. He founded the Zen Center of Los Angeles.

ELAINE MACINNES is a Dharma heir of Koun Yamada. She is a religious of Our Lady's Missionaries living in retirement at her community in Toronto.

BARRY MAGID studied with Eido Shimano and Bernie Glassman. He is a Dharma heir of Joko Beck. He is also a psychiatrist in private practice. He is the teacher at the Ordinary Mind Zendo in New York City.

SUSAN MURPHY studied with Robert Aitken and received Dharma transmission from Ross Bolleter and John Tarrant. She is the founding teacher of the Zen Open Circle in Sydney.

KORYU OSAKA (1901–1987) was a Dharma successor to the Rinzai master Joko Roshi.

DAVID DAE AN RYNICK is a Dharma successor to George Bowman. He is co-founder of Boundless Way Zen, which he currently serves as School Abbot. He works as a life and leadership coach and consultant in Worcester, Massachusetts. He is resident at Mugendo-ji, the Boundless Way Temple in Worcester, Massachusetts.

GRACE SCHIRESON was ordained a Soto priest by and is a Dharma successor to Sojun Weitsman. She continues her studies with the Rinzai master Keido Fukushima. She is the founder and guiding teacher of the Empty Nest Zen Group, the Modesto Valley Heartland Zen Group, and the Fresno River Zen Group.

NYOGEN SENZAKI (1876–1958) was ordained as a Soto priest, but then studied for many years with the Rinzai master Shaku Soyen. He taught for many years, mostly in California through his non-geographical Floating Zendo.

SEUNG SAHN (Seung Sahn Haeng Won Dae Soen-sa) (1927–2004) was a Dharma heir of Ko Bong. He founded the Kwan Um School of Zen, which is the largest mostly convert Zen community in the West. The Providence Zen Center in Cumberland, Rhode Island, is the international headquarters for the KUSZ.

SHAKU SOEN (1859–1919) was a Rinzai master and the first known Zen teacher to visit the West. His student D. T. Suzuki would be the first person to write widely about Zen in the English language.

SHENG YEN (1930–2009) was a Chan monk, scholar, and a Dharma heir in both the Linji (Rinzai) and Caodong (Soto) lineages. He founded Dharma Drum Mountain in Taiwan, with a branch in upstate New York.

ZENKEI SHIBAYAMA (1894–1974) was a scholar and Rinzai Zen teacher, and a prominent Zen figure in both Japan and the West.

EIDO SHIMANO is a Dharma successor to Soen Nakagawa. He founded the Zen Studies Society, which has two centers, the New York Zendo Shoboji and Dai Bosatsu Zendo Kongoji, both in New York.

ELIHU GENMYO SMITH was a student of Taizan Maezumi and the first Dharma heir of Joko Beck. He leads the Prairie Zen Center in Champaign, Illinois.

KURT SPELLMEYER is a Dharma heir in the Obaku lineage having received Inka from Kangan Glenn Webb. He leads the Cold Mountain Sangha in New Brunswick, New Jersey.

JOAN SUTHERLAND is a Dharma heir to John Tarrant and was a co-founder of the Pacific Zen Institute. She is the founding teacher of Awakened Life in Santa Fe, New Mexico, and the Open Source, a network of practice communities in the western United States.

JOHN TARRANT was the first Dharma successor to Robert Aitken. He founded and leads the Pacific Zen Institute in Santa Rosa, California. He wrote *Bring Me the Rhinoceros & Other Zen Koans That Will Save Your Life* as an illustration of new ways to work with koans.

THICH THIEN-AN (1926–1980) was a prominent Vietnamese Thien teacher. He founded the International Buddhist Meditation Center in Los Angeles.

GERRY SHISHIN WICK is a Dharma successor to Taizan Maezumi. A physicist by training, he is president and spiritual teacher of the Great Mountain Zen Center in Lafayette, Colorado.

KOUN YAMADA (1907–1989) is a Dharma heir to Haku'un Yasutani. He was the first lay leader of the Sanbo Kyodan headquartered in Kamakura, Japan.

HAKU'UN YASUTANI (1885–1973) was a Dharma successor to Harada Sogaku. He established the Sanbo Kyodan, which would have enormous influence in the West.

WUMEN HUIKAI (1183–1260) was a Rinzai Zen master and editor of the famous koan collection, the *Wumenguan*, the "Gateless Gate."

NOTE: Chinese names that are found in various transliterations throughout the book are listed here under the Pinyin spelling.

About the Editors

 JAMES ISHMAEL FORD is a Dharma successor to Houn Jiyu Kennett and John Tarrant. He was the founding abbot of the Boundless Way Zen school and continues to serve as a senior guiding teacher. He is also an ordained Unitarian Universalist minister. He is resident teacher at the Benevolent Street Zendo, which is hosted by the First Unitarian Church of Providence, Rhode Island, where he serves as senior minister.

 MELISSA MYOZEN BLACKER is a Dharma successor to James Ishmael Ford. She is a co-founder of Boundless Way Zen, which she currently serves as a senior guiding teacher. She is also the associate director of the Stress Reduction Clinic and a director of professional training at the Center for Mindfulness, University of Massachusetts Medical School. She is resident at Mugendo-ji, the Boundless Way Temple in Worcester, Massachusetts.

About Wisdom Publications

Wisdom Publications, a nonprofit publisher, is dedicated to making available authentic works relating to Buddhism for the benefit of all. We publish books by ancient and modern masters in all traditions of Buddhism, translations of important texts, and original scholarship. Additionally, we offer books that explore East-West themes unfolding as traditional Buddhism encounters our modern culture in all its aspects. Our titles are published with the appreciation of Buddhism as a living philosophy, and with the special commitment to preserve and transmit important works from Buddhism's many traditions.

To learn more about Wisdom, or to browse books online, visit our website at www.wisdompubs.org.

You may request a copy of our catalog online or by writing to this address:

Wisdom Publications
199 Elm Street
Somerville, Massachusetts 02144 USA
Telephone: 617-776-7416 • Fax: 617-776-7841
info@wisdompubs.org • www.wisdompubs.org

The Wisdom Trust

As a nonprofit publisher, Wisdom is dedicated to the publication of Dharma books for the benefit of all sentient beings and dependent upon the kindness and generosity of sponsors in order to do so. If you would like to make a donation to Wisdom, you may do so through our website or our Somerville office. If you would like to help sponsor the publication of a book, please write or email us at the address above.

Thank you.

Wisdom Publications is a nonprofit, charitable 501(c)(3) organization affiliated with the Foundation for the Preservation of the Mahayana Tradition (FPMT).